I0818251

FIGHTING
★ ★ ★ FOR THE ★ ★ ★
FREEDOM
TO LEARN

Edited by James V. Shuls and Neal P. McCluskey

FIGHTING ★ ★ ★ FOR THE ★ ★ ★ FREEDOM TO LEARN

Examining America's Centuries-Old School Choice Movement

Hardcover ISBN: 978-1-964524-81-8
Ebook ISBN: 978-1-964524-82-5

Library of Congress Cataloging-in-Publication Data available.

Library of Congress Control Number: 2025944114

Cover design by Faceout Studio.

Printed in the United States of America.

CATO
INSTITUTE
1000 Massachusetts Ave. NW
Washington, D.C. 20001

www.cato.org

Contents

Introduction

By James V. Shuls and Neal P. McCluskey

Our perception of history is shaped not just by facts but by the words we use to describe those facts. Language provides the foundation for understanding, yet words themselves can be elusive, evolving over time and altering the way we interpret past events.

Consider a simple analogy: *Hot is to cold as up is to [blank].* The answer is obvious—*down*. We grasp the relationship because we know the meanings of the words. Now try this one: *Obsequious is to imperious as parsimonious is to [blank].* This analogy follows the same simple structure—each pair consists of opposites—but unless you are familiar with the words, the relationship is obscured. Without understanding the vocabulary, we struggle to comprehend the idea.

History presents a similar challenge, not only because we may be unfamiliar with certain words, but also because words themselves shift in meaning over time. Take "manufacturing," for example. Today, we associate the term with industrial production—massive factories filled with machines. But historically, the word meant something very different. It comes from the Latin *manu factus*, meaning made by hand. The modern interpretation is nearly the opposite of its original meaning.

In the same way, our contemporary understanding of the term "school choice" is shaped by modern assumptions. Today, when we think of school choice, we think of policies that help students leave traditional public schools. Charter schools—publicly funded but privately operated—are a form of school choice. Vouchers, which allow students to use public funds at private schools, are also a form of school choice, as are scholarship tax credits that make sure people who donate money for children to get private education do not also pay taxes for public schools. Education savings accounts (ESAs), which provide families with flexible funds for tuition or other educational expenses, fit within this definition as well. In short, school choice today refers to a set of policies, typically enacted by state legislatures, that provides students with funding or opportunities to exit the public school system.

With this definition in mind, we might attempt to pinpoint when school choice began. The nation's first charter school law was passed in Minnesota in 1991. Arizona introduced the first tax-credit scholarship program in 1997 and the first ESA program in 2011. The first modern voucher program was created in Wisconsin in 1990. Some critics of school choice point to the desegregation period of the 1950s and 1960s as the true origins of vouchers, citing efforts to use them for segregationist purposes. But similar programs existed well before that era. In 1802, Pennsylvania created a program that paid for poor families to attend "any school in their neighborhood."[1] Vermont and Maine created "town tuitioning" programs in 1869 and 1873, respectively, allowing students in rural areas without public schools to attend private schools with public funding. And various states and jurisdictions funded diverse schools directly, making choice available to families.[2]

This brings us back to where we started. Maine and Vermont did not call their programs vouchers, and they did not frame them as school choice. Their programs were simply a means of ensuring access to publicly funded education. If we define school choice only in modern terms—by the labels we use today—we risk missing the bigger picture. Educational freedom existed long before "school choice" became a formal policy term. The words we use carry connotations shaped by present-day debates, but the fundamental idea—the right of parents to direct their children's education—transcends any single term or policy framework.

That is the theme of this book: educational freedom. You will not find references to "school choice" in early American educational history, yet you will find countless examples of parents, communities, and educators fighting for the right to educate children in accordance with their values and needs. It would make no sense to implement a school choice policy, as we define it today, in a time before public schooling was widespread. Yet the desire for educational freedom has always existed—long before charters, vouchers, or ESAs.

This book explores that long struggle. It examines the historical battles over parental rights in education, the evolving role of government in schooling, and how the fight for educational freedom has shaped the policies we now call "school choice." By looking beyond modern definitions and policy frameworks, we gain a clearer understanding of where we have been—and where we are going.

The Structure of This Book

We have assembled a collection of work from 12 different authors, including the two of us. Each author was asked to tackle a specific period or a particular struggle for educational freedom in the American context. Thus, the book takes a sweeping look from the founding of the American colonies to present day, and examines how the fight for educational freedom took place in these different eras and contexts. Because the authors were not given exact years or dates to examine, some overlap between the chapters is inevitable. Yet each chapter helps contribute to our understanding of the history of education and educational freedom in the United States.

The first three chapters of the book address the period before common schools. Economist Albert Fishlow reported that by 1840, 90 percent of white adults in the United States were literate.[3] Yet Horace Mann, the champion of the common school movement, did not assume office as the first secretary of the Massachusetts State Board of Education until 1837.[4] As the first three chapters explain, these tremendous literacy rates were achieved through a decentralized system of education that was publicly and privately funded and operated. But note that the data are only for "white" adults. During this same period, government—the owner of common schools—in many places prohibited or handicapped reading instruction for African Americans.

This book begins with the development of educational institutions in colonial America. Jane Shaw Stroup examines the diverse and decentralized landscape of education in America before the rise of common schools, challenging the assumption that government-run schooling was the inevitable or superior model. She highlights the variety of educational arrangements that existed—from home instruction and dame schools to church-supported institutions, charity schools, apprenticeships, and academies—and demonstrates how families, religious organizations, and local communities took the lead in providing education. Stroup also critiques the teleological view held by some historians, who frame the rise of public schools as the culmination of educational progress, rather than recognizing the effectiveness and adaptability of earlier systems. Stroup further explores how financial constraints, geographic diversity, and cultural differences shaped schooling in different regions, leading to a rich tapestry of educational options. Ultimately, she argues that the history of American education is not one of steady centralization but of evolving efforts to balance educational freedom, local control, and societal needs.

In a similar vein, William Jeynes explores how the diverse ethnic, linguistic, and religious backgrounds of settlers in the mid-Atlantic region influenced the development of education. Focusing primarily on Pennsylvania, New York, New Jersey, Maryland, and Delaware, he examines how early settlers, despite their differences, prioritized education as a unifying force, emphasizing shared values and religious foundations. This led to the rise of charity schools, denominational schooling, and higher education institutions that expanded educational opportunity and unity while respecting and preserving diversity.

While Stroup and Jeynes focus on the structure and cultural influences of early education, Dick Carpenter shifts the lens to how these schools were funded and sustained. In his chapter, he digs deeper into the financial underpinnings of education before the common school movement, revealing the diverse mechanisms that supported early schooling. Schools and learning environments were maintained through a mix of private contributions, religious institutions, community efforts, and some government assistance. Carpenter challenges the modern notion of a strict division between public and private education, showing how early American schooling was characterized by a blend of funding sources and governance structures.

Chapters 4 and 5 of the book focus on the rise of, and resistance to, the common school movement. The chapters by Charles Glenn and Ashley Berner examine the historical rise of the common school movement and the persistent critiques that have shaped debates over educational freedom. Glenn explores how the common school ideology, emerging in the 19th century, was driven by a desire to unify American citizens under a state-directed educational system that would instill shared values and national loyalty. However, this system often sought to suppress religious and cultural pluralism, positioning itself against denominational and locally controlled schools. Berner builds on this analysis by detailing the arguments made by critics of the common school model, particularly those arguments that highlight the inability of the common school model to remain value-neutral, its tendency to marginalize civil society institutions, and its failure to provide equal access to quality education for all students. Together, Glenn and Berner demonstrate that while the common school ideal was framed as a means of fostering democratic unity, it has faced continuous resistance from those who argue that true educational freedom requires a more pluralistic and decentralized approach.

Though much of this book focuses on the common school movement and resistance to it, it is important to recognize that common schools were not common to all. This theme is explored by Cheryl Fields-Smith. Her chapter examines the historical struggle for educational freedom among black Americans, emphasizing how self-agency, self-determination, and resistance have defined their pursuit of literacy and schooling. From enslaved Africans secretly learning to read despite anti-literacy laws, to the establishment of independent schools during Reconstruction and the resilience of black educational institutions under segregation, the chapter highlights the enduring link between education and liberation. It also explores how black communities navigated systemic barriers, from Freedmen's Bureau schools to Rosenwald schools and beyond, demonstrating a persistent commitment to securing quality education for future generations.

Following the Civil War, there was a lull in the educational freedom movement. Neal McCluskey and Matthew Lee explore the movements that seemingly dampened the demand for educational freedom and those that started to turn the tide. McCluskey examines the period from 1880 to 1955, showing how rising nationalism, industrialization, mass immigration, and centralization of education contributed to a retreat of the school choice movement. The drive to assimilate diverse populations and control society led to efforts that threatened the very existence of diverse educational options, such as the passage of Blaine amendments and attempts to outlaw private schooling altogether. McCluskey then highlights how choice came back from the brink by the mid-20th century, reignited by resistance to government overreach, religious discrimination, and fears of totalitarianism. Lee, meanwhile, focuses on the broader shifts in Protestant and Catholic attitudes toward education, illustrating how the initial Protestant support for public schooling gave way to disillusionment as the government increasingly secularized education and removed parental oversight. As Protestants lost influence in public schools and Catholics fought for their right to maintain independent schools, both groups found common cause in advocating for greater parental control over education. Together, these chapters provide a historical road map for understanding how educational freedom, while suppressed at times, remained a persistent force that eventually resurged in new and powerful ways.

Although there is no doubt that school choice, as we know it today, began to take shape in the 1950s and 1960s, there is some misunderstanding about what actually took place. Milton Friedman's seminal 1955 essay, "The Role of Government in Education," laid the intellectual foundation for modern school choice, advocating for a voucher system to improve education through market competition rather than segregation. But Friedman was not alone. In Chapter 9, James V. Shuls examines the historical framing of educational freedom as a civil rights issue, highlighting the advocacy of Virgil Blum and Citizens for Educational Freedom (CEF) starting in the 1950s. Drawing from archival records, Shuls demonstrates how Blum and CEF positioned school choice as an extension of the broader civil rights movement, arguing that the denial of educational benefits to families who chose religious schools was a violation of fundamental rights under the First and Fourteenth Amendments. Shuls also contextualizes the push for school choice within the history of Catholic advocacy for educational funding, which long predated the desegregation battles of the 1950s and 1960s. Although some critics argue that school choice policies were rooted in segregationist resistance to *Brown v. Board of Education*, Shuls refutes that narrative by showing how school choice was a longstanding movement for educational freedom, one that intersected with but was not defined by segregationist efforts. Through a detailed examination of legal battles, legislative advocacy, and public rhetoric, Shuls underscores how educational freedom has consistently been viewed as a fundamental civil right by its proponents.

Today, critics attempt to cast school choice as a right-wing movement. Ron Matus dispels that idea in his chapter, uncovering deep progressive roots in the school choice movement. He highlights how left-leaning academics, civil rights leaders, and social justice advocates—ranging from Berkeley law professors John Coons and Stephen Sugarman to black leaders like Polly Williams and Howard Fuller—have long championed school choice as a means of empowering marginalized communities. Matus traces how education freedom movements, including the push for community-controlled schools in black neighborhoods and alternative learning models like free schools, have been driven by progressive values of equity, pluralism, and self-determination. By reclaiming this often-overlooked history, Matus reframes the debate over school choice, demonstrating how its motivations have historically transcended political ideology and reflecting a broader struggle for educational freedom and opportunity.

Next, Nicole Garnett examines the legal developments that have paved the way for school choice. She traces the long arc of legal battles, from 19th-century Catholic resistance to Protestant-dominated public schools, to the imposition of Blaine amendments, to the gradual shift in Supreme Court rulings favoring religious liberty and parental choice. Key decisions—including *Pierce v. Society of Sisters* (1925), *Zelman v. Simmons-Harris* (2002), and *Carson v. Makin* (2022)—helped establish the constitutional foundation for school choice by reinforcing that states cannot discriminate against religious schools in publicly funded programs. Garnett highlights how recent legal victories have largely removed federal constitutional barriers to school choice, shifting future battles to state courts and policy debates over regulation. Her analysis underscores that while legal victories have been crucial in expanding educational freedom, ongoing litigation will shape the future of school choice programs and their accessibility to families nationwide.

Jason Bedrick's chapter brings the book into the present, charting the rapid expansion of school choice policies in recent years and the shifting political dynamics that have made it possible. He traces how school choice moved from a fringe idea in the mid-20th century to an incremental policy movement in the 1990s, before finally reaching a tipping point in the 2020s with the adoption of universal choice programs in multiple states. Bedrick argues that the COVID-19 pandemic accelerated the movement but was not the primary cause of its boom. Instead, he highlights the emergence of the "Red State Strategy," in which school choice advocates abandoned the bipartisan approach in favor of a conservative-led effort that linked school choice to cultural concerns, parental rights, and dissatisfaction with public school governance. By leveraging grassroots activism and tying school choice to broader conservative priorities, advocates successfully pushed through universal education savings accounts and other expansive policies across Republican-led states. Bedrick concludes by exploring how these recent gains could reshape the future of American education, potentially normalizing universal school choice and forcing even traditionally resistant states and political factions to reconsider their stance.

Public Versus Private Education

This book helps us understand that recent movements for school choice are really carrying on the long arc of individuals seeking educational freedom. In every era, Americans have fought to educate their children based on their diverse needs and desires. This has looked different depending on the circumstances of the time. Before the common school movement, parents did not need to seek an exit from an unacceptable school where their child had been assigned. And, when progressives were pushing to ban private institutions altogether, it made little sense for anyone to push for universal vouchers. They simply fought for the right of their institutions to exist. As our education system evolved, so too did advocacy for educational freedom.

Beyond broadening our understanding of educational freedom, this book helps us see the blurred lines between "public" and "private" schools. For many decades of American history, not just in modern times, citizens provided funds to private, religious educational institutions. This was common during the same periods in which the Founders enshrined the separation of church and state into the Constitution. They did not see a contradiction. It was later, as progressives sought to build a national identity and reduce the influence of religion, that these activities were quashed. In this sense, modern school choice policies are both an innovation and a restoration, bringing back the pluralistic, community-driven approaches to education that existed long before the common school movement sought to centralize learning under the state.

Notes

1. Mark Storslee, "Church Taxes and the Original Understanding of the Establishment Clause," *University of Pennsylvania Law Review* 169 (2020): 162.
2. "School Choice Timeline," Cato Institute, accessed March 21, 2025.
3. Albert Fishlow, "Levels of Nineteenth-Century American Investment in Education," *Journal of Economic History* 26, no. 4 (1966): 418–36.
4. Jonathan C. Messerli, "Localism and State Control in Horace Mann's Reform of the Common Schools," *American Quarterly* 17, no. 1 (1965): 104–18.

Chapter 1

The Years Before Common Schooling

By Jane Shaw Stroup

Before the establishment of "common" or public schools in the United States, children and young people attended many types of schools and received many kinds of education. However, historians have tended to be dismissive of the diverse education options that were available. Some historians have viewed education teleologically; that is, they have viewed a common or public school, which is financed by taxes and open to all children, as the result of a long struggle for reform. This struggle gradually replaced an unorganized and free-wheeling supply of education options with formal "public" schools run by a government, local or state. The most famous of these historians, the mid-20th-century writer Ellwood Cubberley, said that the creation of the US Constitution made a public school education possible because it freed education from religion. However, "the struggle to establish that general education required the best efforts of those interested in the highest welfare of the Republic for more than half a century to come."[1]

In 1978, education historian R. Freeman Butts put a different spin on the story. He credited the American Revolution for starting the concept of common schools—long before there were any. In his view, the American Revolution led to the idea that America was different, a new republic that must maintain the loyalty of a broad range of people. To create this vision of national unity, he wrote, "public education was proposed to strengthen the new Republic and bind together the increasingly heterogeneous population into a viable political community."[2] This laid the foundation, says Butts, for the common school movement, although it took a long time to achieve it.

Bernard Bailyn had another idea altogether. In 1960, he castigated historians of education for seeing public schools as the culmination of an ongoing process of improvement of education, as implied by Cubberley (and by Butts). Their incorrect view, he summarized, was that the public school came about from the early "delicate seeds of the idea and institutions" because "nineteenth-century reformers, fighting bigotry and ignorance, cleared the way for their full flowering."[3]

To Bailyn, this view of schools moving inch by inch to an ideal, public, and "American" education system missed what was really happening in the colonial period and thereafter. Americans were, of necessity, slowly giving up their European inheritance and cultural traditions, including family and church-based education, that had been controlled through the tightly knit family and kinship groups of European village life.

In America, the stress of living in a new "wilderness"; the freedom, opportunity, and sometimes necessity of moving away from home to open lands; and the need to be ready to change one's life and career as conditions changed, all led to the separation of education from the family. Thus, education at what we call the K–12 level took the shape of formal institutions outside the family more than it had in Europe. But these schools, and other forms of education, were far from uniform.

Bailyn considered the many laws that were passed in the 17th century—especially in Massachusetts, but elsewhere, too—as signs of the breakdown of traditional family control and hierarchy under the pressures and opportunities of the new, vast surroundings. "Within a decade of their founding all of the colonies passed laws demanding obedience from children and specifying penalties for contempt and abuse," he wrote.[4] Nothing like this would happen in Europe until Europe, too, began to experience an "opening up" of the traditional family and religion.

For New England, Bailyn's claim is amplified by historian Perry Miller. The Puritans became increasingly worried that their children were straying from religious and moral precepts. Instead of being a "shining city on a hill" (as Gov. John Winthrop had promised), subsequent generations were not living up to the example of their great Puritan leaders and were turning the land into "a moral quagmire." In 1647, this concern resulted in a law being passed that required every town of 50 or more families to provide reading and writing instruction, and every town of 100 or more families to provide a grammar school. The law is known as the Old Deluder Satan Act because it refers to Satan (the "Old Deluder"), who is always trying to pull people off the moral and religious track. How well the law worked is uncertain: In 1679, the leaders of the Puritan Synod "published a long and detailed inventory of sins, crimes, [and] misdemeanors."[5]

However, insistence that parents teach their children was not limited to Massachusetts, even in the 1600s. In Virginia, 1646 saw a law passed that "empowered local authorities to round up and send to public workhouses boys and girls who, whether by parental neglect or absence, were not being instructed 'in some good and lawful calling.'"[6]

Despite such anxiety about the children, and little public schooling—at least outside of New England—Americans became literate during the colonial and early republic periods. Historian Albert Fishlow calculates that about 90 percent of white adults in America could read and write by 1840, only a few years after the push for common schooling began in earnest with Horace Mann becoming the first secretary of the Massachusetts State Board of Education in 1837. Fishlow says that early "popular" education, described above, "successfully preceded an extensive system of publicly supported and controlled schools."[7]

The Changing Educational System

It is difficult to generalize about the prevailing educational system before common schools. For one reason, the gradual separation of education from the family to outside institutions placed more responsibilities on private teachers, the church, missionary groups, and communities, including town and state governments. One could call this separation a move to "public" education, but in Bailyn's view, it was a move to relying on outside sources for education.

Perhaps the biggest obstacle to robust private education funding in this new land of pioneers was that there were few ready sources of financial support for education outside the family. In England, where most of the settlers came from, education outside the home (primarily college and secondary level) had relied on endowments from the wealthy. In England, land had been extremely valuable, so large landowners could start schools somewhat easily. In contrast, in the colonies, land was widely available and could not be counted on to provide a valuable return. Thus, there was a continual need for funds for education. Such funds came from many sources, including parents paying to send their children to a "dame" school (a small school for young children, usually taught by a woman in her home), churches that sponsored charity schools, and lotteries authorized by colonial legislatures, to name just a few.

Historian Lloyd Jorgenson has emphasized the diversity of school funding in terms of private, charitable, and government finances. "Colonial and early national schools were neither wholly public nor wholly private," he has written."[8] In early years, "government financial support for voluntary (including denominational) schools, so common during the colonial period, continued well into the national period."[9] Jorgenson's book, *The State and the Non-Public School,* is partly intended to show that support for private or religious schools could, and did, include funds from government sources.

Bailyn and Jorgenson both emphasize the similarity of the experience faced by all the colonies: separation of education from the family and a move to reliance on the community in one way or another. But each region handled education differently, reflecting the culture and background of the colonists who settled there, as well as the varied regional geography, which determined the feasibility of local schools and school financing.

Perhaps the best way to see the structures of education—from teaching at home to dame and "parson's" schools as well as others—is to look at schooling in the major geographical areas during the colonial times and the early republic. We will, as with most education histories, start with New England. The region has been repeatedly studied and described and has often—incorrectly, perhaps—been viewed as providing something close to a public school system, although one deeply entwined with religion. Then we will look at the Middle Colonies and the South.

New England: Yes, Puritan

The Massachusetts Bay Colony was founded by Puritans in 1630. The group, dissenting from, but still a part of, the Anglican Church, was united by its religious fervor. (The Pilgrims at Plymouth were similarly united, but Massachusetts Bay was a more open society, which grew much larger and had a bigger impact.) The Puritans believed that Christians should be able to read the Bible, thus literacy was fundamental to their religion. According to historians Wayne J. Urban and Jennings L. Wagoner Jr., Puritans believed that only by understanding the Bible could the individual Christian "approach God in prayer and confession, without the intercession of a priest or minister."[10] The leaders—"saints" or "elders"—of the colony were by and large educated men themselves, some having attended universities in England.

Parents were responsible for education at the start. This responsibility was indicated by a 1642 law, sometimes called the first "school" law, but as Urban and Wagoner point out, it was more of an apprenticeship law. The statute "compelled heads of households to provide occupational training and ensure that their children learned 'to read and understand the principles of religion and the capital laws of this country.'"[11] A town had the authority to take children away from their parents if town officials thought the parents were not teaching them properly and "put them out for apprenticeship"—practical skills, not just literacy.

In 1647, the colony went beyond making education the responsibility of the family. The legislature decreed (with the passage of the Old Deluder Satan Act) "that towns with fifty or more families must make provision for instruction in reading and writing." Reading the Bible was essential to resist and evade the devil.

Furthermore, the law said, if a town grew to 100 families, it would have to create a school to prepare young men for Harvard College, the first college in the United States (founded in 1636). Such a preparatory school was called a grammar school, but it was more like a private high school that taught Latin and Greek. Towns that didn't follow the 1647 law could be fined, and some of them were. The law left it up to a town's citizens to decide who should pay the teachers—parents or the local community (in the latter case, presumably through taxation).

So what were the schools like in this highly coalesced, religious community? They varied. The family still had a major role in education, with parents and siblings often teaching the smaller children to read. "Children in households without a literate adult could sometimes attend a nearby 'dame school' if they lived in a village or town," Urban and Wagoner write.[12] A woman in the town would teach children to read, possibly along with her own children. Initially, wrote Ellwood Cubberley, the dame school—also called a "petty" school—was "a very elementary school, kept in a kitchen or living room by some woman who, in her youth, had obtained the rudiments of an education." Each child paid a few pennies a week. In Cubberley's view, the dame school became "the primary school of colonial New England."[13] Attending a dame school was the typical way children prepared for the more demanding grammar school.

The Boston Latin School was the first grammar school in America. Created in 1635, a year before Harvard, Boston Latin describes itself as the "oldest school in America." It was a college prep school, following "classical lines." Relatively few people were able to meet the demands of such schools, both financially and intellectually.

Clearly some entrepreneurial schools were private, but who owned the town schools mandated by law? In New England, religion and polity were difficult to separate. According to Urban and Wagoner, "the Puritan or Congregational churches in the [Massachusetts] Bay colony became officially established or state-sponsored institutions. The intertwined relationship of church and civil government was symbolized by the fact that often a single building—termed a meeting house rather than a church—was used for both religious services and town business."[14]

Urban and Wagoner contend that this close connection of church and state in the Massachusetts colony has led historians into a "Massachusetts myopia," seeing the colony's highly controlled education as the model for the future common school.[15] Indeed, the emblematic public education defender Ellwood Cubberley saw the New England school as moving "from a church into a state school."[16] In Cubberley's view, this was the spark that eventually lit up state schooling.

By the end of the 1600s (especially after King Philip's War of 1675–1676, which pitted Native Americans against colonists and their own Indian allies), Massachusetts colonists began to expand outside of town centers. This expansion meant that it was more difficult for children to attend school. The solution was for the towns to develop school districts similar to districts governing such needs as road construction and military recruitment. Thus, districts began to arrange for their own small teaching units. Cubberley quotes a public record of Worcester, Massachusetts, from 1731, which stated that many children could not attend school in "ye center of ye town," so the town voted that "a suitable number of school dames, not exceeding five, be provided by ye selectmen, at ye charge of ye town, for the teaching of small children to read."[17]

The Middle Colonies and the South

New England did not necessarily start public schools. From 1891 to 1893, two prominent school officials—Andrew S. Draper from New York and George H. Martin from Massachusetts—debated in educational publications whether the Dutch in New York or the Puritans in Massachusetts sowed the first seeds of public education.[18] Draper defended the role of the Dutch in New York on the grounds that the Dutch West India Company, which settled New Amsterdam to develop trade, started a "town school" (Urban and Wagoner's term) in 1638. Dutch settlers lived near New Amsterdam in small towns, and by 1664, 11 of the 12 Dutch towns had set up schools. By 1659, a "classical secondary school" had been created.[19] When the English took over New Amsterdam in 1664 and made it New York, the Dutch were allowed to live pretty much unhampered.

Martin disagreed with Draper, citing the close, state-like control by the religious state of the Massachusetts Bay Colony as the model for the future. At the time (the late 19th century), both Martin and Draper were trying to push the proper locus for public school control—the state or the town. To do so, each was trying to lay claim to the origin of public education. Furthermore, as Ronald M. Johnson wrote in a PhD thesis, it was "a supposedly historical argument but actually revealed a mutual desire to trumpet public education." And, "Their major concern, apart from magnifying their respective states, was professional and involved a desire to bend the record in support of public education."[20]

In any case, New York did have a long history of colonial education. The Middle Colonies also included New Jersey, Delaware, and Pennsylvania. Unlike New England, these colonies were composed of many ethnic groups with distinctive cultures and varieties of Christianity. No single religious denomination was as pervasive as were the Puritans in New England. Write Urban and Wagoner, "Here localized settlements of Dutch, Germans, English, Scots, Swedes, French, Norwegians, Irish, and other immigrants tended to isolate themselves from other groups and to establish groups and to establish church-related schools to preserve their linguistic, religious, and cultural distinctiveness."[21] However, the pull of opportunity (and necessity) led to more vocationally oriented education, such as evening schools.

Evening schools were first started by the Dutch as early as 1661 along with day schools. By 1690, evening schools for English-speaking students appeared in New York. Often called winter schools because they were open during the winter months, these started as schools for apprentices who were working during the day to learn a trade but who needed "rudimentary" learning as well—that is, reading, writing, and arithmetic. Robert Francis Seybolt examined apprentice indentures (agreements) in New York City during the colonial period. He found 108 indentures that mentioned attending evening school.[22] An example from 1705 stated that the apprentice would have "in Every Winter three Months Learning att any Evening School within this City, and to pay for the same."[23] Young women were invited to attend evening schools, sometimes in sessions just for them, and other times in coed classes.

Over the years, the schools expanded into a variety of trade-related skills. For example, a New York newspaper in 1759 advertised its evening school as offering "Writing and Arithmetic both Vulgar and Decimal, Interest and Annuity, Extraction of Roots of All Powers." Another school, in 1765, offered simple and compound interest.[24] Other subjects taught included "surveying, levelling, gauging, mensuration, dialling, geography, spherics, conics . . . architecture, fortification, gunnery," and much more.[25] Clearly, these schools were training young people for a variety of careers.

In addition, writing schools for young men were offered. These schools might have been viewed as trade schools because they did not normally lead to college. However, readable cursive writing was a prized skill in colonial times because of the need to prepare and copy legal, financial, and other documents. "Penmanship was considered a craft and was largely a male concern," write Urban and Wagoner.[26]

The South

The South had its own distinctions. Except for Maryland, the Southern colonies (those below New York and Pennsylvania) were not founded with a religious goal. As a result, the New England–type of church or town school was not available. Furthermore, the Anglican Church did not encourage outside schools because, say Urban and Wagoner, Anglicans "tended to regard schooling as a private matter."[27] In addition, in North Carolina and in parts of Virginia, the Anglican Church was not very strong, especially away from the seacoast. Nevertheless, individual clergymen could start "parson's schools," and their services were paid for by parents, many of whom wanted to be sure there was a religious element to the schooling. "In these schools," write Urban and Wagoner, "the quality of instruction mattered less than the fact that a minister served as the teacher."[28]

South Carolina and Virginia had large plantations. Initially, some of these plantations cultivated tobacco, rice, and indigo, but many became cotton plantations after the invention of the cotton gin in 1793. These family-based plantations were distant from one another, which meant that in much of the South, "town" schools were not feasible and plantation owners hired tutors to teach their children privately. Nevertheless, other kinds of schools could be found in the South.

In fact, a few Virginia planters founded schools as early as the 17th century, following the tradition of English endowments. In 1642, a school opened (at no charge) in Elizabeth City, Virginia, the result of a bequest by Benjamin Syms, a planter. In 1659, Thomas Eaton, a physician, left a bequest that led to another school in Elizabeth City, open to all. In time, others followed, although such bequests were not a major source of school funding.[29]

"Old-field" schools, or rural schools, were built on worn-out tobacco fields and were extremely simple in style and construction. Parents paid the fees, and it was common for the teacher at these schools to be someone who had "turned up" in the locale to start a school. Ellwood Cubberley said, "These schools were of all types, though mostly not unlike those of rural schools of elementary grade elsewhere."[30] These schools taught the basics, at most.

Schools Proliferate

Throughout the colonies, many people were concerned that poor children would not be taught the "rudiments" of reading, writing, and arithmetic. As a result, there was a move toward support of charity schools, which took different forms. Some of these schools were sponsored by churches for children of their own denomination. Some served only children whose families could not afford to pay, while other charity schools allowed some families to pay tuition and others to attend without paying. In the colonial period, the need for at least elementary education was widely recognized. And although the Anglican Church did not provide education outside the home, a missionary arm of the Anglican Church did.

The Society for the Propagation of the Gospel in Foreign Parts (SPG) set up and funded schools not only in the American colonies but throughout the British Empire. Founded in 1701 in England, its goal was to provide clergymen, books, and supplies to teach children in the British colonies, both colonists and Indigenous populations. In general, those who could afford it would pay tuition fees, while indigent children could attend without charge.

The SPG's work in the American colonies has been highly praised. Lloyd Jorgenson cited two writers who said in 1947 that the society was "the most important religious and philanthropic agency operating in the American Colonies."[31] Although the size and population of the society's schools are not known, Jorgenson found records of the number of clergymen who were sent by the society. These records give an idea of the geographical dispersion of the schools. He reports that between 1702 and 1785, the SPG sent 197 clergymen to the South, 149 to the Middle Colonies, and 84 clergymen to New England (despite its Puritan domination).

Another effort to supply elementary education was the Sunday School movement. Not a formal organization for the most part, the movement began in England when Robert T. Raikes, a newspaper editor in Gloucester, hired a few women to teach indigent children on Sundays. Teaching on Sundays made sense because many children worked in textile mills or other factories every day except Sunday. The movement became immensely popular.

The first Sunday school of this kind in America was started in 1785 in Virginia; soon thereafter, additional Sunday schools were started in Virginia, as well as in Boston, Massachusetts; Charleston, South Carolina; and New York. In 1827, one estimate indicated that the Sunday School movement had taught 200,000 children.[32]

The Free School Society of New York, formed in 1805 by a group led by New York Mayor DeWitt Clinton, was another successful education effort. Although New York had charity schools and religious schools, Clinton thought those schools were not reaching some children—possibly because these children were wandering the streets. These children had not been instilled with religious values, so Clinton and others wanted a "religious but nonsectarian" school.[33] The Free School Society expected, and obtained, funds from the state legislature to pay its teachers. "By 1814, the combination of private philanthropy and public cooperation sustained almost 800 students in free schools established by the society, and the growth continued in subsequent decades."[34]

Controversies arose with a group of Baptists, who wanted to do something similar to what the Free School Society had done—reach out to the nonreligious, but in a more sectarian way, and be paid by state funds. The legislature did provide funds for the teachers, but the fight for funding became complex because the Free School Society received some special benefits in land and buildings and the Baptists wanted those benefits, too. By 1824, the legislature had had enough. To end the controversy, it stopped providing funds for the teachers. Even without those funds, the Free School Society continued to sponsor schools in New York until a public school system began in 1853.

A Broader Picture

From the colonial period to the Civil War, academies conducted a great deal of education. Although the term "academy" has been applied loosely, it meant primarily a grammar school (what we would call a high school today), but this type of education lacked the emphasis on the classics—on learning Latin and Greek. It was sometimes called an English grammar school.

The Philadelphia Academy, started by Benjamin Franklin in 1751, appears to be the first such school. It consisted of three separate divisions: the Latin School, the English School, and the Mathematical School.

Given his background, Benjamin Franklin uniquely illustrates how Americans embraced education. Benjamin Franklin was the son of a candlemaker (another description was as a "soap boiler"), 1 of 10 children. Thus, he had a relatively humble beginning compared with most of the elite politicians he joined with later. Benjamin Franklin's father sent him to grammar school briefly because Benjamin showed intellectual promise. However, his father decided that because he could not afford to send Benjamin for enough years to prepare him for college, Benjamin should learn at home. His father hired a visiting tutor, George Brownell, who taught Benjamin arithmetic and writing.

"With less than two years of formal schooling, Benjamin Franklin became one of the most learned, original, and respected men of the Revolutionary generation," write Urban and Wagoner.[35] He accomplished this through self-education, entrepreneurship, and changing apprenticeships until he found one he liked: printing. By age 28, Franklin owned his own printing shop.

Franklin furthered his and his friends' education by starting a discussion and debating society called the Junto, in 1727, when Franklin was 21. Once a week, a group of young men, apparently professional men, tradesmen, and artisans of high intellectual caliber, would meet to debate and discuss a variety of subjects such as science and morals. Every three months, each participant was required to write an essay on the topic of his choosing. This club was a valuable education source for Franklin and his friends, and it lasted for nearly 40 years. In the 1760s, it helped spawn the American Philosophical Society, which became a leading organization for the study and exposition of science.

Similar organizations sprang up throughout the colonies, illustrating the American interest in self-education. So did the subscription library that Franklin and his friends developed. They started with donations of books and then members were assessed fees to expand the library.

Even so, in Franklin's day, to be "educated" meant attending a classical grammar school (like Boston Latin) and probably college as well. Franklin recognized that he was not at the social level of many people in Philadelphia, in part because his schooling had been so informal. To help others in the same predicament, he believed an American school that was not as classics-dependent as the college preparatory schools was needed. In 1749, he anonymously wrote a plan for this school. An excerpt from his rather charming, anonymous proposal follows:

> As to their STUDIES, it would be well if they could be taught every Thing that is useful, and every Thing that is ornamental: But Art is long, and their Time is short. It is therefore propos'd that they learn those Things that are likely to be most useful and most ornamental.[36]

Yes, the time might be short, but Franklin managed to propose approximately 20 subjects, ranging from modern history to horticulture and agriculture (with time for swimming). He thought that students should read some of the best English writers, such as Joseph Addison and Alexander Pope. Learning Latin and Greek, as required by the classical schools, would not be necessary, except for those pupils whose careers, such as divinity or medicine, required them, or if the students wanted to learn them for other reasons:

> And though all should not be compell'd to learn Latin, Greek, or the modern foreign Languages; yet none that have an ardent Desire to learn them should be refused; their English, Arithmetick, and other Studies absolutely necessary, being at the same Time not neglected.[37]

Franklin also sprinkled his proposal with references to admired writers, such as John Locke and John Milton, because they seemingly agreed with him on various points. Thus, he persuaded a group of leading citizens to support the creation of the Philadelphia Academy.

In 1751, Franklin laid out a more specific curriculum for the new trustees of the school. But the trustees never fully accepted or understood Franklin's reasons for his plan. As time went on, they restored more classical curricula. As David Tyack wrote in 1966, "He [Franklin] was useful as publicist and promoter, but the trustees seemed little disposed to honor his opinions. After a political disagreement in 1756, they displaced him as president of the Board, though he continued to serve as trustee until his death."[38] Over time, the school became part of Philadelphia College and later became the University of Pennsylvania.

Conclusion

The landscape of K–12 education in the colonial and early republic periods was a varied one. You could say that Americans made up their schooling as they went along. We see the forces of charity, self-interest, and community spirit all contributing to a complicated but customized education system. Many actors—clergy, dames, and entrepreneurs, to name a few—found places where their services were needed. The evidence that 90 percent of white Americans could read by 1840 is a testament to the success of a largely spontaneous system.

Notes

1. Ellwood P. Cubberley, *Public Education in the United States: A Study and Interpretation of American Educational History* (Riverside Press, 1919; Riverside Press, 1947), p. 91.

2. R. Freeman Butts, *Public Education in the United States: From Revolution to Reform* (Holt, Rinehart and Winston, 1978), p. 6.

3. Bernard Bailyn, *Education in the Forming of American Society: Needs and Opportunities for Study* (University of North Carolina Press, 1960), pp. 10–11.

4. Bailyn, *Education in the Forming of American Society*, p. 23.

5. Perry Miller, "Errand into the Wilderness," in *American Religious History*, ed. Amanda Porterfield (Blackwell Publishers, 2002), p. 33.

6. Wayne J. Urban and Jennings L. Wagoner Jr., *American Education: A History*, 5th ed. (Routledge, 2014), p. 22.

7. Albert Fishlow, "Levels of Nineteenth-Century American Investment in Education," *Journal of Economic History* 26, no. 4 (1966): 418.

8. Lloyd P. Jorgenson, *The State and the Non-Public School, 1825–1925* (University of Missouri Press, 1987), p. vii.

9. Jorgenson, *The State and the Non-Public School*, p. 4.

10. Urban and Wagoner, *American Education*, p. 30.

11. Urban and Wagoner, *American Education*, p. 33.

12. Urban and Wagoner, *American Education*, p. 35.

13. Cubberley, *Public Education in the United States: A Study*, p. 27.

14. Urban and Wagoner, *American Education*, p. 29.

15. Urban and Wagoner, *American Education*, p. 12.

16. Cubberley, *Public Education in the United States: A Study*, p. 73.

17. Cubberley, *Public Education in the United States: A Study*, p. 71n1.

18. Bailyn, *Education in the Forming of American Society*, p. 11.

19. Urban and Wagoner, *American Education*, p. 44.

20. Ronald Maberry Johnson, "Captain of Education: An Intellectual Biography of Andrew S. Draper, 1848–1913," (PhD diss., University of Illinois at Urbana-Champaign, 1970), pp. 115–16.

21. Urban and Wagoner, *American Education*, p. 42.

22. Robert Francis Seybolt, *The Evening School in Colonial America* (University of Illinois, 1925), p. 10.

23. Seybolt, *Evening School in Colonial America*, p. 24.

24. Seybolt, *Evening School in Colonial America*, p. 26.

25. Seybolt, *Evening School in Colonial America*, p. 28. Seybolt quotes a 1771 advertisement in the *Philadelphia Gazette.*

26. Urban and Wagoner, *American Education*, p. 38.

27. Urban and Wagoner, *American Education*, p. 44.

28. Urban and Wagoner, *American Education*, p. 20.

29. Urban and Wagoner, *American Education*, p. 21. The two schools merged to become Hampton Academy, and in 1855, the academy became a district public school in Elizabeth City County (now the city of Hampton).

30. Cubberley, *Public Education in the United States: A Study*, p. 425.

31. Jorgenson, *The State and the Non-Public School*, p. 8.

32. Jorgenson, *The State and the Non-Public School*, p. 13.

33. Jorgenson, *The State and the Non-Public School*, p. 14.

34. "New York Free School Society," Philanthropy Roundtable, accessed April 27, 2025.

35. Urban and Wagoner, *American Education*, p. 46.

36. Benjamin Franklin, *Proposals Relating to the Education of Youth in Pensilvania* [*sic*] (Philadelphia, 1749).

37. Franklin, *Proposals Relating to the Education of Youth in Pensilvania.*

38. David Tyack, "Education as Artifact: Benjamin Franklin and Instruction of 'A Rising People,'" *History of Education Quarterly* 6, no. 1 (1966): 10.

Chapter 2

Developing a Strong Education System in the Diverse Mid-Atlantic

By William H. Jeynes

Overview of the Situation

Pennsylvania, New York, New Jersey, Maryland, and Delaware were a diverse group of mid-Atlantic colonies and later states that were a great example of the United States' motto, *e pluribus unum* ("out of many, one"). There was also much diversity *within* these colonies and states. As historian Richard Bernstein observes, "The United States was a fragile nation seeking to hold itself together despite physical strife."[1] Given that fragility, there was a tendency in the early days of the country to seek peace and harmony, which were greatly honored qualities.[2] As the port towns of New York and Philadelphia grew into diverse cities, it became increasingly important to overcome whatever differences existed and to build unity and consensus on issues of central importance to the mid-Atlantic region.[3]

The ethnic, linguistic, and religious diversity of the mid-Atlantic colonies and states greatly affected education, with the kind of diversity that existed in a certain state or colony changing with time.[4] For example, in the 1600s, Dutch settlements dominated New York City.[5] As time passed, however, it would be accurate to say that both English and Dutch families dominated New York City.[6] In Pennsylvania, in about the same period, English Quakers, Anglicans, German Moravians, Mennonites, and Dunkers were among those who settled the area.[7]

The Keys to Victory

Those in the Middle Colonies were able to overcome their differences in language and ethnicity largely because of several factors. First, they realized they had common goals. Some of the foremost goals included wanting (a) a loving and civil society, versus the religious persecution that had been present for many decades in Europe, and (b) a strong and prosperous nation that would enable the colonies and eventually states to become like a new Europe, in contrast to the poverty that most Americans faced on their arrival in the New World. These goals were a direct result of their suffering both in Europe and in their initial situations in America. Suffering often softens people who choose a road of hope and faith. What emerges frequently is an attitude of "we need to make this work."

Second, even though those who came to the Middle Colonies were religiously diverse to some extent, they were nearly all from the Judeo-Christian tradition and therefore all honored all, or the vast majority, of the Bible. Ultimately, as people of different denominations were exposed to each other more, they realized they had far more commonalities than they had differences.

Despite the general commonality of denominations, some religious groups were afraid of certain denominations because they had been severely persecuted by those denominations in Europe for many decades (or even centuries). Those denominations were some of the more powerful in Europe, and the fear was therefore understandable. When one has been persecuted and learned to live in fear, it is neither easy nor wise to simply change locale and trust the same group that had persecuted you. With this in mind, it is laudable that denominational differences were often laid aside to emphasize commonalities.

This chapter examines the effects of these realities—common goals and a shared Judeo-Christian tradition—on developing a strong education system among the diverse populations in the mid-Atlantic.

Common Goals

At first glance, the mid-Atlantic settlements had little in common.

Pennsylvania

Pennsylvania grew at a brisk pace during the colonial period, throughout the 1700s and into the 1800s. This steady growth contributed to its role as a major center for government and business, and it attracted diverse groups of people from England, Germany, Ireland, and Scotland. By the mid-1700s, one-third of people in Pennsylvania were German and many of the schools taught in the German language.[8]

Maryland, Pennsylvania, and Delaware: Catholics Arrive on Mid-Atlantic Shores

As part of the diversity in the mid-Atlantic, Catholics settled in the area, especially in Maryland and Pennsylvania.[9]

Catholics named Maryland primarily to honor Mary, the mother of Jesus. In spite of Maryland being designed as a refuge for Catholics, people of many different denominations settled there.[10] Jesuits would travel around the Chesapeake Bay, spreading the word of Christ.[11] Catholics were also present in southeast Pennsylvania, where 9,000 of them lived.[12] In Delaware, the town of Canterbury, south of Dover, was popularly known as Irish Hill.[13]

New York

A number of historical highlights contributed to the geographical population diversity in New York and New Jersey. The first historical highlight was Henry Hudson's (1565–1611) journey through the New World in 1609. Hudson was English, but he sailed on behalf of the Dutch East India Company. He sailed up the Hudson River, which was later named after him. The second historical highlight was the Dutch purchase of Manhattan Island in 1626 from the Native Americans. Manhattan then became the centerpiece of what is now New York City, and it is the borough that is now home to Wall Street, Grand Central Station, the United Nations, and most of the nation's highest skyscrapers, among other landmarks.[14]

New England influences also seeped into New York. "By the 1740s an overflow of New England Puritans shared New York with an older immigrant population of Reformed Dutch and French Huguenots," writes historian Milton Coalter.[15] The Puritans believed that the father had a special role in a child's spiritual development.[16] This focus became influential in the New York area, while the Dutch initially "financed a town school in New Amsterdam in 1638."[17] While the degree of educational emphasis of the Dutch did not rival that of the Puritans and Pilgrims, it was nevertheless present.

By about 1815, New York had become the largest city in the Western Hemisphere, at more than 200,000 people. With the building of the Erie Canal in 1825, it became the nation's trading center as well. No other place in the United States could rival New York City's importance. As author Richard Platt shared, New York City was "simply the brightest, brashest, richest, loudest, fastest city on the continent."[18] Philadelphia also grew, in part, because it was protected by New York to the north and Baltimore to the south.[19]

The world's biggest ships went through New York. As Platt points out, in the early years as a state, "New York is now a financial center too, with major banks and two stock exchanges."[20] The New York Stock Exchange was founded in 1792, and New York became both the American financial center and one of the country's foremost ports.[21] By 1720, New York had already become a crucial center port, and as business became brisk, New York's harbor area was home to a number of the city's most crowded streets.

Finally, New York did not wish to fall behind in experiments in factory production. For example, a group of Oneida County businesspeople established cotton and wool factories in 1809.[22] By 1850, most workers in New York were in factories. The explosion of technological innovations in this period transformed the nation. National systems of transportation (railroads and steamship lines) and communication helped create a large, unified economic system.

New Jersey

New Jersey was home to distinct groups that settled in various parts of the state. From the 1600s into the 1700s, settlers from the Netherlands and those belonging to the Dutch Reformed Church settled in the northern portion of the state, across the Hudson River from New York

City. In southern New Jersey and to a degree in central New Jersey, there was a high concentration of Presbyterians. This distinction is especially interesting because even to this day, the culture of northern New Jersey is very different from what one witnesses in southern New Jersey. It is fascinating that cultural distinctions that existed a few centuries ago likely contribute to differences that exist today.[23]

Examples of Common Goals

Because Europeans came from several areas of the continent, where various languages were spoken, the mid-Atlantic region was linguistically diverse. Those who lived in the Middle Colonies developed an impressive balance in terms of addressing their linguistic diversity. On the one hand, they founded a copious number of schools that used a language other than English as their primary means of communication. On the other hand, there was a consensus that for both the country and its people to flourish, people had to be able to communicate with each other. Those in the Middle Colonies acknowledged that English was the primary language of the people. They realized that for both the nation and one's family members to thrive, everyone needed to learn English.

Educational practices of the inhabitants of the Middle Colonies reflected the diversity of the region. Essentially, each religious group sought to educate its children within the confines of the home, church, and community.[24]

In spite of the diversity, these groups adhered to certain axioms that helped the country become knit together. First, there was a real consensus among these different groups that cooperation had to prevail for Americans to reach their fullest potential. Given that the United States, even upon its founding in 1776, was a new and weak nation, working together for the common good was a necessity. New York became the most powerful city in the country and Philadelphia the most industrialized.[25] Philadelphia was also perhaps the most important center of science and technology.[26] Quakers, who were heavily involved in the establishment of Pennsylvania, believed that God had given human beings minds to understand the environment God had created.[27] New York and Philadelphia became the most urbanized states in the country, and there was a growing awareness among Americans that for the United States to succeed, its largest and most prominent cities had to succeed. That had been true in New England with the city of Boston. People in the mid-Atlantic realized that this was true regarding New York and Philadelphia, and they realized that education was at the heart of any common goals for economic growth, prosperity, and unity.

Second, in many cases, Americans had a shared vision, which was enunciated explicitly in the Northwest Ordinance of 1787. The original vision appeared in Article 3, "Religion, morality, and knowledge being necessary to good government and the happiness of mankind, schools and the means of education shall forever be encouraged." In this spirit, James Reed and Ronnie Prevost note, "Each religious group established its own school, the local minister was often the teacher as well. Those parochial schools served children in the middle colonies until the mid-1830s."[28] Wayne Urban and others observe that "Presbyterians, Baptists, Catholics, Dutch Reformed, Jews, and Quakers also established schools in their communities when population density warranted."[29] The authors go on to state, "Over time, however, as contact among groups increased, so too did tolerance for diversity and recognition of the need for civility and accommodation."[30]

People who lived in the Middle Colonies admired New England for its high literacy rate. They realized that "the high rate in Massachusetts in 1860 was achieved mainly by the fact that children attended private- or church-sponsored schools before 1830."[31]

Third, a number of these early settlements in the North attempted to do what they could to eliminate slavery. The Puritans and Quakers especially believed that providing schooling for African Americans was the key to eventual emancipation. In the cities of New York and Philadelphia, there was a belief that for the nation to reach its fullest potential, every individual needed to reach his or her greatest potential. This included slaves. Not only did the peoples of the mid-Atlantic area believe that slaves should be emancipated; they also maintained the conviction that emancipation was not sufficient.[32] It was important for the churches and the country as a whole to educate African Americans both in the North and the South. Those in New York and

Philadelphia believed that most of this education should occur before emancipation, because schooling—especially under the tutelage of those most passionate about freedom for all—would likely contribute to emancipation.[33]

Regarding the Middle Colonies, the early abolitionist movement in America was led by itinerant Quakers such as John Woolman (1720–1772). Many of the schools in Pennsylvania and other Northern colonies were largely integrated by 1700.[34] However, other schools were designed specifically to help African American families, who had escaped from slavery. Perhaps the most salient school for African Americans was the African school that Anthony Benezet (1713–1784) established in Philadelphia.[35] Benezet, a Quaker, called for his fellow Quakers to go more public and be more forceful with their anti-slavery convictions, especially with reference to eliminating slavery in the South, which was well beyond where Quakers lived. Largely because of his emphasis, the Quakers, including Benezet and Woolman, confronted Virginia about slavery and urged it to end the practice. In a Pennsylvania annual meeting, the Quakers asserted that it was not enough simply to free the slaves; members needed to educate them.[36]

To develop a strong education system among the diverse populations that lived in the mid-Atlantic area, common values were vital.

The Judeo-Christian Tradition

Many of the developments that transpired to advance education in the mid-Atlantic area were a result of the vast majority of the region's citizenry coming from the Judeo-Christian tradition.

Charity Schools

One of the most noteworthy developments in American educational history was the expansion of charity schools. These were private schools usually established by churches, beginning with the first grade, in which the vast majority of students attended for free. This was made possible by the generosity of upper-class and upper-middle-class citizens, who paid the tuition. The Puritans initially established these schools in the

1600s, but they expanded throughout the North following the Revolutionary War.

DeWitt Clinton (1769–1828) operated the largest organization of free schools in New York. He was not merely an influential educator, but also one of the most noteworthy American politicians in the early 1800s.[37] When he became a political leader, he earned a reputation for maintaining a presence in copious spheres of influence. Before becoming the head of the New York Free School Society, Clinton served simultaneously as mayor and lieutenant governor of New York City and State, respectively.[38]

One of the most incredible educational happenings following the Revolutionary War was Americans' desire to embrace the charity school concept on a broader scale. Although charity schools had been present since the days of the Puritans, these schools enjoyed unprecedented support after the Revolutionary War.

One of the foremost goals of the charity school was to reduce poverty and crime. These educational institutions were founded with the idea of developing stronger character among America's young. The schools operated with the conviction that a weak family structure contributed significantly to potential problems and criminal inclinations among America's youth. If these schools could help develop strong moral character and enable children to stay away from crime, the schools could perform an indispensable service for the community.[39]

The idea for charity schools has deep roots, dating back to the early 1600s in Europe.[40] The Puritans in Europe believed it was crucial to make schooling accessible to all and decoupled from one's ability to pay.[41] The movement was specifically a church-sponsored one with several goals in mind: (a) to reduce some of the social and moral ills often associated with a lower socioeconomic status; (b) to spread the gospel; and (c) to school children in the reading, writing, and mathematical skills they needed to succeed in society.[42] In fact, M. G. Jones notes, "The schools were of greater consequence to religion than any other design which had been on foot since the Reformation."[43]

Given that the immigrants who came to America at the time were largely from England, it is no surprise that they brought the charity school with them to the New World. America's first charity schools were actually founded early in America's colonial history. Probably the largest organization sponsoring charity schools was the society for the Propagation of the Gospel in Foreign Parts.[44] The society originated in England and soon expanded to the United States.[45]

Soon after the establishment of Harvard University and Boston Latin School, New England educators made it a priority to establish charity schools. The Puritans in England were the people most dedicated to the free school concept.[46] It is therefore only logical that the Puritans were the most committed to the free school concept in the United States.[47] Within early American society, it was understood that the small number of wealthy people that existed had a responsibility to support other members of society.[48] Therefore, wealthy settlers would pay for 20, 50, or 100 students.[49]

One of the most remarkable aspects of the charity school is the extent to which each teacher was adopted by the child's family and vice versa. In today's society, most families know teachers only from a distance. However, in colonial New England, teachers went to church with their students and often sat side by side.

One facilitating factor that enabled the Massachusetts free school model to proliferate was that many Puritans migrated and settled in Connecticut and, to a lesser extent, in other areas of New England. Once the Massachusetts model had spread to other parts of New England, it spread to the mid-Atlantic states, including New York and Pennsylvania. It then spread to other Eastern states as well. The Massachusetts model soon became the exemplary charity school model in the country.[50]

In this context, there arose an innovative Englishman named Joseph Lancaster, who had a considerable impact on American schools. Lancaster was born in England in 1778.[51] He was a school systematizer, as opposed to an originator. Lancaster greatly respected the Puritan charity schools, as he saw them operate in England. As a Quaker, he had a great deal of appreciation for the dual emphasis the Puritans placed on moral and academic education.[52]

A key factor in Lancaster's success, from a financial standpoint, was the willingness of many religious philanthropists to fund the establishment and operation of his charity schools.[53] Christians were enthusiastic about those schools because one of Lancaster's emphases was that children be given a "Scriptural education."[54] Consistent with this support, Christians were some of the first to apply the Lancaster model in their charity schools.[55]

The Place of DeWitt Clinton

As great an influence as Joseph Lancaster was on the American education system, he would not have had the influence he did had DeWitt Clinton not embraced his methods.

Clinton argued forcefully in Albany for a strong system of charity schools and the building of the Erie Canal.[56] Historians generally regard the building of the Erie Canal as the most important public works project in the 19th century.[57]

Clinton believed that the New York Free School Society should emulate many of the aspects of church charity schools that made them thrive. He was particularly interested in the success that churches enjoyed in educating African Americans.[58]

Given that churches undertook most of the country's education, the New York Free School Society emulated religious schools in many respects.[59] The religious inspiration was especially prominent in the society's moral education program.[60] Both Clinton and Lancaster believed in teaching the Bible in the classroom in a nonsectarian fashion.[61] They averred that this teaching should serve as the foundation for a school's moral education program. Over time, Clinton became very proud of the effectiveness of the moral education program. He stated:

> Of the many thousands who have been instructed in our free schools in the City of New York, there is not a single instance known of anyone being convicted of a crime.[62]

It would be hard to imagine a mayor of a major American city making this statement today.

Free Schools and African Americans

African Americans in the North quickly emerged as one of the primary beneficiaries of free schools.[63] Most African Americans in the North were freed slaves who did not have much money with which to pay for education.[64] Consequently, free schools emerged as the ideal means through which many could capitalize on their first taste of freedom.

Higher Education in the Middle Colonies

The momentum toward collaboration, cooperation, and unification in the Middle Colonies and states not only applied to elementary and secondary school education but also existed in higher education. For example, via a certain level of "compromise and conciliation, Columbia University (King's College) and the University of Pennsylvania (the College of Philadelphia) were founded by an interdenominational sponsorship."[65] Regarding Princeton University (1746), Columbia (1754), and Penn (1755), Roger Geiger states, "The new colleges of the New York-Philadelphia axis were products of the rapid growth of the economies and population of the Middle Colonies, although each reflected the distinctive demography and religious character of its surroundings."[66] The momentum of the Great Awakening (1730–1755) was the catalyst of evangelism that got these colleges going.[67]

Just as Christian groups led the way in the effort to start schools and colleges in New England (e.g., Harvard College [1636], and Yale College [1701]), the same was true in the more diverse mid-Atlantic states. Geiger observes that "Historians have accorded the Awakening a large role in shaping colonial colleges."[68] And Reed and Prevost note that "The movement was propelled by famous preacher Jonathan Edwards (1703–1758)."[69] In fact, Edwards was the third president of Princeton.

Meanwhile, Quaker schools "were free and open to all, including Blacks" and Native Americans.[70] "Quaker schools were also coeducational. Strict instructions were also used concerning disputes with Native Americans, which were to be arbitrated between six whites and six Indians with everyone treated equally before the law."[71]

There were Presbyterian churches, academics, and colleges throughout Pennsylvania.[72] Founding Father and Presbyterian Benjamin Rush was very active in education and asserted that the schooling of females should be just as vigorous as that for males.[73] He and other Presbyterians were asked to found a college in western Pennsylvania: Dickinson.

Technically, Dickinson was interdenominational, but its board was dominated by Presbyterians. As Judith Ridner states, "Through it all and regardless of their class stood their religion."[74]

New Light Presbyterians wanted a seminary nearby. Early in the 1700s, the American seminaries were located north and south of the New York, New Jersey, and Philadelphia area. The seminaries were at Harvard, Yale, and William & Mary. Presbyterians, cut out of the Great Awakening mold, were the primary founders of Princeton in 1746. George Whitefield started going on American tours beginning in 1739, and the effect of those revival services was tremendous. Governor John Hamilton signed the charter for Princeton, initially called the College of New Jersey.[75] It was a college for all religious denominations and included Native Americans.[76] The college started its operation in Elizabethtown, New Jersey, in 1746 and moved to Princeton in 1754. Presbyterian clergyman Gilbert Tennent helped the establishment of Princeton with fundraising in the United Kingdom. Nearly half of the university's first graduates in its first 22 years were ministers.

Religion remained the most important component of life, "even in the South."[77] Many Presbyterians and people from other groups known for their love, leadership, kindness, and intellect also contributed to the American public's embracing of the Great Awakening. It was not merely Jonathan Edwards, George Whitefield, John Wesley (1703–1791), and Gilbert Tennent. Others who had these attributes were William McGuffey, the primary author of the textbooks used in America's public schools, and Benjamin Rush.

John Wesley was a strong believer in educating children in order to increase harmony and "early piety" in American society. He was one of the founders of Methodism and modern-day Evangelicalism. Some people in the late 1700s and early 1800s focused on educating adults, but John Wesley believed it was also important to help build a more unified future. Reed and Prevost assert that "Wesley was concerned with the spiritual nurture of children and based his approach in education on the principles of sense realism and universal education."[78]

Wesley was an acquaintance and supporter of Robert Raikes, and Wesley and Methodism supported the growth of the Sunday School movement in England and the United States. "Wesley valued the home in the Christian education of children."[79]

The Great Awakening contributed to the founding of the nation. In the Second Great Awakening (1790–1840), people from colleges including Princeton, Brown, and Dartmouth often were powerful leaders in education and ministry.[80]

Concluding Thoughts

The history of American schooling before the vast expansion of public schools was in many respects a direct response to the extent of the diversity that existed in the United States.[81] Ironically, after this period, the answer of American government was to back public schools and to make it more difficult, especially through steadily increasing taxation for parents, to send children to religious and other private schools. One would think, realistically speaking, that increased centralization and bureaucracy were the antithesis of what was needed for a diverse population. With the United States having increased its degree of diversity since that time, it would seem the logical action to allow greater diversity in school options. This is especially reasonable because meta-analyses and the examination of nationwide data sets indicate that the pupils who benefit the most from faith-based schools, both academically and behaviorally, are African American, Latino, and poor children.[82] Will government and society respond logically and affirmatively to more school choice during this period in history? Time will tell.

Notes

1. Richard B. Bernstein, *The Education of John Adams* (Oxford University Press, 2000), p. 184.
2. Bernstein, *Education of John Adams*, p. 181.
3. Wayne J. Urban et al., *American Education: A History* (Routledge, 2019), p. 40.
4. James E. Reed and Ronnie Prevost, *A History of Christian Education* (Broadman & Holman, 1993), p. 296.
5. Catherine Reef, *Education and Learning in America* (Facts on File, 2009), p. 6.

6. Richard Middleton and Alan Lombard, *Colonial History: A History to 1763,* 9th ed. (John Wiley & Sons, 2011), p. 467.

7. Reed and Provost, *History of Christian Education*, p. 6.

8. Reed and Provost, *History of Christian Education*, p. 6.

9. Kevin Starr, *Continental Ambitions: Roman Catholics in North America* (Ignatius Press, 2016), p. 523.

10. Middleton and Lombard, *Colonial History*, p. 122.

11. Starr, *Continental Ambitions*, p. 503.

12. Starr, *Continental Ambitions*, p. 507.

13. Starr, *Continental Ambitions*, p. 507.

14. Richard Platt, *Through Time: New York City* (Kingfisher, 2010), pp. 15–19.

15. Milton Coalter, *Gilbert Tennent, Son of Thunder: A Case Study of Continental Pietism's Impact on the First Great Awakening in the Middle Colonies* (Greenwood Press, 2018), p. xvii.

16. Middleton and Lombard, *Colonial History*, p. 270.

17. Urban et al., *American Education*, pp. 40–41.

18. Platt, *Through Time*, p. 14.

19. Middleton and Lombard, *Colonial History*, p. 178.

20. Platt, *Through Time*, p. 19.

21. Platt, *Through Time*, pp. 19–25.

22. Janet W. Greene, *From Forge to Fast Food: A History of Child Labor in New York State* (AFL-CIO, 1995), p. 49.

23. Maxine N. Lurie, "Colonial Period: The Complex and Contradictory Beginnings of a Mid-Atlantic Province," in *New Jersey: A History of the Garden State*, eds. M. N. Lurie and R. F. Veit (Rutgers University Press, 2012), pp. 33–63.

24. Urban et al., *American Education*, p. 40.

25. Gary B. Nash, *First City: Philadelphia and the Forging of Historical Memory* (University of Pennsylvania Press, 2002); Judith Ridner, *The Scots Irish of Early Pennsylvania: A Varied People* (Temple University Press, 2018), p. 98.

26. Middleton and Lombard, *Colonial History*, p. 329.

27. Middleton and Lombard, *Colonial History*, p. 329.

28. Reed and Prevost, *History of Christian Education*, p. 296.

29. Urban et al., *American Education*, p. 41.

30. Urban et al., *American Education*, p. 40.

31. Larry K. Monteith, *In Pursuit of Prosperity: Education in North Carolina as the United States Becomes a Wealthy Nation* (North Carolina State University Libraries, 2020), p. 305.

32. James Proud, *William Penn's "Holy Experiment": Quaker Truth in Pennsylvania, 1682–1781* (Inner Light Books, 2019), pp. 301–14.

33. William H. Jeynes, *American Educational History: School, Society, and the Common Good* (Sage Publications, 2007), pp. 82–84.

34. Reed and Prevost, *History of Christian Education*, p. 296.

35. Reed and Prevost, *History of Christian Education*, p. 296.

36. James Proud, *William Penn's "Holy Experiment,"* pp. 301–14.

37. Jeynes, *American Educational History*, pp. 48–53.

38. Dorothie Bobbe, *DeWitt Clinton* (Minton, Balch & Company, 1933), pp. 69–78.

39. William Jeynes, "What We Should and Should Not Learn from the Japanese and Other East Asian Education Systems," *Educational Policy* 22, no. 6 (2008): 900–27.

40. M. G. Jones, *The Charity School Movement: A Study of Eighteenth Century Puritanism in Action* (Cambridge University Press, 1964), pp. 55–63.

41. Jeynes, *American Educational History*, p. 47.

42. William H. Jeynes, *School Choice: A Balanced Approach* (Praeger, 2014), pp. 32–33, 122–23; and Jones, *Charity School Movement*, pp. 57–61.

43. Jones, *Charity School Movement*, p. 59.

44. Bernard Bailyn, *Education in the Forming of American Society: Needs and Opportunities for Study* (University of North Carolina, 1960), pp. 13, 69–73, 106; and Jeynes, *American Educational History*, pp. 11, 38, 82, 84.

45. Ellwood P. Cubberley, *The History of Education* (Houghton Mifflin, 1920).

46. Charles Benton Eavey, *The History of Christian Education* (Moody Press, 1964), pp. 30–55.

47. Jeynes, *American Educational History*, p. 47.

48. Jones, *Charity School Movement*, pp. 55–63.

49. Jones, *Charity School Movement*, pp. 55–63.

50. Bailyn, *Education in the Forming of American Society*, pp. 26–27, 79–80.

51. Carl Kaestle, *Pillars of the Republic: Common Schools and American Society, 1780–1860* (Hill & Wang, 1983), pp. 34–38.

52. Kaestle, *Pillars of the Republic*, pp. 34–38.

53. Kaestle, *Pillars of the Republic*, pp. 31–38.

54. Kaestle, *Pillars of the Republic*, p. 36.

55. Kaestle, *Pillars of the Republic*, pp. 35–38.

56. Evan Cornog, *The Birth of Empire: DeWitt Clinton and the American Experience* (New York: Oxford University Press, 1998), pp. 48–53.

57. Cornog, *The Birth of an Empire,* pp. 104–16.

58. Edward A. Fitzpatrick, *The Educational Views and Influence of DeWitt Clinton* (Arno Press, 1969), pp. 52–53.

59. Robert Ulich, *A History of Religious Education: Documents and Interpretations from the Judaeo-Christian Tradition* (New York University, 1968), pp. 8–25;

and Stephen M. Yulish, *The Search for a Civic Religion: A History of the Character Education Movement in America, 1890–1935* (University Press of America, 1980), pp. 12–24.

60. Fitzpatrick, *Educational Views and Influence of DeWitt Clinton*, pp. 54–58, 152; and Ulich, *History of Religious Education*, pp. 8–25.

61. Ulich, *History of Religious Education*, pp. 8–25; and Yulish, *Search for a Civic Religion*, pp. 12–31.

62. Fitzpatrick, *Educational Views and Influence of DeWitt Clinton*, p. 54.

63. Charles C. Andrews, *The History of the New York African Free Schools: From Their Establishment in 1787, to the Present Time (1830)* (Negro Universities Press, 1969), pp. 10–56.

64. P. Wilson, "Discrimination Against Blacks in Education: An Historical Perspective," in *Social Justice and Preferential Treatment*, eds. William T. Blackstone and Robert D. Heslep (University of Georgia Press, 1977), pp. 161–75.

65. Urban et al., *American Education*, p. 40.

66. Roger L. Geiger, *The History of American Higher Education* (Princeton University Press, 2015), p. 33.

67. Geiger, *History of American Higher Education*, p. 33.

68. Geiger, *History of American Higher Education*, p. 33.

69. Reed and Prevost, *History of Christian Education*, p. 303.

70. Urban et al., *American Education*, p. 41.

71. Middleton and Lombard, *Colonial History*, p. 177.

72. Ridner, *The Scots Irish of Early Pennsylvania*, p. 49.

73. Jeynes, *American Educational History*, pp. 111–15.

74. Ridner, *The Scots Irish of Early Pennsylvania*, p. 5.

75. Coalter, *Gilbert Tennent*, p. 143.

76. Coalter, *Gilbert Tennent*, p. 143.

77. Middleton and Lombard, *Colonial History*, p. 309.

78. Reed and Prevost, *History of Christian Education*, pp. 275–76.

79. Reed and Prevost, *History of Christian Education*, p. 276.

80. Reed and Prevost, *History of Christian Education*, pp. 303–4.

81. William H. Jeynes, "School Choice and the Achievement Gap," *Education and Urban Society* 46, no. 2 (2014): 163–80.

82. William H. Jeynes, "Assessing School Choice: A Balanced Perspective," *Cambridge Journal of Education* 30, no. 2 (2000): 223–41; and William Jeynes, "A Meta-Analysis on the Effects and Contributions of Public, Public Charter, and Religious Schools on Student Outcomes," *Peabody Journal of Education* 87, no. 3 (2012): 265–305.

Chapter 3

Education Funding Prior to the Advent of the Common School

By Dick M. Carpenter II

Introduction

This chapter examines how schools in America were supported before the advent of the common school in the mid-19th century. In so doing, it focuses on the years beginning in the early colonial period and extending into the early republic. Although the chapter concentrates on educational funding, by necessity it also describes the types of schools or learning environments available to students of the time. It considers only schools or environments below the collegiate level.

It is important to note from the start that this chapter pays particular attention to schools (or other designated places of learning) rather than education as more broadly defined by historian Bernard Bailyn and others.[1] In seeking to expand the early 20th-century historical literature of education beyond its dominant focus on schools and systems by the likes of scholars such as Ellwood Cubberley,[2] mid-20th-century historians advocated for a broader understanding of education to include the entire process by which culture is transmitted across generations, including families, churches, and communities.[3] I do not discount the value of such an approach, but for the purposes of this chapter, my approach is more akin to Cubberley's than to Bailyn's.

A few brief historical reminders might provide helpful context. First, the period in question operated under a belief in and practice of laissez-faire government, particularly compared to the present age.[4] It was not until well into the 19th century that industrialization and organized social policymaking developed, both of which played a role in the common school movement.[5] Second, during these years, almost everyone in America lived on a farm or in a small village. For most people, life was essentially agricultural and pioneer. As Cubberley notes, as late as 1820 there were only 13 cities of 8,000 inhabitants or more in all 23 states at that time, and those 13 cities contained a mere 4.9 percent of the total national population.[6] Third, in Europe, Christian churches and schooling had been intimately connected for more than 1,000 years, and this connection was retained in much of the New World.[7] Of course, there were exceptions, such as apprenticeships, and those exceptions grew more common over time, but in most of the learning types described in the following sections, faith-based groups, churches, religious leaders, and religious content unapologetically played some role.[8]

Given this historical framework, the period in question can generally be understood as one dominated by a great diversity of schooling options funded by a loose blend of private and public sources.[9] The education landscape included home schools, town schools, dame schools, church schools, charity schools, old-field schools, academies, and Latin grammar schools, to name the more prevalent types. Depending on the geographic location and time period, most of these would have been funded by private or public sources or an eclectic combination of both. Indeed, as Bailyn describes, "the modern conception of public education, the very idea of a clean line of separation between 'private' and 'public,' was unknown before the end of the eighteenth century."[10] Moreover, as James Carper notes, "[a] school was public if it served a public purpose. . . . Public education did not require public support and control" as we understand it today.[11]

A Diversity of Educational Institutions

In the New England and mid-Atlantic regions, church schools, dame schools, town schools, Latin grammar schools (primarily in New England), charity schools, academies, and apprenticeships tended to dominate the landscape.[12] As the principal unit of early colonial society, families, particularly fathers, were the first and primary sources of learning the basics of reading and writing, among other things.[13] But outside the home, church schools were among the earliest educational institutions in the colonies.[14] They taught students not only religious subjects but also the basics of reading and writing.[15] Religious schools were typically funded by the congregations that established them. Church members contributed to the maintenance of the school through donations and tithes, and in some cases the church itself provided land or a building for the school. In addition to financial support from the church, parents were often required to pay tuition fees to cover the costs of their children's education. However, these fees were usually modest, and some church schools offered free education to children from poor families, reflecting the charitable missions of the overseeing religious organizations.[16]

Dame schools, also known as petty schools, were informal institutions typically run by women in their homes.[17] The dame school taught small groups of young children—boys and girls—for whom it often represented the first stage of education.[18] Instruction at dame schools focused on basic literacy and religious teachings, with students learning to read and recite prayers.[19] Although some dame schools eventually received modest public support,[20] most did not; instead, parents paid a small fee to the woman who operated the school.[21]

Town schools were more formal institutions designed to provide basic education in reading, writing, and arithmetic, and they were generally reserved for boys, though in some instances girls could attend as well. Throughout the colonial period, town schools grew in prominence as the centrality of religious life and dominance of church schools waned.[22] Town schools were funded through a combination of fees (waived for poor children), gifts, and taxes and were overseen by town officials.[23] As the colonies grew, town schools evolved into district schools. These schools were established as growing towns divided into smaller districts, each responsible for maintaining its own school.[24] District schools were funded through a combination of local taxes and contributions from the families who used the schools.[25] In some cases, parents were required to provide material goods, such as wood for the schoolhouse or food and lodging for the teacher.[26] This decentralized approach to education funding often resulted in disparities between districts, with wealthier areas able to provide better facilities and higher-paid teachers than poorer ones.

For (male) students who showed academic promise—and who satisfactorily completed dame schools or town/district schools[27]—Latin grammar schools offered more advanced education.[28] These schools were preparatory institutions for college and later the ministry, law, or medicine.[29] The curriculum at Latin grammar schools focused on Latin, Greek, and classical literature, along with advanced mathematics and theology. These schools were typically funded through tuition fees paid by the families of the students, though in some cases towns provided additional support.[30]

By the mid-18th century, academies began to emerge as an alternative to traditional grammar schools, eventually replacing grammar schools as the primary form of secondary education for boys and increasingly for girls.[31] Unlike grammar schools, which offered more elite content, academies offered a broader curriculum perceived as more "useful"—modern languages, science, arts, mathematics, rhetoric, and subjects related to commerce or business such as navigation and accounting.[32] The latter were increasingly seen as important as economic and social life in the colonies and later the states grew more complex and sophisticated.[33] Academies remained popular well into the 19th century, eventually giving way to and providing a model for modern high schools.[34]

Academies were private schools supported by churches, endowments, and fees, and sometimes by self-sustaining activities, as in the manual-labor academies popular in the South.[35] Governments at various levels sometimes contributed to academies, but the amount was rarely large and tended to take the form of assisting in the founding of new schools.[36] During the early 19th century, a number of states, including Kentucky, Indiana, Georgia, and Texas, adopted legislation to encourage the formation of academies. As one example, Indiana's state legislature passed the County Seminary Law of 1818, which granted the governor power to appoint a trustee in each county responsible for using county funds to support a local academy.[37] In another example, as early as 1792, the New York State legislature provided money to the state's academies and in 1813 established a permanent fund for support of academies. During the 1830s and 1840s, the state's academies received between 12.5 and 16.4 percent of their total revenues from the public treasury.[38]

The greater state contribution tended to be providing land for school buildings and granting charters for the creation of new academies.[39] In 1791, the Massachusetts General Court, for example, issued its first land grant to Hallowell Academy, which sold it in 1802 for $2,099. Later, a half-dozen academies (Bridgewater, Bristol, Framingham, Fryeburg, Milton, and Washington) had land grants stipulated in their acts of incorporation.[40] In the 1830s, Indiana and Iowa facilitated the creation of academies by providing land on which academies were built.[41] In 1857, Wisconsin passed "an act for the encouragement of academies and normal schools," which disseminated one-fourth of the proceeds of the sale of state-owned swamplands to academies.[42]

As for charters, the first chartered academy is believed to have been formed by Benjamin Franklin in 1753 in Philadelphia, but others were soon to follow.[43] In 1766, the colonial assembly introduced a bill to incorporate an academy in New Bern, North Carolina, the second in the English-speaking colonies after Franklin's.[44] Charters continued in the early republican era, with one in Granville County, North Carolina, in 1779;[45] Liberty Hall Academy in Virginia in 1782;[46] the aforementioned Milton Academy in 1798;[47] Episcopal Academy of Connecticut in 1801;[48] and Maine's Gorham Academy in 1805.[49] Edgar Knight provides a documentary history of charters in Southern states dating as late as 1858.[50]

Despite such state recognition, however, the schools saw little to no government oversight.[51] States' perspectives on academies are illustrated by New York State, where no restrictions upon the founding of academies were written into law. Instead, state law plainly said that no person or persons should be deprived of the right to erect such schools.[52] This was, of course, a period of national development and laissez-faire government.[53] Consequently, academies spread rapidly, particularly after the Revolution.[54] By the middle of the 19th century, nationwide at least 6,000 schools employed more than 12,000 teachers serving more than 260,000 students.[55]

Given such proliferation of academies, it's not surprising that many, although not all, educational options required some kind of payment by families. Because many families could not afford such payments, religious and philanthropic organizations—motivated by social reform—opened and operated charity schools for poor children.[56] These schools and other educational support for poor children had begun as early as the Pilgrims, but the late 18th and early 19th centuries saw the greatest activity in this sector.[57] Wealthy benefactors, religious organizations such as the Society for the Propagation of the Gospel, and free school societies were among the dominant funders,[58] but local governments also provided support, recognizing the public benefit of educating the poor.[59] Charity schools most often focused on basic literacy and religious instruction, with many using the Lancasterian or monitorial method,[60] but they also taught practical skills that could help students find employment.[61]

In addition to formal schools, apprenticeship programs were a common method of education, particularly for boys (although girls were also apprenticed) from poorer families.[62] Apprenticeships began in the earliest days of the colonial period and extended well into the 19th century.[63] In the usual custom, apprenticeship was an exchange in which the master received the service of an apprentice for anywhere from five to seven years, and the apprentice received instruction, room, board, and clothing.[64] While the primary focus of apprenticeships was vocational training, apprentices were often required by law to receive basic education in reading, writing, and arithmetic as part of their agreement.[65]

Such basic education did not, however, need to be provided by the master. Indeed, illiteracy among masters was not uncommon.[66] Some apprentices were sent to free town schools or fee-based schools, the latter paid sometimes by the master and other times by the local government.[67] Additionally, many apprentices learned reading and writing in Sunday schools. As the name implies, these schools operated on Sundays to provide basic literacy and religious instruction, particularly for apprentices and other working-class children who could not attend school during the week.[68] These schools often attracted large numbers of students, reflecting the demand for education among the working poor. In the early republican period, Sunday schools grew in popularity throughout all the states, eventually totaling approximately 6,000 schools.[69] Sunday schools were funded primarily by donations from religious organizations and individual benefactors, although some schools were supported with public funds.[70] They were typically free to attend, making them accessible to children who might otherwise have been excluded from formal education.[71]

In Southern colonies, a few of these same types of opportunities existed in larger cities, particularly charity schools funded by the Society for the Propagation of the Gospel or religious schools supported by churches.[72] But home-based education was more prevalent, largely due to greater interest in the South in reproducing English institutions, including education.[73] Southerners favored the English precept that education was primarily a private rather than public matter. Accordingly, very little legislation was adopted in the Southern colonies to create tax support for education.[74] Geography also hindered the development of schools in the South, which was significantly less densely populated than the North and dominated by farms and plantations.[75] Thus, home-based education, sometimes called mansion schools or family schools, predominated and often took the form of tutors instructing the children of one or more families.[76] Southern colonies and states also saw the establishment of field schools or old-field schools, which were typically small, makeshift structures located on unused or unproductive land, often in a field, hence the name.[77] Although field schools could be found in the Northern colonies (and later states), they were more common in the South due to the abundance of rural areas where formal schools were not feasible.[78] Field schools were usually funded by the local community, with parents pooling resources to hire a teacher and provide supplies, not unlike the microschools growing in popularity as of this writing.[79] The curriculum was rudimentary, focusing on basic literacy and arithmetic.[80]

Funding of Schools

Just as the types of schools offered in the period were diverse, so too were the funding mechanisms, which could include, among others, taxation, land grants, tuition fees, charitable donations, and community contributions.[81] Perhaps the most common form of support was tuition, fees, or other forms of direct payment such as material goods to schools or teachers.[82] Rate bills, whereby families paid for schooling based on the number of children attending and the number of days in attendance, also fall into this category, although the money was typically collected through the standard taxing mechanism.[83]

Schools—particularly charity schools and religious schools—were also commonly supported through charitable donations such as endowments, bequeathals, or direct payment.[84] These donations, which most often took the form of property (land or structures) or money, were seen as acts of public service and were motivated by both religious and social considerations.[85] Such support offset, either in part or in full, the cost of schooling and allowed children to attend without charge.

Although public funding of schools is often associated with the common school movement, such funding actually began early in most New England colonies, where laws required towns of certain sizes to establish and maintain schools.[86] Often this support took the form of taxation but was not limited to such.[87] Public support also included building and maintaining schoolhouses, paying teachers with agricultural commodities, and providing land that could be used to generate revenue or on which to house a school.[88] To these were added a variety of license taxes, sales taxes, occupational taxes, lotteries, bank taxes, fines for misdemeanor offenses, and proceeds from the sale of prizes of war to raise money for schools.[89] Such public support, particularly taxation, was initially less common in the mid-Atlantic colonies but grew more so throughout the 18th century.[90] In Southern colonies (later states), public support was rarer still and remained so well into the 19th century.[91]

The 18th and 19th centuries also saw an increasing number of towns, cities, and colonies/states across all the regions (including the South) create permanent school funds.[92] These funds (a) collected assets through donations, the sale of public lands, grants from colonial/state governments, and other sources, (b) invested the assets, and (c) paid for various types of educational costs.[93]

Perhaps one of the most consequential forms of public support was land grants. During the colonial period, commonly held or public lands were often dedicated to schools, and this practice was greatly expanded in the early republic when the Continental Congress appropriated federally held public lands to establish and support schools.[94] Although first implemented in the Northwest Ordinance, land grants continued under different legislation governing the admission of new states and eventually totaled 77,630,000 acres.[95] To support schools, land was (and in some places still is) exploited in different ways, including selling the land, leasing it, or building schools on it.[96]

Although this chapter has presented private and public support as distinct from each other, it is important to reemphasize that before the mid-19th century, the separation between them was unheard of.[97] From the earliest colonial times and extending into the 19th century, private schools, including church schools, were supported by public charters and appropriations of land and money.[98] And even as nonreligious schools began to proliferate, aid to private and church schools persisted. In Pennsylvania, for example, this continued until 1834. In New Jersey, laws in 1830 and 1831 permitted private and parochial schools to share in state appropriations. Massachusetts granted aid to parochial schools until the 1830s.[99]

In the 18th and early 19th centuries, schooling was a concern of churches, towns, entrepreneurs, and philanthropic groups, with some aid and encouragement from government in the form of charters, land, grants, taxes, and the like. Indeed, Americans of that era were not used to thinking of a division between public and private in support of schooling.[100] Consequently, it was simply not unusual for schools of all types to receive a mixture of private and public support.[101] In an era dominated by a belief in laissez-faire government, there was a vast difference between the principle of government support for schooling and a government system of schooling.[102] Paying for something did not, by definition, require providing it. Thus, to the extent that similar arguments are made today in advocacy of educational choice, it is an idea as old as and even older than the republic.

Notes

1. Bernard Bailyn, *Education in the Forming of American Society: Needs and Opportunities for Study* (University of North Carolina Press, 1970); and Lawrence A. Cremin, *American Education: The Colonial Experience, 1607–1783* (Harper and Row, 1970).

2. Ellwood P. Cubberley, *School Funds and Their Apportionment* (Teachers College, Columbia University, 1906); Ellwood P. Cubberley, *Public Education in the United States: A Study and Interpretation of American Educational History* (Houghton Mifflin, 1919); and Ellwood P. Cubberley, *The History of Education: Educational Practice and Progress Considered as a Phase of the Development and Spread of Western Civilization* (Houghton Mifflin, 1948).

3. Bailyn, *Education in the Forming of American Society*; and Cremin, *American Education.*

4. Michael Les Benedict, "Laissez-Faire and Liberty: A Re-Evaluation of the Meaning and Origins of Laissez-Faire Constitutionalism," *Law and History Review* 3, no. 2 (Autumn 1985): 293–331; Sidney Fine, *Laissez Faire and the General-Welfare State: A Study of Conflict in American Thought, 1865–1901* (University of Michigan Press, 1964); R. M. Havens, "Laissez-Faire Theory in Presidential Messages During the Nineteenth Century," *Journal of Economic History* 1, S1 (December 1941): 86–95; and Calvin Woodard, "Reality and Social Reform: The Transition from Laissez-Faire to the Welfare State," *Yale Law Journal* 72, no. 2 (December 1962): 286–328. But see Brian Balogh, *A Government Out of Sight: The Mystery of National Authority in Nineteenth-Century America* (Cambridge University Press, 2009).

5. Michael B. Katz, *Reconstructing American Education* (Harvard University Press, 1987).

6. Cubberley, *History of Education.*

7. Harry Gehman Good, *A History of Western Education* (Macmillan, 1960).

8. Good, *History of Western Education.*

9. James C. Carper, "Pluralism to Establishment to Dissent: The Religious and Educational Context of Home Schooling," *Peabody Journal of Education* 75, no. 1/2 (2000): 8–19.

10. Bailyn, *Education in the Forming of American Society*, p. 11.

11. Carper, "Pluralism to Establishment to Dissent," 11.

12. Sol Cohen, *Education in the United States: A Documentary History* (Random House, 1974); Cubberley, *History of Education*; Good, *History of Western Education*; Karolina Korytkowska-Ogrodowczyk, "Education in Colonial America During the 18th Century," *Studia Z Historii Spoleczno-Gospodarczej* 9 (2011): 29–42; and Maris A. Vinovskis, "Schooling and Poor Children in 19th-Century America," *American Behavioral Scientist* 35, no. 3 (1992): 313–31.

13. Bailyn, *Education in the Forming of American Society*; Carper, "Pluralism to Establishment to Dissent"; Hyman Kuritz, "Education and the Poor in 18th Century America," *Educational Forum* 35, no. 3 (1971): 367–74; Cohen, *Education in the United States*; Cubberley, *Public Education in the United States*; Frederick Rudolph, ed., *Essays on Education in the Early Republic* (Belknap Press, 1965); and Vinovskis, "Schooling and Poor Children in 19th-Century America."

14. Cohen, *Education in the United States.*

15. Cohen, *Education in the United States.*

16. Cohen, *Education in the United States.*

17. Cohen, *Education in the United States*; Cremin, *American Education*; and Jennifer C. Madigan, "The Education of Women and Girls in the United States: A Historical Perspective," *Advances in Gender and Education* 1, no. 1 (2009): 11–13.

18. Cohen, *Education in the United States*; and Madigan, "Education of Women and Girls."

19. Good, *History of Western Education.*

20. Cohen, *Education in the United States.*

21. Walter Herbert Small, *Early New England Schools* (Arno Press, 1969).

22. Cubberley, *History of Education.*

23. Cohen, *Education in the United States*; and Carl F. Kaestle, *Pillars of the Republic: Common Schools and American Society, 1780–1860* (Hill and Wang, 1983).

24. Cohen, *Education in the United States*; and Good, *History of Western Education.*

25. Cohen, *Education in the United States*; and Good, *History of Western Education.*

26. Kaestle, *Pillars of the Republic*; and Small, *Early New England Schools.*

27. Cohen, *Education in the United States*; and Madigan, "Education of Women and Girls."

28. Cubberley, *School Funds*; and Good, *History of Western Education.*

29. Cohen, *Education in the United States*; and Cubberley, *History of Education.*

30. Cohen, *Education in the United States*; Cremin, *American Education*; and David L. Madsen, *Early National Education, 1776–1830* (John Wiley and Sons, 1974).

31. Cubberley, *History of Education*; Good, *History of Western Education*; Edgar Wallace Knight, *A Documentary History of Education in the South Before 1860*, vol. 1, *European Inheritances* (University of North Carolina Press, 1949); Madsen, *Early National Education*; and Madigan, "Education of Women and Girls."

32. Cubberley, *History of Education*; and Madsen, *Early National Education.*

33. Kaestle, *Pillars of the Republic.*

34. Good, *History of Western Education.*

35. Cubberley, *History of Education*; Good, *History of Western Education*; Edgar Wallace Knight, *A Documentary History of Education in the South Before 1860*, vol. 4, *Private and Denominational Efforts* (University of North Carolina Press, 1953); and Madsen, *Early National Education.*

36. Cubberley, *History of Education*; and Good, *History of Western Education.*

37. Kim Tolley, "Mapping the Landscape of Higher Schooling, 1727–1850," in *Chartered Schools: Two Hundred Years of Independent Academies in the United States, 1727–1925*, eds. Nancy Beadie and Kim Tolley (Routledge, 2002), pp. 19–43.

38. Christine A. Ogren, "Betrothed to the State?: Nineteenth-Century Academies Confront the Rise of the State Normal Schools," in *Chartered Schools: Two*

Hundred Years of Independent Academies in the United States, 1727–1925, eds. Nancy Beadie and Kim Tolley (Routledge, 2002), pp. 284–303.

39. Good, *History of Western Education*; and Knight, *Documentary History of Education*, vol. 4.

40. Richard G. Durnin, "New England's Eighteenth-Century Incorporated Academies: Their Origin and Development to 1870" (doctoral dissertation, University of Pennsylvania, 1968).

41. Kim Tolley, "The Rise of the Academies: Continuity or Change?," *History of Education Quarterly* 41, no. 2 (Summer 2001): 225–39.

42. Ogren, "Betrothed to the State."

43. Good, *History of Western Education.*

44. Tolley, "Mapping the Landscape."

45. Knight, *Documentary History of Education*, vol. 4.

46. Knight, *A Documentary History of Education*, vol 4.

47. Durnin, "New England's Eighteenth-Century Incorporated Academies."

48. Durnin, "New England's Eighteenth-Century Incorporated Academies."

49. Durnin, "New England's Eighteenth-Century Incorporated Academies," p. 188.

50. Knight, *Documentary History of Education*, vol. 4.

51. Good, *History of Western Education*; Knight, *Documentary History of Education*, vol. 4; and Madsen, *Early National Education.*

52. Good, *History of Western Education.*

53. Good, *History of Western Education*; and Knight, *Documentary History of Education*, vol. 4.

54. Good, *History of Western Education*; and Knight, *Documentary History of Education.*

55. Cubberley, *History of Education*; and Madsen, *Early National Education.*

56. Clinton B. Allison, *Present and Past: Essays for Teachers in the History of Education* (Peter Lang, 1995).

57. Cubberley, *History of Education*; and Kuritz, "Education and the Poor in 18th Century America."

58. Cohen, *Education in the United States*; and Cubberley, *History of Education.*

59. Allison, *Present and Past*; Cubberley, *History of Education*; and Vinovskis, "Schooling and Poor Children in 19th-Century America."

60. Good, *History of Western Education*; Madsen, *Early National Education*; and Vinovskis, "Schooling and Poor Children in 19th-Century America."

61. Kuritz, "Education and the Poor in 18th Century America."

62. Cohen, *Education in the United States*; Knight, *Documentary History of Education*, vol. 1; and Robert Francis Seybolt, *Apprenticeship and Apprenticeship Education in Colonial New England and New York* (Teachers College, Columbia University, 1917).

63. Knight, *Documentary History of Education*, vol. 1.

64. Seybolt, *Apprenticeship and Apprenticeship Education.*

65. Knight, *Documentary History of Education*, vol. 1; and Seybolt, *Apprenticeship and Apprenticeship Education.*

66. Seybolt, *Apprenticeship and Apprenticeship Education.*

67. Seybolt, *Apprenticeship and Apprenticeship Education.*

68. Cubberley, *History of Education*; Madsen, *Early National Education*; and Vinovskis, "Schooling and Poor Children in 19th-Century America."

69. Madsen, *Early National Education.*

70. Madsen, *Early National Education.*

71. Kaestle, *Pillars of the Republic.*

72. Cohen, *Education in the United States*; and Good, *History of Western Education.*

73. Cohen, *Education in the United States.*

74. Cohen, *Education in the United States.*

75. Cohen, *Education in the United States.*

76. Good, *History of Western Education*; Cohen, *Education in the United States*; Korytkowska-Ogrodowczyk, "Education in Colonial America During the 18th Century"; Knight, *Documentary History of Education*, vol. 1; and Madsen, *Early National Education.*

77. Cohen, *Education in the United States.*

78. Good, *History of Western Education.*

79. Andrew Atterbury, "'Microschools' Could Be the Next Big School Choice Push. Florida Is on the Cutting Edge," *Politico*, July 24, 2024; Michael Matsuda, "The Rise of Microschools: A Wake-Up Call for Public Education," *EdSource*, August 19, 2024; and Ron Matus, "The Education Choice Revolution Is About More than Schools," Opinion, *The Hill*, July 21, 2024.

80. Cohen, *Education in the United States*; and Corliss Hines Edwards Jr., "Richard Malcolm Johnston's View of the Old-Field School," *Georgia Historical Quarterly* 50, no. 4 (December 1966): 382–90.

81. Bailyn, *Education in the Forming of American Society*; and Cubberley, *History of Education.*

82. Small, *Early New England Schools.*

83. Seybolt, *Apprenticeship and Apprenticeship Education.*

84. Bailyn, *Education in the Forming of American Society*; Cohen, *Education in the United States*; Good, *History of Western Education*; Kaestle, *Pillars of the Republic*; and Knight, *Documentary History of Education*, vol. 1.

85. R. Freeman Butts and Lawrence A. Cremin, *A History of Education in American Culture* (Holt, Rinehart and Winston, 1953).

86. Cubberley, *Public Education in the United States*; and Madsen, *Early National Education.*

87. Kaestle, *Pillars of the Republic.*

88. Cubberley, *History of Education*; Kaestle, *Pillars of the Republic*; and Small, *Early New England Schools.*

89. Cohen, *Education in the United States*; Cubberley, *School Funds*; Cubberley, *History of Education*; and Madsen, *Early National Education.*

90. Cubberley, *Public Education in the United States.*

91. Butts and Cremin, *History of Education in American Culture*; Good, *History of Western Education*; and Madsen, *Early National Education.*

92. Butts and Cremin, *History of Education in American Culture*; Cubberley, *School Funds*; and Madsen, *Early National Education.*

93. Butts and Cremin, *History of Education in American Culture*; Cubberley, *School Funds*; Kaestle, *Pillars of the Republic*; and Madsen, *Early National Education.*

94. Cubberley, *School Funds*; Cubberley, *History of Education*; Good, *History of Western Education*; Madsen, *Early National Education*; and Alexandra Usher, "Public Schools and the Original Federal Land Grant Program," Center on Education Policy, April 2011.

95. Sally K. Fairfax, Jon A. Souder, and Gretta Goldenman, "The School Trust Lands: A Fresh Look at Conventional Wisdom," *Environmental Law* 22, no. 3 (1992): 797–910; and David B. Tyack, Thomas James, and Aaron Benavot, *Law and the Shaping of Public Education, 1785–1954* (University of Wisconsin Press, 1987).

96. Peter W. Culp, Diane B. Conradi, and Cynthia C. Tuell, *Trust Lands in the American West: A Legal Overview and Policy Assessment* (Lincoln Institute of Land Policy/Sonoran Institute, 2005).

97. Bailyn, *Education in the Forming of American Society*; Cohen, *Education in the United States*; and Good, *History of Western Education.*

98. Cubberley, *History of Education.*

99. Cubberley, *History of Education*; and Madsen, *Early National Education.*

100. Madsen, *Early National Education.*

101. Bailyn, *Education in the Forming of the American Society.*

102. Madsen, *Early National Education.*

Chapter 4

Emergence of the Common School Ideology

By Charles L. Glenn

The "common school" was not so much a new phenomenon in the 1830s and 1840s as it was the slogan for an emerging way of thinking about popular schooling, one which has continued powerfully to influence public discussion. Notably, it has served as a primary rhetorical device for those opposed to supporting parental choice within a pluralistic education system.

This ideology drew in part from developments occurring in Europe in the 1830s, in the wake of the disruptions of revolutions and continent-wide war, as statesmen sought to build a sense of national loyalty through popular schooling.[1] The Kingdom of Prussia, patched together from disparate territories whose populations were traditionally Catholic, or Lutheran, or Reformed, had taken the lead in this respect during the previous century; American reformer Horace Mann would express strong admiration of the Prussian model. This nation-building project was emulated in Austria, France, and the Netherlands; French Prime Minister François Guizot wrote of teachers that "the state obviously needs a great lay body . . . exercising on youth that moral influence which shapes it to order, to rules."[2] Later in the 19th century, the successful leader of the Italian *Risorgimento* (national unification) was famously reputed to say, "now that Italy has been created, it is necessary to create Italians!"[3]

Horace Mann and his allies believed that it was necessary to create Americans on the basis of a model that left no room for significant differences over values and loyalties, or for the structural pluralism in society's institutions that permits genuine freedom and responsibility.[4] Notably, they lacked confidence in the common sense of their fellow citizens, "the capacity to educate themselves and their children."[5] Unfortunately, as Bob Pepperman Taylor notes,

> the American experience with mass education has been and continues to be importantly shaped by the kind of democratic anxiety that drove Mann to work so tirelessly. . . . It has also politically perverted and distorted this education from time to time in the past, threatens to do so in the present, and will likely continue to do so in the future as well.[6]

The Arguments for State-Directed Schooling

For 16 and more centuries in the West, it had not been government but churches that made sporadic efforts to provide schooling for the general population. Education under church auspices was—and is still, in most cases—a continuation or confirmation of the education provided in the home, a widening and deepening of fundamental convictions held by the family. Schooling under state auspices in the 19th century increasingly aimed instead at a fundamental transformation, substituting government-approved loyalties and perspectives for those with which children came to school and which were supported by local communities.

This emerging agenda rested on a conviction that society could be reformed—indeed completely remade—through the use of schooling as an instrument of policy. Immanuel Kant had observed, as an obvious truth, that "man can only become man by education. He is merely what education makes of him."[7] Here we see expressed the idea of the "makeability" of human beings and of society that would come to its full expression in totalitarian schemes of indoctrination in the 20th century.[8]

In both Continental Europe and North America, influential voices in the early 19th century argued that social cohesion and the preservation of national identity and purpose required that all children, or at least all children of the "common people" (since it was assumed that children of wealthy families did not require such intervention), attend government-operated schools. These schools should have as a primary purpose the fostering of government-approved dispositions and loyalties so that whichever school children happened to attend, they would emerge with the same civic virtues and orientation.

A crucial factor in the development of the state role in education was an expansion of the concept of the citizen. With increased discussion of alternative forms of political authority, there was a renewed appreciation of Aristotle's argument that citizens should be shaped by state-directed education to match the form of government under which they would live.[9] While this applied to all forms of government, it was especially the case in republics, according to French *philosophe* Montesquieu whose *The Spirit of the Laws* was widely read by American political leaders.

> It is in republican government that the full power of education is needed. . . . One can define this virtue as love of the laws and the homeland. This love, requiring a continual preference of the public interest over one's own, produces all the individual virtues; they are only that preference . . . in a republic, everything depends on establishing this love, and education should attend to inspiring it.[10]

During the radical phase of the French Revolution, in the early 1790s, it was an article of faith that "as long as you have not molded on the same form of virtue all the children of the Republic, it is in vain that your laws proclaim the holy law of equality."[11]

The United States seemed fragile to many during the first decades of its existence. As in Europe, many political theorists called for the use of schooling to solidify the sense of nationhood and commitment to social order. Samuel Harrison Smith, editor of the official newspaper of the Jefferson administration, wrote, in 1795, that "it is the duty of a nation to superintend and even to coerce the education of children." In light of this duty, "high considerations of expediency not only justify but dictate the establishment of a system which shall place under a control, independent of and superior to parental authority, the education of children."[12] This education, Smith argued, must be compulsory and not left up to the decision of parents.

James Gordon Carter of Massachusetts wrote, in his influential *Essays upon Popular Education*, that "[u]pon this topic of popular education, a *free* government must be *arbitrary*." The objective of educational action by government had little to do with economic or egalitarian goals; it was to shape future citizens to a common pattern. Like Rousseau and educational theorists during the French Revolution, Carter turned to the model of Sparta to illustrate what the state could and should do. "If the Spartan could mold and transform a nation to suit his taste, by means of an early education, why may not the same be done at the present day?"[13]

The "common school revival" that began in the late 1820s and received definitive form in the 1840s under the leadership of Horace Mann, Henry Barnard, and their allies in the Midwest was primarily a struggle over *education,* over the role of schooling in shaping the character of the American people, not over *instruction*, the imparting of skills and objective knowledge.

Ralph Waldo Emerson commented, in September 1839, that Horace Mann was promoting "the modern gloomy view of our democratical institutions, and hence the inference to the importance of schools."[14] What was troubling Mann and his allies in Massachusetts and elsewhere in the North? Partly it was the rapid social changes that accompanied economic development, concentrated in commercial centers like Boston and new industrial cities like Lowell. At first this involved native New Englanders moving from their unproductive farms, but by the 1840s that was eclipsed by a massive immigration of poverty-stricken Irish families.

Also important was the belief in an emerging "scientific pedagogy," based in part on the theories of Scottish phrenologist George Combe, whose book *The Constitution of Man* exerted a great influence on Mann and others. This new approach, Mann and others believed, would offer the means to effect transformations in human nature never previously possible. Mann asked, in 1846,

> How shall the rising generation be brought under purer moral influences [so that] when they become men, they will surpass their predecessors, both in the soundness of their speculations and in the rectitude of their practice? . . . The same nature by which the parents sank into error and sin, preadapts the children to follow in the course

> of ancestral degeneracy. Still, are there not moral means for the renovation of mankind, which have never yet been applied?[15]

Mann and his allies were determined to apply such means to shaping America's children, and its future. Mann argued, in his *Lectures on Education*, that "our greatest political hopes and energies . . . should be focused on the civic education of children," and he stressed "that the intellectual content of education has a foundational but strictly subordinate instrumental importance to our moral goals."[16] Thus for him, what we are calling *instruction* was far less important than was *education*, rightly understood and directed.

Implementing the State Role

Prior to the 1830s, schooling in New England and the Upper Midwest—which was settled by New Englanders—was provided primarily by local townships; the role of the state was to ensure that local government met its obligations. In the mid-Atlantic states, most schooling was denominational, with Pennsylvania and other states sometimes providing vouchers for children from low-income families to attend these schools. In the South, popular schooling of white children was sporadic at best (though North Carolina would make some significant efforts[17]), and that of black children usually forbidden.

Histories of American education cite Thomas Jefferson's 1778 "Bill for the More General Diffusion of Knowledge" as a landmark, though they do not always mention that the bill failed to pass the Virginia legislature. In fact, Jefferson's state did not implement anything like a universal system of public education for white children—not to mention black children—for another 100 and more years. Ambitious proposals for education reform bear no necessary relationship to actual provision of effective schooling!

Despite its limited practical effect, Jefferson's advocacy was largely in line with the goals of the movement that emerged in New England and the Upper Midwest. A proposal for schooling that he spelled out in 1817 was devoted entirely to the goal of forming citizens, stipulating that no one over the age of 15 would be considered a citizen of Virginia "until he or she can read readily in some tongue, native or acquired."[18] This was consistent with the concern he had expressed, 35 years earlier, in his *Notes on the State of Virginia*, that immigrants "will bring with them the principles of the governments they leave, imbibed in their early youth; or, if able to throw them off, it will be in exchange for an unbridled licentiousness. . . . In proportion to their numbers, they will share with us the legislation. They will infuse into it their spirit, warp and bias its direction, and render it a heterogeneous, incoherent, distracted mass."[19]

The actual implementation of Jefferson's program was not in his Virginia but in New England and the Upper Midwest. With James Carter playing a key legislative role, Massachusetts created a school fund in 1834. The following year, a bill specifying how income from the fund would be distributed stipulated that only those towns that furnished detailed information about their schools would receive aid, thus introducing an instrument for coercion by the state. Following up, in 1837, the legislature voted to create a state Board of Education to provide advice on how schools could be improved.

At the beginning of the 19th century, the *instruction*—reading, writing, and arithmetic, as well as local behavioral norms—provided in Massachusetts and other northern states was in general quite adequate to the economic needs of the day. There is little evidence of grassroots demand for fundamental reform of the schooling available. To the extent that parents were dissatisfied, they made their views known locally, and if these were not addressed adequately, they turned to the private academies that were widely available.

The primary contribution of Horace Mann and his allies in other states to American popular schooling was in the elaboration of new justifications for and structures of state influence over local schools and the local government that managed them, in the interest of an ambitious state-guided agenda of *education*. The actual reforms that gathered momentum in the 1830s, by contrast, "the demand for better teachers and school houses, the use of publicity and publication, even teachers' institutes, appeared in New England and the Midwest prior to Mann's appointment to his position of state leadership."[20]

There can be no question, however, that the publicity that he and Henry Barnard of Connecticut gave to the achievements of popular schooling in German states—most notably, Prussia, where the state took the lead in promoting and controlling its development, and the skillful use which they made of the collection and publication of data about schools—gave a new prominence to state action. In a decisive shift of focus, the 1830s and 1840s saw legislation proposed and sometimes adopted in state after state, which strengthened considerably the oversight of state government over local schools; indeed, "the common school revival should perhaps more accurately be titled state initiative or interference."[21]

In a sense, the emergence in the United States of the common school ideology did not change much in the actual provision of schooling for some years. In the Northeast and Upper Midwest, elementary schools continued—and continue to this day—to be operated by local districts, which selected the teachers and oversaw the instruction provided. Cities generally included a number of districts, each with its own school or schools. It was only gradually that the new agenda imposed itself through state regulations and state provision of teacher training.

In several states, the public was reluctant to support an enhanced state role in overseeing the schooling provided—and paid for—at the local level. In the long run, however, anxiety about immigration and the growing role of Catholicism produced broad political support for state supervision of public schools.[22] Connecticut, having abolished Henry Barnard's position as state superintendent in 1840, restored it in 1845 and "under a strongly nativist government in the 1850s, passed laws to strengthen consolidation and central supervision" of schools.[23]

Historians of American popular education agree that "by 1850 almost every northern state was well on the way to a permanent and systematic provision for common schools controlled by state officials and supported largely if not exclusively by public monies."[24] Twenty-four of 30 states had appointed a state official responsible for encouraging and overseeing local efforts to provide schools. In most cases, there was a state fund to supplement the efforts of local communities, and this in turn "hastened centralization of power by the states," since state legislatures could make compliance with their directives a condition for the receipt of this support. "States imposed requirements for participation in the funds, including the submission of statistical reports, the raising of local taxes, the hiring of only certified teachers, and the holding of school sessions for the term set by law."[25]

Calvin Wiley in North Carolina, Charles Fenton Mercer and Henry Ruffner in Virginia, William Perry in Alabama, Robert Breckinridge in Kentucky, and others less well known did their best to create adequate schooling in the South; in the Midwest, John Pierce and Isaac Crary of Michigan, Caleb Mills of Indiana, Samuel Lewis and Calvin Stowe of Ohio, John Mason Peck and Ninian Edwards of Illinois, and many others labored with rather more success. Many of the reformers were themselves transplanted New Englanders who sought to reproduce the model of schooling that they had known in Massachusetts or Connecticut.

It was Horace Mann, with his *Annual Reports of the Secretary of the Board of Education* (read in Europe and Latin America as well as among American reformers), who articulated most persuasively the state's role in guiding popular schooling. Perhaps the key to his influence was the conviction with which he asserted the wonders that properly guided public schools could accomplish. In 1841, he claimed enthusiastically that

> the Common School is the greatest discovery ever made by man. . . . Other social organizations are curative and remedial; this is preventive and an antidote. . . . Let the Common School be expanded to its capabilities, let it be worked with the efficiency of which it is susceptible, and nine tenths of the crimes in the penal code would become obsolete; the long catalogue of human ills would be abridged.[26]

Similarly, in 1846, he insisted that "as an innovation upon all preexisting policy and usages, the establishment of Free Schools was the boldest ever promulgated, since the commencement of the Christian era."[27]

What could be accomplished through a state-directed system of schooling, Mann and his allies believed, was almost unlimited. In its *Third Report*, drafted by Mann, the Board of Education stressed that "the state, in its sovereign capacity, has the deepest interest in this matter" of popular enlightenment. In this way, the state could "call into existence an order of men" who would be unlike any before.[28] One is reminded of efforts a century later to use schooling to create the "New Soviet Man" and parallel efforts in Nazi Germany and Fascist Italy.

In his last report as secretary of the Board of Education, Mann reported, on the basis of a survey of some of his fellow reformers (as if they were impartial judges!),

> their belief, that, if all the children in the community, from the age of four years to that of sixteen, could be brought within the reformatory and elevating influences of good schools, the dark host of private vices and public crimes, which now embitter domestic peace and stain the civilization of the age, might, in ninety-nine cases of every hundred, be banished from the world. . . . without any miracle, without any extraordinary sacrifices, of costly effort, but only by working our existing Common School system with such a degree of vigor as can easily be put forth, and at such an expense as even the poorest community can easily bear.[29]

And he affirmed his own conviction that the common school was "the most effective and benignant of all the forces of civilization," in large part because of the "universality of its operation."[30] That is, because it was intended to allow no variation of mission to accommodate the demands of a pluralistic society, and one growing more so with immigration.

Despite these high ambitions for a coherent, centrally directed popular schooling, almost all the initiative and the responsibility to provide schooling remained at the local level. Even toward the end of the 19th century, the state departments of education were usually staffed only by the superintendent or commissioner and his clerk; the former "distributed money to districts from the common school fund, collected statistics, prepared annual reports, and gave speeches to arouse greater enthusiasm for the latest improvements in schooling. But even the most eminent superintendent had little direct power to regulate education."[31]

Despite this limited state jurisdiction, Mann and other reformers were deeply opposed to any rivals to the common school and saw the defeat of private schooling as a high priority. Although this is commonly attributed to anti-Catholicism, it was already evident before immigrants began to establish Catholic schools. In a long series of articles that he wrote for his new *Common School Journal*, Mann urged "the professional men of Massachusetts" to put their own children in the common schools rather than in private academies, warning that, otherwise, "the distinctions of the dark ages, and of aristocratic governments, will be revived on these happy shores."[32]

Controversy over Religion in Popular Schooling

Mann was even more urgently opposed to schools representing a distinctive religious viewpoint, warning, in his first annual report as secretary of the Board of Education, that

> the tendency of the private school system is to assimilate our modes of education to those of England, where churchmen and dissenters . . . maintain separate schools, in which children are taught, from their tenderest years, to wield the sword of polemics with fatal dexterity; and where the gospel, instead of being a temple of peace, is converted into an armory of deadly weapons, for social, interminable warfare. Of such disastrous consequences, there is but one remedy and one preventive. It is the elevation of the common schools.[33]

Not that he was opposed to religion in public schools; to the contrary, he insisted that he promoted it, arguing that it would be provided more consistently in the state-guided common schools, and in a form that would be broadly acceptable. Mann asked in his 1845 *Annual Report,*

> How many are there of those, who swarm in our cities, and who are scattered throughout our hundreds of towns who, save in the public schools, receive no religious instruction? They hear it not from the lips of an ignorant and a vicious parent. They receive it not at the sabbath school, or from the pulpit. And, if in the Common School, the impulses of their souls are not awakened and directed by judicious religious instruction, they will grow up, active in error, and fertile in crime.[34]

Before the bitter controversies that would arise over Catholic schools, Mann was strongly critical of the Shaker community of the rural community of Shirley, which refused to allow the town authorities to examine their teacher or inspect their school. Mann considered this a very dangerous precedent:

> If a difference of opinion, on collateral subjects [of course, the Shakers did not consider their religious beliefs "collateral"] were to lead to secession, and to exclusive educational establishments among us, it is obvious that all the multiplication of power which is now derived from union and concert of action would be lost. . . . If once the principle of secession be admitted, because of differences in religious opinion, all hope of sustaining the system itself must be abandoned. . . . Our school system—alike the glory of the past, and the hope of the future—would be broken into fragments. . . . Civilization would counter-march, retracing its steps far more rapidly than it had ever advanced . . . whoever would instigate desertion, or withdraw resources, from the common cause is laboring, either ignorantly or willfully, to shroud the land in the darkness of the middle ages, and to reconstruct those oppressive institutions of former times, from which our fathers achieved the deliverance of this country.[35]

If this seems rather extreme language to apply to the desire of the world-shunning little Shaker community to be left alone to raise the foster children they had taken in, it is an indication of how much Mann believed was at stake when he insisted on the importance of creating a single system of elementary education for all children under state supervision.

The common school was intended to be deeply religious—indeed, Mann argued, *more* authentically religious than "sectarian" schools—in an optimistic mode that had no place for sin and redemption. This, he contended, would usher in an age of unprecedented social and personal felicity. Mann was indignant when his efforts were resisted by some stubbornly orthodox Protestants, as they would be more notably by Catholics as their growing presence took institutional form. One of his early Protestant opponents wrote, "I have not accused Mr. Mann with being opposed to what *he calls* religion in the schools. On the contrary, I charge him with being a dogmatist—a sectarian, zealous and confident, as all sectarians are. . . . If I may not teach native depravity in schools, because the Constitution forbids it, may you teach native holiness?"[36]

One of the most thoughtful critics of Mann's common school agenda, Orestes Brownson, charged in 1839 that these educational reforms, as Christopher Lasch explained, "far from democratizing intelligence, would create a modern form of priesthood by setting up an educational establishment empowered to impose the 'opinions now dominant' on the common schools. 'We may as well have a religion established by law,' Brownson maintained, 'as a state-defined system of education.'"[37] He did not "deny that there is a role for the state government in public education, but he would confine this to raising revenue. When it comes to curriculum and teacher selection, power should be left in the hands of the parents in their local districts."[38]

As was occurring around the same time in France and the Netherlands, such attempts by the state to form the character and convictions of its young citizens came into conflict with religious institutions and with parents.[39] It was as the state sought to impose uniformity of values and loyalties that conflicts over education—conflicts that have continued, in one form or another, down to the present—became a constant theme of American politics. In fact, despite his fine rhetoric, "an intolerance for substantive ambiguity, debate, and disagreement haunted Mann's common schools. . . . Because Mann aimed to promote an education that would eliminate significant democratic disagreement, he failed to plan for precisely the kind of skills required by democratic citizens in a real democratic society."[40]

Summary

Horace Mann and his allies, in promoting the ideology of the common school, were consciously setting themselves against three assumptions that, working together in various configurations, had shaped the purposes and functioning of schools in Europe and its colonies for centuries.

The first was that families would have the primary role in shaping the values and the loyalties—the "settled dispositions"—of youth, as well as teaching them those skills most immediately necessary for a productive life. These skills included some basic mathematics, but not necessarily reading, much less writing.

The second assumption was that local communities would be concerned if any children were "running wild," and might intervene to chastise or, in extreme cases, even to replace their parents. The appropriate nurturing of children was thus to some extent a shared community responsibility. This nurturing might include providing some formal schooling.

The third was that the local church would be a focal point for such schooling and that, in areas where there were competing churches, there might be competing schools. Thus, the Prussian government expected Protestant and Catholic pastors to supervise local Protestant and Catholic schools on behalf of the state,[41] while in Scotland and in New England, pastors commonly played a leading role in selecting teachers and supervising schools.

Schools would naturally vary in quality and assumptions about what their pupils would learn, depending on the demands of the local economy as well as on cultural expectations that were often based on the prevailing local religious tradition. Thus, many studies have found that in Europe, the literacy level achieved was higher in predominantly Protestant than in predominantly Catholic areas as a result of the Protestant expectation that adults—women as well as men—would read the Bible as well as devotional materials for themselves.

Families, local communities, and religious institutions together provided not only the instruction in skills and knowledge considered necessary for the future lives of children, but also supplied an education in family, local, and religious traditions. These necessarily diverse influences competed with the agenda of the common school as articulated by Mann and his allies. The objection of the reformers was not to a failure to teach basic literacy or the prerequisites for blacksmithing or farming, but to the likelihood that allowing children in different communities and from families of varied religious and other perspectives would foster societal pluralism and thus frustrate their effort to create a unified and improved model of citizen.

In contrast to families, local communities, and religious institutions, the common school was intended by its advocates to serve a higher purpose that previous generations had been insufficiently "enlightened" to embrace. Whereas schooling had been thought of primarily as a means of passing on to children the habits, the skills, and the loyalties that had served previous generations, it now was to have a transformative role, liberating children from the influence of their families and their communities. Just as, a century later, totalitarian regimes in Germany and the Soviet Union would seek to reshape their subjects through schooling, so did Horace Mann and his allies, though without the unlimited authority necessary to achieve their goal.

This agenda was frustrated by the strong localism of American society, especially with regard to deeply held values. Alexis de Tocqueville noted, during his visit in the early 1830s, that "one encounters no one among the inhabitants of New England . . . who recognizes in the government of the state the right to intervene in the direction of interests that are purely the township's."[42] As a result of this tradition of localism, today, with some 13,000 school districts employing and evaluating school staff, the common school program of institutional uniformity in the interest of societal and cultural uniformity has never been realized.

The more persistent effect of this ideology has been a remarkably effective resistance to government support of alternatives to the local public school. Long after the European models of state direction of schooling so admired by Horace Mann began to accommodate and provide government funding to nonpublic schools, the education establishment in the United States was able to wield the ideology of the common school as the only guarantor of social unity and citizenship.[43] Only in recent years has the misleading and indeed dangerous effect of this ideology become apparent, and a healthy educational pluralism begun to take its place.

Notes

1. See Charles L. Glenn, *The Myth of the Common School* (University of Massachusetts Press, 1988); Charles L. Glenn, *Contrasting Models of State and School: A Comparative Historical Study of Parental Choice and State Control* (Continuum, 2011).

2. Pierre Rosanvallon, *Le moment Guizot* (Gallimard, 1985), pp. 232–33.

3. Although usually attributed to Massimo d'Azeglio in this form, in fact, the idea first appears negatively in his posthumous memoirs *I miei ricordi* (1867): "pur

troppo s'è fatta l'Italia, ma non si fanno gli Italiani," in Simonetta Soldani and Gabriele Turi, *Fare gli italiani: Scuola e cultura nell'Italia contemporanea. I. La nascita dello Stato nazionale,* (Il Mulino, 1993), p. 17.

4. See Ashley Rogers Berner, *Educational Pluralism and Democracy: How to Handle Indoctrination, Promote Exposure, and Rebuild America's Schools* (Harvard Education Press, 2024).

5. Christopher Lasch, *The True and Only Heaven: Progress and Its Critics* (W. W. Norton, 1991), p. 190.

6. Bob Pepperman Taylor, *Horace Mann's Troubling Legacy: The Education of Democratic Citizens* (University Press of Kansas, 2010), pp. 14–15.

7. Immanuel Kant, *Education* (University of Michigan Press, 1960), p. 6.

8. See Charles L. Glenn, *Educational Freedom in Eastern Europe*, 2nd ed. (Cato Institute, 1995).

9. Aristotle, *Politics,* trans. H. Rackham (Harvard University Press, 1944), book 8, chapter 1, section 1337a, p. 635.

10. Montesquieu (Charles Louis de Secondat), *The Spirit of the Laws*, trans. and ed. Anne M. Cohler, Basia Carolyn Miller, and Harold Samuel Stone (Cambridge University Press, 1989), p. 72.

11. Carol Blum, *Rousseau and the Republic of Virtue: The Language of Politics in the French Revolution* (Cornell University Press, 1986), p. 187; see Glenn, *Myth of the Common School*, pp. 19–29.

12. Samuel Harrison Smith, "Remarks on Education," in *Essays on Education in the Early Republic*, ed. Frederick Rudolph (Harvard University Press, 1965), p. 210.

13. James G. Carter, *Essays upon Popular Education, Containing a Particular Examination of the Schools of Massachusetts, and an Outline of an Institution for the Education of Teachers* (Bowles and Dearborn, 1826), pp. 48, 16.

14. Quoted from Emerson's *Journals* for September 14, 1839, in Arthur Burr Darling, *Political Change in Massachusetts, 1824–1848: A Study of Liberal Movements in Politics* (Yale University Press, 1925), p. 250n.

15. Horace Mann, *Ninth Annual Report of the Board of Education, Together with the Ninth Annual Report of the Secretary of the Board* (Dutton and Wentworth, 1846), pp. 64–65.

16. Taylor, *Horace Mann's Troubling Legacy*, pp. 31, 52.

17. Luther L. Gobbel, *Church-State Relationships in Education in North Carolina Since 1776* (Duke University Press, 1938).

18. Lorraine Smith Pangle and Thomas L. Pangle, *The Learning of Liberty: The Educational Ideas of the American Founders* (University Press of Kansas, 1993), p. 115.

19. Thomas Jefferson, *Writings*, ed. WMerrill Peterson (The Library of America, 1984), p. 211.

20. Edith Nye MacMullen, *In the Cause of True Education: Henry Barnard and Nineteenth-Century School Reform* (Yale University Press, 1991), p. 341.

21. MacMullen, *In the Cause of True Education,* p. 119.

22. Glenn, "Social Anxiety and the Common School," chap. 3 in *Myth of the Common School.*

23. Carl F. Kaestle, *Pillars of the Republic: Common Schools and American Society, 1780–1860* (Hill and Wang, 1983), p. 219.

24. Rush Welter, *Popular Education and Democratic Thought in America* (Columbia University Press, 1962), p. 119.

25. David Tyack et al., *Law and the Shaping of Public Education, 1785–1954* (University of Wisconsin Press, 1987), p. 42.

26. Glenn, *Myth of the Common School*, p. 80.

27. Sol Cohen, ed., *Education in the United States: A Documentary History*, vol. 2, 1660–1885 (Random House, 1974), pp. 1096–97.

28. Horace Mann, *Third Annual Report of the Board of Education, Together with the Third Annual Report of the Secretary of the Board* (Boston: Dutton and Wentworth, 1840), p. 96.

29. Cohen, *Education in the United States,* p. 1107.

30. Cohen, *Education in the United States*, p. 1107.

31. David Tyack and Thomas James, "State Government and American Public Education: Exploring the 'Primeval Forest,'" *History of Education Quarterly* 26, no. 1 (Spring, 1986): p. 49.

32. Horace Mann, "The Advantages of Common Schools, and the Dangers to Which They Are Exposed," *Common School Journal* 1, no. 18 (1839), p. 200.

33. Horace Mann, *First Annual Report of the Board of Education, Together with the First Annual Report of the Secretary of the Board* (Dutton and Wentworth, 1838), p. 56.

34. Horace Mann, *Eighth Annual Report of the Board of Education, Together with the Eighth Annual Report of the Secretary of the Board* (Dutton and Wentworth, 1845), pp. 16–17.

35. Horace Mann, *Fifth Annual Report of the Board of Education, Together with the Fifth Annual Report of the Secretary of the Board* (Dutton and Wentworth, 1842), pp. 66–68.

36. Taylor, *Horace Mann's Troubling Legacy*, pp. 50–51.

37. Christopher Lasch, *The Revolt of the Elites and the Betrayal of Democracy* (W. W. Norton, 1995), p. 65.

38. Taylor, *Horace Mann's Troubling Legacy*, p. 69.

39. Glenn, *Myth of the Common School*; Glenn, *Contrasting Models of State and School.*

40. Taylor, *Horace Mann's Troubling Legacy*, pp. 72–73.

41. Glenn, *Contrasting Models of State and School.*

42. Alexis de Tocqueville, *Democracy in America*, ed. and trans. Harvey C. Mansfield and Delba Winthrop (University of Chicago Press, 2000), p. 62.

43. Charles L. Glenn and Jan De Groof, eds., *Balancing Freedom, Autonomy, and Accountability in Education*, vols. 1–4 (Wolf Legal Publishing, 2012).

Chapter 5

Against the Common School: Three Centuries of Arguments

By Ashley Rogers Berner

The previous chapter examined the 19th-century advocates of the common school, who feared that the widespread practice of funding denominational schools (especially Catholic schools) would foster social divisions. Those proponents also held high hopes that the common school would make possible a united citizenry such as the world had never seen. Resistance to the common school, born of religious particularism and the habit of local control, has ebbed and flowed throughout American history, though as we'll see in subsequent chapters, demands for alternatives have emerged at different times.[1]

The current chapter turns to the arguments of those who opposed the common school model from the 19th into the 20th and 21st centuries. The primary arguments against the common school model itself can be categorized in four related themes: (a) the nonneutrality of education, (b) the role of civil society organizations in the delivery of education, (c) civil rights and equal access, and (d) the empirical record. These strands overlap but are delineated here for the purpose of clarity.

First, though, we need to distinguish two kinds of critiques: those that sought to control rather than undo the common school and those that demanded alternative, state-funded options, such as charter schools, vouchers, or tax credits. Many of the so-called schooling wars with which we are familiar—for instance, over religion or sex education—fall in the first category.

For instance, although designed to defund *Catholic* faith formation, the early common schools were, essentially, Protestant institutions. The same legislatures that had removed funding from overtly "sectarian" schools required a generalized Protestantism in the common schools. States that required that the Protestant Bible be read in school, for instance, included Pennsylvania in 1913, Delaware and Tennessee in 1916, Alabama in 1919, Georgia in 1921, Maine in 1923, Kentucky in 1924, Florida and Ohio in 1925, and Arkansas in 1930.[2]

Eventually, the Supreme Court struck down public (Protestant) prayers, Bible reading for moral or spiritual purposes, the recitation of the Lord's Prayer, and posting of the Ten Commandments for nonpedagogical reasons.[3] Many Protestants, particularly Evangelicals, experienced this secularization as a profound loss, which some still seek to reverse.[4]

Another area of conflict has been parents' objections to specific curricular content. As of April 2025, the Cato Institute's Public Schooling Battle Map charts 4,408 public school conflicts tracked since 2005, of which 872 (almost 20 percent) were about parents' objections to their school district's curriculum.[5] Historically, parents' dissent is not always honored. In one landmark case, *Mozert v. Hawkins Public School District*, the Sixth Circuit held for the district against parents' objections to the district's reading curriculum.[6]

Book bans and curricular protests constitute attempts to control the district school—not to opt out of it. What have been the primary arguments against the common school itself?

Argument 1: Education Cannot Be Values-Neutral

One objection to a democratic government's funding of only one school type is that schooling cannot be neutral with respect to values. As Charles Glenn put it,

> Formal education . . . presents pictures or maps of reality that reflect, unavoidably, particular choices about what is certain and what in

> question, what is significant and what unworthy of notice. No aspect of schooling can be truly neutral.[7]

In this view, it is impossible to select teachers, recruit families, create a student disciplinary code, or even conduct classroom conversations without drawing on some kind of normative claims about the world, however implicit. Even the questions we do *not* ask in the classroom ("Is there a God?") are instructive for young people.[8] If Horace Mann's vaguely Protestant, Unitarian vision for the common school seemed unobjectionable to him, it did not to the general public—at least not in the 1830s and early 1840s.[9]

It wasn't that early reformers such as Horace Mann doubted the moral valence of education, or that early-20th-century legislators had not enshrined a faintly Protestant tenor; he did, and they had. In fact, because of the recognized morals that animated common schools, Catholics established their own parallel educational institutions. The Supreme Court of the United States, too, implicitly underscored the values in common school practices with their decision in *West Virginia v. Barnette*, the case in which Jehovah's Witnesses obtained the right not to salute the flag in school:

> If there is any fixed star in our constitutional constellation, it is that no official, high or petty, can prescribe what shall be orthodox in politics, nationalism, religion, or other matters of opinion, or force citizens to confess by word or act their faith therein. If there are any circumstances which permit an exception, they do not now occur to us.[10]

Indeed, *because* of the religiosity of the common schools, the Supreme Court effectively secularized them in the 1960s, as previously noted.[11]

The secularization of common schools, however merited on Constitutional grounds, did not resolve the values issue but rather shifted it to new terrain. Which nonreligious approach to values could be leveraged in this context? Whose values could be reinforced, if any? The values clarification model began to fill the vacuum in the mid-1960s, becoming a powerful approach to ethical formation and one that putatively avoided indoctrination.

As proponents of values clarification explained, the method aimed *not* to impose any particular version of ethics but rather to eschew absolutes and "teach a valuing *process*. . . . Responses are not judged as better or worse; each student's views are treated with equal respect" [italics mine].[12]

The theory came from New York University professor Louis Raths's coauthored *Values and Teaching: Working with Values in Classrooms*, which became a national bestseller and "a staple in university teacher education programs and innovative urban schools."[13] Values clarification experienced a "rapid rise in popularity," with a proliferation of new books, professional learning sessions, and presentations across the country.[14]

In a 2017 retrospective, Stanford University education professor emeritus Larry Cuban, who had used *Values and Teaching* to prepare teachers in the 1960s, described a typical values clarification lesson of that time. The teacher poses the following question and three options from which to choose:

Which would you find hardest to do?

1. Drop a bomb on Vietnam?
2. Electrocute a man who has been judged to die in the electric chair?
3. Run over someone who is threatening you with harm while you are driving a car?[15]

As Cuban explained, the role for students in this exercise included weighing the various consequences, choosing the right path, and owning the decision publicly; the role for teachers was accepting students' choices and relinquishing any belief in the "rightness" of different answers.[16]

But was this new, popular approach to values clarification—and its successor, the character education movement—really neutral? Or were they both merely a replacement paradigm for the older "Protestant light," and every bit as morally instructive?

Two legal scholars, John Coons and Stephen Sugarman, argued that the values clarification approach was emphatically not ethically neutral. They also claimed it damaged students' developmental process. How so?

In *Education by Choice: The Case for Family Control*, Coons and Sugarman claimed that the search for moral neutrality reinforced something specific—namely, "the emptiness of all values." This in turn encouraged "riskless noncommitment" and a "flaccid legitimation of ethical detachment."[17] Ethical detachment, these progressives wrote, constituted a *position* about the world—and one that unintentionally reinforced the consumer culture of America.

They also thought ethical detachment undermined moral development, citing Lawrence Kohlberg's theory of the developmental need for "ego strength."[18] It is important, posited Coons and Sugarman, that children observe "trusted adults gripped by a moral concern which is shared and endorsed by [their] own family," which creates a stable foundation from which to question any and all philosophies.[19] The end result should be an "emotionally secure individual [who] is likely not only to be more tolerant, but also to be concerned with maintaining the social order which has respected him."[20] Values clarification simply could not produce this desired developmental success.

A similar complaint could be made about the character education movement, which in the 1980s came to replace values clarification in public schools.[21] University of Virginia sociologist James Hunter noted in his analysis of the movement that, because it resisted the "why" questions ("Why should I be good?" "Why should I *not* cheat?"), the character education movement unwittingly reinforced the culturally dominant ethic of self-interest.[22] And while it is too early to tell, the more recent social and emotional learning may bring similar results.[23]

Even this brief survey illustrates why some maintain that, whether tacit or explicit, the values of the common school affect the moral formation of students. The policy consequence is that, rather than reinforce majoritarian culture, the state should fund a variety of educational institutions that reflect the diverse commitments of democratic citizens.[24]

As Charles Glenn wrote in 2017,

> Structural pluralism consists of legal and policy arrangements that provide space for coherent understandings of the human good to take institutional form, to flourish, to adapt to new circumstances, and to be transmitted to new generations and (in some cases) to adults who choose to associate themselves with the group.[25]

Argument 2: Non-State Institutions Matter for Democracy

A second objection to the common school has always been that democracy requires the effective presence of non–state institutions such as the individual (or the family) and civil society organizations in the delivery of public education, rather than an exclusive reliance on the state. This argument has two tangents: a pluralist case and a libertarian one.[26]

The pluralist case follows Alexis de Tocqueville, who argued that the voluntary sector—civil society—acts as a hedge against the equal tyrannies of the state and the individual. Surveying the early and still fragile republic in the 1830s, this Frenchman worried about both.[27] Tocqueville found solace, however, in the protective nature of the voluntary activities so abundant in the United States:

> Americans of all ages, all stations in life, and all types of disposition are forever forming associations. There are not only commercial and industrial associations in which all take part, but others of a thousand different types—religious, moral, serious, futile, very general and very limited, immensely large and very minute. Americans combine to give fetes, found seminaries, build churches, distribute books, and send missionaries to the antipodes. Hospitals, prisons, and schools take shape in that way. Finally, if they want to proclaim a truth or propagate some feeling by the encouragement of a great example, they form an association.[28]

For Tocqueville, the associations of civil society protected modern democratic life from the potentially isolating effects of individual liberty on the one hand and the hegemonic power of the state on the other.

Tocqueville's view was shared by contemporary American legislators and educational leaders. As Glenn points out in *The Myth of the Common School*, Mann's vision of state oversight generated resistance from rural communities and the Democratic Party of the 1830s and 1840s. In 1840, for instance, Massachusetts's legislature issued a blistering Majority Report opposing the controlling power of the Board of Education, calling its oversight of schools, books, and data collection a "catastrophe" for liberty, pluralism, and political freedom.[29] Although Massachusetts did not abolish the Board of Education—as Connecticut did in 1842—the conflict between religious particularism and a vague Protestantism "was the leading drama in Massachusetts for more than a generation, until abolition and immigration came to replace it . . . in the late 1840s."[30]

A contemporary political theorist, James Skillen, notes that institutional pluralism seeks "to avoid or overcome the absolutization of the family, the state, the market, and the individual in order to promote societal differentiation and integration."[31] Another theorist, William Galston, argues in favor of civil society and a "parsimonious" use of state power to define and cultivate academic and civic success in young people.[32]

With respect to schooling, then, the pluralist assigns the delivery of education in the first instance to the voluntary sector. Churches, synagogues, mosques, pedagogical societies, community organizations, and other entities ought to provide public education, even as the state funds and regulates schools, and individual families should be able to choose the ones they want.

The pluralist model constitutes the international norm, with 171 out of 204 nations surveyed by UNESCO in 2021 operating with "public-private partnerships" for the delivery of education, even as governments are tasked with funding and overseeing all of them.[33] As I and many others have written, educational pluralism attempts to bolster civil society as an independent democratic good, to affirm parental rights, and to ensure school quality.[34]

Analogies in the United States would be charter school laws in states such as New Jersey, New York, and Massachusetts, which assign a high value to academic quality, or, for private schools, scholarship laws that allow public funds to flow to non-state schools if participating students take common assessments.[35]

For its part, a libertarian approach narrows the scope of the state to oversight of basic safety standards or minimal academic standards, or both. This stance sometimes emphasizes educational markets in which "consumer sovereignty" and competition drive success.[36] Other voices, such as that of Howard Fuller, derive from profound mistrust of government on the basis of the historical experience of families of color.[37]

Current examples of "light-touch" or even "no-touch" regulations include some of the recent education savings account programs that allow public funds to flow, through parents, to a wide range of curricular, pedagogical, or recreational options.[38] As one advocate put it in 2023 with respect to education savings accounts having minimal oversight:

> I am quite skeptical of the idea of benevolent regulators finding the right balance between preventing objectively inappropriate uses (which there are already controls to limit) and giving parents wide latitude to experiment with subjective uses. I've seen enough regulatory capture and risk aversion to be skeptical.[39]

Both pluralist (civil society) and anti-state (libertarian) positions acknowledge the risks inherent in assigning all educational power to the state, even though pluralists assign more value to the voluntary sector and libertarians assign it to individual families. In sum, this argument rests on the risks inherent in a statist approach to education.

Argument 3: Democracy Requires Equal Access to Excellence—for All Students

Others have argued that the common school inevitably reinforces society's existing inequalities on the basis of race, class, or both. How so?

First, there is the matter of residential assignment, or mandatory attendance at a school near one's home. This practice often consigns students to schools that reflect their families' current socioeconomic status, without exposure to peers with higher social capital and ambition. Residential assignment's negative effects are compounded by its overlay with racist redlining and the United States' practice of funding schools via local property taxes. The result can be divergent opportunities in even geographically contiguous common schools.

Some advocates promote open enrollment policies as the antidote. Unlike vouchers or charters, open enrollment does not offer an alternative to the common school per se. It does, however, enable access to a wide range of common schools within or even between specific district boundaries.

In 2023, 43 states permitted districts to allow students to enroll in common schools for which they are not zoned. The phenomenon is growing, and early research shows promising results on student achievement.[40] In some states, such as Wisconsin, more students participate in open enrollment policies than use private school scholarships or attend charter schools. Enabling within-district and between-district transfers is popular, with some 73 percent of parents supporting it.[41] And the right to travel across residential boundaries is the specific mission of a coalition, launched in February 2024, called No More Lines:

> Imagine a world where ZIP code no longer dictates a child's educational journey—where parents have the power to decide, and diverse, tailored experiences are not just a goal, but a reality. Too often, kids are separated from a school that works for them because of how much money their family makes.[42]

While No More Lines does not endorse specific legislation, it does convene advocates who believe that "every student deserves access to the public school that best serves their needs regardless of race, home address, socioeconomic status, ability, or the location of the school."[43]

As Coons and Sugarman noted, residential assignment to schools is fundamentally at odds with other government-funded goods such as housing, medical care, and food, which allow recipients to choose providers.[44] Enabling "family choice for the non-rich" would not only bring education into alignment with public policy generally but would also end the "American double standard" of private schools for some and "compulsory assignment" for others.[45] Furthermore, as philosopher of education Harry Brighouse noted, not only the right to *join* a school but also the right to *leave* it remain important markers of parents' agency and voice.[46]

Second, others, such as Carter G. Woodson, the first black American to have received a PhD from Harvard, have focused on the common school as a locus of racist theories that diminish cultural minorities in general and black Americans in particular. In his 1933 book *The Mis-Education of the Negro,* Woodson argued that even high schools managed and staffed entirely by black administrators and teachers were subject to distortions; black teachers had been "trained to devalue their heritage" and to dismiss "African civilizations and African folklore and history."[47] Woodson coauthored a high school history textbook called *The Story of the Negro Retold* to highlight the accomplishments of African and African American contributions to the United States and the world.[48]

Civil rights advocates of the 1960s explicitly cited Woodson's views to support alternatives to the "inner-city schools [that] had failed black children."[49] Left-leaning advocates made a "leading contribution to the development of choice" based on "liberal educational reform movements, the civil-rights movement, and black nationalism."[50]

Emblematic of the frustration with the chronic undereducation of black students is the nation's first modern voucher program, launched in 1990 in Milwaukee with leadership from the city's representative to the state assembly, Annette "Polly" Williams, and superintendent Howard Fuller. In a 1992 interview, Williams noted the "problem with the education institutions in the entire nation in educating our children. . . . African-American and other ethnic minority children are failing." Furthermore, Williams said, the racial integration of schools had changed nothing; "mixing children doesn't automatically require that they are going to be educated."[51] For this reason, she sponsored a bill to provide public funds for low-income Milwaukeeans to attend private schools with a track record of accelerating success for black and Hispanic students—including 98 percent attendance rates and 92 percent college-going rates.[52]

Fuller, a professor emeritus at Marquette University, defended and still defends giving low-income families access to private schools in terms of civil rights. A former Black Panther, in 2017 he wrote that

> today's pain is not new for black people. But sometimes the pain and the scars reach down and touch the very depths of our souls. How deep was the pain when we were told to move to the back of the bus?

> How jagged were the scars when they told us, "Niggers ain't allowed to eat here"? How much did the wounds ache when they told us to train a white person for the job they said we were not qualified to do? Yes, all these dehumanizing acts left scars and caused pain. But today, there is nothing more painful than seeing so many of our children being denied the quality education they need and deserve.[53]

So, too, Charles Glenn, former "community activist in Boston" and "[conscientious prisoner] in North Carolina in 1963," who "walked across that Selma bridge with Dr. King in 1965," sees a straight line between these activities and his support for school vouchers.[54]

And last, the major international human rights documents acknowledge the rights of parents to direct the education of their children according to their cultural, linguistic, and ethical values, noting specifically, for instance, that "parents have a prior right to choose the kind of education that shall be given to their children.[55] The justice of enabling all families, especially low-income families and those from cultural minorities, to enroll their children in the Catholic school down the street, the Waldorf pre-K by their place of work, or an arts-focused magnet across town, constitutes a prominent argument against the status quo of the zoned common school.

Argument 4: Empirical Record—Both Negative and Positive

The viewpoints listed thus far may be compelling to some Americans, but they are insufficient to override the long-standing experiences and the financial interests that identify the common school as the exclusive carrier of public education.[56]

What, then, has enabled states in the United States to actually depart from the uniform delivery system put in place in the late 19th century? What has led legislatures to support not only open enrollment policies but also voucher programs (1990), charter schools (1991), tax credits (1997), and education savings accounts (2011)? And what has accounted for the rapid proliferation of programs that challenge the exclusive delivery system of the common school?[57]

Part of the answer lies in empirical findings about the unequal outcomes of US education.

Exhibit A is the work of sociologist James Coleman, author of the first post–civil rights evaluation of American education in *Equality of Educational Opportunity*, otherwise known as *The Coleman Report*. The field still refers to Coleman's sober finding that American education *in the aggregate* did not change students' expected life outcomes.[58] Put differently, the best predictor of young people's academic outcomes and social mobility is family background; what "goes into" the schoolhouse is what "comes out."

Since *The Coleman Report*, the questions asked of every educational intervention and every new type of school are, "Does it beat the odds? Does it change students' trajectory and allow social mobility?" As researchers are at pains to argue, the right answer is always, "It depends." The factors influencing outcomes include funding, neighborhood, teaching staff, hiring practices, curriculum, school size, school culture, peer effects, and parent involvement. There is substantial variability of outcome *within* school sectors (e.g., between one charter school and another, or between one district school and another) and even within a single school. And no type of school is immune from financial malfeasance and other scandals.[59]

These caveats notwithstanding, there does seem to be an advantage (in the aggregate) to leaving low-performing public schools and attending charters and private schools. For instance, after his 1966 report, Coleman went on to study the comparative effect of attending Catholic and other private schools. His findings, explained in *High School Achievement: Public, Catholic, and Private Schools Compared*, include positive Catholic-school effects such as better graduation rates, more rigorous courses, and higher overall achievement, in some cases virtually erasing the achievement gap across four years of high school.[60] Coleman and his team's conclusion sets the common school model on its head:

> Thus, we have the paradoxical result that the Catholic schools come closer to the American ideal of the "common school," educating all alike, than do the public schools. Furthermore . . . a similar result holds for race and ethnicity. The achievement of blacks is closer to

that of whites, and the achievement of Hispanics is closer to that of non-Hispanics, in Catholic schools than in public schools.[61]

Former *Ramparts* editor Sol Stern recounts similar findings in New York City in *Breaking Free: Public School Lessons and the Imperative of School Choice*. The 2003 book chronicles, for instance, the expensive two-year effort required to remove teachers deemed physically and verbally abusive from the classroom, the negative effect of labor contracts on teachers' professionalism, and seniority rules that kept principals from hiring the staff they wanted.[62] By contrast, the city's Catholic schools, which Stern also studied in depth, helped their low-income students succeed academically at vastly higher levels, at a lower cost, than the district schools.[63] Stern found this contrast ultimately persuasive; he found in school choice "a new civil rights movement that was completing the unfinished business of the 1960s movement I had once been part of."[64]

Woeful public school outcomes also led Joe Williams, a journalist and the founder of Democrats for Education Reform (DFER), to advocate for a rapid increase in the number of charter schools, which are publicly funded but independently governed, as an exit strategy from low-performing, bureaucratic public schools. *Cheating Our Kids: How Politics and Greed Ruin Education* includes data on students' underperformance and accounts of teachers' union protectionism that led Williams to conclude, of young people's prospects, "Even our best and brightest are getting a substandard education."[65] DFER became a driving force behind pro-charter legislation, teacher evaluations, and academic accountability across the country and at the US Department of Education.[66]

Charter schools' academic outcomes have been mixed. Virtual charters underperform, as do some urban centers such as Fort Myers, Fort Worth, and Phoenix.[67] Nevertheless, Stanford's Center for Research on Education Outcomes (CREDO) found in 2015 that, in the aggregate, urban charter students learned significantly more than their "virtual twins" in traditional public schools, such that "[the] results translate to urban charter students receiving the equivalent of roughly 40 days of additional learning per year in math and 28 additional days of learning per year in reading." CREDO's academic results were particularly strong for "Black, Hispanic, low-income, and special education students."[68]

Test scores aren't the only outcomes that matter. What about students' civic capacities, such as their political knowledge, attachment to country, and tolerance of beliefs with which they disagree? A 2020 meta-analysis of civic outcomes found that, of 86 statistically significant findings, 50 showed a clear private school advantage, 33 found a neutral effect, and only 3 showed a public school advantage.[69] This pattern pertained with respect to political tolerance, political participation, and civic knowledge and skills.[70] What about students' college attendance and graduation? A 2019 Urban Institute study found that students who participated in Florida's private school scholarship (tax credit) program had higher rates of enrollment and completion in higher education than their matched public school peers. Furthermore, those impacts increased with every year of enrollment in private school.[71] What about pro-social outcomes? A 2019 study of Milwaukee's voucher program found that middle school participants had lower rates of criminal convictions in early adulthood.[72]

Again, no school system is perfect; neither is any one type of school. But the chronic underachievement of many public systems, and the academic, civic, and social benefits that can follow charter and private school attendance, have led individuals across the political spectrum to embrace alternatives to the common school.[73]

Summary

The case against the United States' common school model includes its inherent (if variable) moral claims that privilege some beliefs at the expense of others; the vital role of civil society in mediating the potential ills of the overweening state and the isolated individual; the justice claims of low-income families and cultural minorities to exercise agency in determining their children's education; and research findings that are generally positive about non-public school outcomes. A large majority of US students, however—83 percent in 2021–2022—attend traditional public schools.[74] The landscape of K–12 education is changing to encompass a veritable mosaic of state-funded educational models that respond to political arguments, empirical findings, and crises such as COVID-19. The question of how to ensure the best academic and civic outcomes for the next generation while establishing a shared understanding of what it means to be a citizen of the United States, however, remains as pressing as it was 200 years ago.

Notes

1. See chapter 4 of this volume. Charles L. Glenn, "Emergence of the Common School Ideology," in *Fighting for the Freedom to Learn: Examining America's Centuries-Old School Choice Movement,* eds. James L. Shuls and Neal P. McCluskey (Cato Institute, 2025).

2. Charles L. Glenn, "The Discriminatory Origins of New Hampshire's 'Blaine' Amendment," unpublished testimony, April 29, 2013. Copy in author's files.

3. *Abington Township, Pennsylvania v. Schemp*, 374 *United States Reports* 203 (Supreme Court of the United States, 1963); *Chamberlin v. Dade County Public Schools*, 377 *United States Reports* 402 (Supreme Court of the United States, 1964); *Stone v. Graham*, 449 *United States Reports* 39 (Supreme Court of the United States, 1980); Geoffrey R. Stone, "In Opposition to the School Prayer Amendment," *University of Chicago Law Review* 50, no. 2 (1983): 823–48, 826; Editorial staff, "Banning Prayer in Public Schools Has Led to America's Demise," *The Forerunner* (blog), May 1, 1988.

4. "Florida Prayer in Schools Initiative (2024)," database, Ballotpedia, 2023; Steven Dial, "Texas Senate Passes Bills Allowing Time for Prayer in Schools, Requiring Ten Commandments in Classrooms," Fox 4 News, April 21, 2023; Arkansas Legislature, "A Day of Prayer for Arkansas Students," Pub. L. No. 902, § 6-10-135, Title 6-Education Subtitle 2-Elementary and Secondary Education Arkansas Code of 1987 (2021).

5. "Public Schooling Battle Map," Cato Institute, November 1, 2024.

6. Eric A. DeGroff, "Parental Rights and Public School Curricula: Revisiting Mozert After 20 Years," *Journal of Law & Education* 38, no. 1 (2009): 83.

7. Charles Leslie Glenn, *The Myth of the Common School* (University of Massachusetts Press, 1988), p. 11.

8. For more on this subject, see Ashley Berner, *Pluralism and American Public Education: No One Way to School* (Palgrave Macmillan, 2017), pp. 7–28.

9. Glenn, *Myth of the Common School*, pp. 124–25, 130.

10. *West Virginia State Board of Education v. Barnette*, 319 *United States Reports* 624 (Supreme Court of the United States, 1943), p. 319.

11. Abington Township, *Pennsylvania v. Schemp*, 374 *United States Reports*; *Chamberlin v. Dade County Public Schools*, 377 *United States Reports* 402; *Stone v. Graham*, 449 *United States Reports* 39.

12. Howard Kirschenbaum et al., "In Defense of Values Clarification," *Phi Delta Kappan* 58, no. 10 (June 1977): 743–46.

13. Larry Cuban, "Whatever Happened to Values Clarification?," *Larry Cuban on School Reform and Classroom Practice* (blog), October 4, 2017.

14. Kirschenbaum et al., "In Defense of Values Clarification," 743.

15. Cuban, "Whatever Happened to Values Clarification?"

16. Cuban, "Whatever Happened to Values Clarification?"

17. John E. Coons and Stephen D. Sugarman, *Education by Choice: The Case for Family Control* (University of California Press, 1978), p. 82.

18. Lawrence Kohlberg, "Stages of Moral Development as a Basis for Moral Education," in *Moral Education: Interdisciplinary Approaches*, ed. C. M. Beck, B. S. Crittenden, and E. V. Sullivan (University of Toronto Press, 1971), pp. 23–91, 83, cited by Coons and Sugarman, *Education by Choice*, p. 83.

19. Coons and Sugarman, *Education by Choice,* pp. 82–87.

20. Coons and Sugarman, *Education by Choice,* p. 99.

21. James Davison Hunter, *The Death of Character: Moral Education in an Age without Good or Evil* (Basic Books, 2000), p. 90.

22. Hunter, *Death of Character,* pp. 86–89, 151–52, 212.

23. Ashley Berner, *Schools, Character and the Charassein: A Study in Student Development*, R Street Institute's Character Education Series (R Street Institute, 2020).

24. Elmer John Thiessen, *Teaching for Commitment: Liberal Education, Indoctrination, and Christian Nurture* (McGill-Queens University Press, 1993), 194–95.

25. Charles L. Glenn, "Structural Pluralism in Education: Can We Stop Fighting over Schools?," *Johns Hopkins Institute for Education Policy* (blog), December 15, 2017, p. 4.

26. See also Ashley Berner, "Educational Pluralism: Distinctive Schools and Academic Accountability," in *Religious Liberty and Education: A Case Study of Yeshivas vs. New York*, ed. Jay Greene, Jason Bedrick, and Matthew Lee (Rowman & Littlefield, 2020), pp. 15–30.

27. Alexis de Tocqueville, *Democracy in America*, ed. J. P. Mayer, trans. George Lawrence (Harper Collins, 1988), pp. 506, 512.

28. Tocqueville, *Democracy in America*, pp. 513, 515, 517.

29. Glenn, *Myth of the Common School*, pp. 120–21.

30. Glenn, *Myth of the Common School*, p. 161.

31. James W. Skillen, *In Pursuit of Justice: Christian-Democratic Explorations* (Rowman & Littlefield, 2004), p. 30.

32. William A. Galston, *Liberal Pluralism: The Implications of Value Pluralism for Political Theory and Practice* (Cambridge University Press, 2002), p. 20.

33. UNESCO (United Nations Educational, Scientific, and Cultural Organization), "Non-State Actors in Education: Who Chooses? Who Loses?," Global Education Monitoring Report (UNESCO, 2021); see also the four-volume series, Glenn, et al., *Balancing Freedom, Autonomy and Accountability* (Wolf Legal Publishers, 2012).

34. See, for instance, Glenn, et al., *Balancing Freedom, Autonomy and Accountability*; Charles Glenn, *Contrasting Models of State and School: A Comparative Historical Study of Parental Choice and State Control* (Continuum, 2011); and Ashley Rogers Berner, *Educational Pluralism and Democracy: How to Handle Indoctrination, Promote Exposure, and Rebuild America's Schools* (Harvard Education Press, 2024).

35. CREDO (Center for Research on Education Outcomes), *Urban Charter School Study: 41 Regions Workbook* (CREDO, 2015); or see the database linked in Colyn Ritter, "2024 EdChoice Share: Exploring Where America's Students Are Educated," *Engage by EdChoice* (blog), January 17, 2024.

36. Kevin Currie-Knight, *Education in the Marketplace: An Intellectual History of Pro-Market Libertarian Visions for Education in Twentieth Century America* (Palgrave Macmillan, 2019), pp. 53, 147.

37. Howard Fuller, "Advancement—the Second 'A' in NAACP—Should Apply to Our Children Too," The 74, August 2, 2017; Howard Fuller, "Fuller: Call It 'Ed Reform' or Don't—the Fight to Make Schools Work for Our Poorest Families Must Go On. To Stop Is to Dishonor King's Memory," The 74, January 17, 2019; and Derrell Bradford et al., "Bradford, Fuller & Stewart: Liberating Black Kids from Broken Schools—by Any Means Necessary," The 74, June 26, 2017.

38. "Arizona: Empowerment Scholarship Accounts," EdChoice, January 2025.

39. Adam Peshek, "ESAs Don't Need the Charter Treatment," *Permissionless Education* (blog), February 21, 2023.

40. Jude Schwalbach, "Public Schools without Boundaries: Examining Every State's Open Enrollment Policies," *Reason* (blog), October 26, 2023.

41. Jude Schwalbach, "The Hidden Role of K–12 Open-Enrollment Policies in US Public Schools," *Education Next* 24, no. 4 (December 2024).

42. Yes. Every Kid., "Coalition Launches to Eliminate Exclusionary Public School Boundary Lines in All 50 States by 2030," Yes. Every Kid., February 13, 2024; Yes. Every Kid., "No More Lines: How Ending Exclusionary School Boundary Lines Will Revolutionize Education," Yes. Every Kid., February 20, 2024.

43. Yes. Every Kid., "No More Lines."

44. Coons and Sugarman, *Education by Choice*, p. 66.

45. Coons and Sugarman, *Education by Choice*, pp. 2–3.

46. Harry Brighouse, *School Choice and Social Justice* (Oxford University Press, 2000), pp. 56–58, 109.

47. David Levine, "Carter G. Woodson and the Afrocentrists: Common Foes of Mis-Education," *High School Journal* 84, no. 1 (October/November 2000): 5–13, 6.

48. Levine, "Carter G. Woodson," 9.

49. Levine, "Carter G. Woodson," 9.

50. James Forman Jr., "The Secret History of School Choice: How Progressives Got There First," *Georgetown Law Journal* 93, no. 4 (2004): 1287–89.

51. Arthur Wellington Conquest III, "Taking Control of Our Schools: Ending Educational Oppression in Urban America: An Interview with Rep. Polly Williams," *Journal of Experiential Education* 15, no. 3 (November 1992): 17.

52. Conquest III, "Taking Control of Our Schools," 18.

53. Claudio Sanchez, "Lessons on Race and Vouchers from Milwaukee," *NPR ED* (blog), May 16, 2017; Fuller, "Advancement—the Second 'A' in NAACP—Should Apply to Our Children Too"; and Fuller, "Fuller: Call It 'Ed Reform.'"

54. Charles L. Glenn, "Anti-Religious Education," *First Things* 312 (April 2021).

55. "Universal Declaration of Human Rights," United Nations General Assembly, December 10, 1948, articles 26.3 and 27.1; Office of the High Commissioner, "International Covenant on Civil and Political Rights" (United Nations, 1976), articles 18.4 and 27; and Office of the High Commissioner, "International Covenant on Economic, Social and Cultural Rights" (United Nations, 1976), articles 13.1, 13.3.

56. Glenn, "Structural Pluralism in Education," p. 2.

57. Ray Domanico, "A Reformation in Public Education School Choice in Theory and Practice," Manhattan Institute: Issue Brief, August 22, 2024.

58. James S. Coleman, "Equality of Educational Opportunity," US Department of Health, Education, and Welfare, 1966; and Eric A. Hanushek, "What Matters for Student Achievement: Updating Coleman on the Influence of Families and Schools," *Education Next* 16, no. 2 (April 2016): 18–26.

59. See examples in Berner, *Educational Pluralism and Democracy*, p. 112.

60. James S. Coleman et al., *High School Achievement: Public, Catholic, and Private Schools Compared* (Basic Books, 1982), pp. 37–41, 141–44.

61. James Coleman, *High School and Beyond* (Basic Books, 1986), p. 144.

62. Sol Stern, *Breaking Free: Public School Lessons and the Imperative of School Choice* (Encounter Books, 2003), pp. 44, 113.

63. Stern, *Breaking Free*, pp. 175–76.

64. Stern, *Breaking Free*, p. 13.

65. Joe Williams, *Cheating Our Kids: How Politics and Greed Ruin Education* (Palgrave Macmillan, 2005), pp. 1–3.

66. "Democrats for Education Reform: Our Story," Democrats for Education Reform, accessed November 14, 2024.

67. James Woodworth, *Online Charter School Study* (Center for Research on Education Outcomes, Stanford University, October 2015); CREDO (Center for Research on Education Outcomes), *Urban Charter School Study: 41 Regions Workbook*, (Center for Research on Education Outcomes, Stanford University, March 2015), p. 9.

68. CREDO (Center for Research on Education Outcomes), *Urban Charter School Study: Report on 41 Regions* (Center for Research on Education Outcomes, 2015), pp. v, vi.

69. Patrick Wolf, "Myth: Public Schools Are Necessary for a Stable Democracy," in *School Choice Myths: Setting the Record Straight on Education Freedom*, ed. Corey A. DeAngelis and Neal P. McCluskey (Cato Institute, 2020), pp. 46–68, 56.

70. Wolf, "Myth," pp. 59, 60.

71. Matthew Chingos et al., *The Effects of the Florida Tax Credit Scholarship Program on College Enrollment and Graduation*, Urban Institute, February 4, 2019.

72. Corey DeAngelis and Patrick Wolf, "Private School Choice and Character: More Evidence from Milwaukee," EDRE Working Paper No. 2019-03, Social Science Research Network, February 26, 2019, p. 1.

73. For an example of district system underperformance, see Johns Hopkins Institute for Education Policy, "Providence Public School District: A Review," Johns Hopkins Institute for Education Policy, June 2019; and for an example of progressive support for alternatives, see Ashley Berner, "The Progressive Case for Educational Pluralism," Cardus Perspectives Paper, May 2024.

74. Katherine Schaeffer, "US Public, Private and Charter Schools in 5 Charts," Pew Research Center, June 6, 2024.

Chapter 6

Not Common to All: The Education of Black Americans

By Cheryl Fields-Smith

Introduction

African Americans were largely excluded from the 19th-century common school movement, yet they have persistently pursued education as a path toward freedom from slavery to today. Throughout history, African Americans conceptualized education as freedom itself. Frederick Douglass is credited as once saying, "Once you learn to read, you will be forever free."[1] The famed abolitionist deeply believed that literacy would empower African Americans.

Professor Jarvis R. Givens asserted that education and freedom have been inextricably bound together for black Americans, who secured schooling to realize their dreams of freedom and ultimately to undo the social structure that oppressed them.[2] Indeed, the onslaught of antiliteracy laws enacted against allowing enslaved Africans to read indicates slave owners' fear of the empowerment that literacy would provide. As professor Heather Williams explained, "The presence of literate slaves threatened to give lie to the entire system [slavery]."[3] Imagine the contradiction of slaves having been considered less than human, yet slave owners fearing them becoming literate. What nonhuman things can read as humans do? Indeed, the system of slavery depended on the existence of an ignorant free source of labor.

However, enslaved Africans fought for freedom through self-agency, self-determination, and resistance; they created educational opportunities despite the oppression they faced. This chapter examines selected historical examples of African Americans' ongoing struggle for educational freedom, viewed through the lens of self-agency, self-determination, and African American Resistance Theory. The chapter employs significant, yet lesser known, historical exemplars of African Americans' quest for educational freedom.

Defining Self-Agency, Self-Determination, and African American Resistance

Throughout history, African Americans have demonstrated self-determination, self-agency, and resistance, especially in their pursuit of educational freedom. Self-determination—the right of people to set their own goals—has been fundamental to black history. Malcolm X urged African Americans to engage in self-determination, described as taking control of their destinies rather than relying on government support, which he believed would enable them to overcome systemic oppression.[4] Similarly, black self-agency refers to the cultural practices demonstrated throughout African American educational history, where they persistently pursue education despite obstacles.[5] Further, self-agency among African Americans has been, and remains, predominantly communal in nature rather than individualistic.[6] Self-determination and self-agency represent key features of African American resistance, which operates outside existing systems to bring about change.[7] As an example, pushing for the racial integration of schools would represent a protest, rather than African American resistance, because the aim was focused on access to the existing government-run school system. Conversely, enslaved Africans' actions to gain literacy while under government mandates against their literacy represents resistance because their activism operated outside the social order. Combined, the communal concepts of self-agency, self-determination, and resistance represent educational freedom-seeking.

Educational Freedom-Seeking During Slavery

Contrary to the history that is taught in most public K–12 schools, enslaved Africans resisted the system of slavery. Self-ascribed owners of enslaved Africans varied in their opinions regarding allowing slaves to learn to read and write. But enslaved people equated literacy and learning with freedom.[8] Thankfully, due to the insight of researchers living shortly after Emancipation, we know what learning to read and write in English meant to enslaved Africans.[9] In 2002, while working on my doctoral degree at Emory University, I had the opportunity to hear a portion of the slave narrative recordings, where a formerly enslaved person who had been blinded for learning to read chillingly shared that he would risk his sight—and life—again because to him, learning to read was freedom. Literate enslaved Africans sometimes created their own freedom papers, which quite literally led them to freedom.[10] Therefore, even though laws prevented enslaved Africans to learn to read and write, they employed self-agency, self-determination, and resistance to find ways to do so. To help us understand why they would be willing to take such risks, Amira Dehmani, explained that

> The ability to read and write gave enslaved people power. On the one hand it gave them skills . . . to write passes for all persons of color. These passes could be travel passes used to sneak to the North for freedom, or they could be curfew passes for persons of color to be out past dark. . . . Additionally, it allowed them to have a personal freedom that they rarely experienced [and] . . . allowed them to imagine "a world beyond the bondage."[11]

Some states, such as Georgia, passed laws that banned enslaved people from learning to read and also mandated that free persons of color could not learn to read.[12]

Learning to Read in Secret

Because of the anti-literacy laws, enslaved Africans and free persons of color had to use secretive strategies to conceal their pursuit of freedom through literacy. In Heather Williams's book, *Self-Taught*, she recounts multiple strategies used to learn to read, including secretly entering the home of free black women who knew how to read. Some wives of slave owners held religious beliefs that compelled them to teach enslaved people.[13] Further, enslaved Africans used their Sunday downtime to focus on learning to read as soon as slave owners left to attend church.[14] Some enslaved people dug pits in the forest to create secret spaces where those who knew how to read and write would teach others to do so late into the night.[15] Other forms of clandestine learning during the slavery era included disguising reading classes as sewing classes, learning as slave owners' children learned, and even attending underground schools in the homes of free black people.[16] Fredrick Douglass learned to read by bartering with the white children while running errands. He wrote, "The plan which I adopted, and the one by which I was most successful, was that of making friends of all the little white boys whom I met in the street. As many of these as I could, I converted into teachers."[17] At times he would pay the children in bread. As Heather Williams described, enslaved people "truly had to 'steal' an education" and they "put the resources they could garner to maximum use."[18] More than 100 years after slavery, archaeologists found the "remains of graphite pencils and writing slates, some with words and numbers still written on them" among slave cabin artifacts.[19] Enslaved people did whatever they had to do to learn to read, and they did so in collaboration with each other.

Learning to Read from Each Other for Freedom

Most importantly, enslaved Africans learned from one another; they usually kept their ability to read and write secret from their owners, but they willingly shared their abilities with each other. As formerly enslaved women Harriet Jacobs and Elizabeth Keckly explained:

> Literate slaves passed their skills on to others and enslaved parents often taught their children when far removed from the master or overseer; some slaves held underground "schools" in secret hiding places—often deep in the woods—late at night or very early in the morning before or after the workday. "I have seen the Negroes up in

> the country going away under large oaks, and in secret places, sitting in the woods with spelling books," former slave Charity Bowery of North Carolina told an interviewer decades after Emancipation. In sum, African Americans were very creative in finding a way to learn to read and write because they knew that literacy was key to knowledge, freedom and personal power.[20]

By sharing their reading and writing skills among themselves, a larger number of enslaved Africans were able to gain the knowledge they needed to create greater practices of resistance. For instance, James Curry began to craft arguments against slavery.[21] Curry secretly went into his master's home, read the Bible, and discovered a passage stating that one man owning another was against God's will. "Curry interpreted the Apostle Paul's message to mean that since God had made all people, no one group was justified in enslaving another. While his owners attended 'divine worship,' Curry used the words in their own revered Bible to fashion his own condemnation of their unjust practice."[22] Literacy then, enabled enslaved black Americans to garner knowledge and skills necessary to engage in the fight for abolition.

Research on slavery documents the many ways that enslaved Africans resisted laws against their literacy. These people equated freedom with literacy and therefore pursued literacy fervently, although they did so in secret and under duress. Those who were able to gain literacy ultimately used it to help undo the institution of slavery through their abolitionist work.

Educational Freedom-Seeking During Reconstruction

Immediately following the Emancipation of enslaved black Americans, there may have been joy in obtaining freedom, but there were also new challenges. Formerly enslaved people had to decide where to live and how to earn a living once they left the plantations. The institution of slavery began in colonial America in 1619 and legally ended in the United States in 1865. It had endured for 246 years; that's generations of enslaved Africans far from their native lands and their culture. Slavery purposed to make them forget their culture and to believe that they were inferior—not even human. But now that they had become free people, who were they? And how could they survive in their freedom?

Amid the challenges brought on by their new freedom, education remained a priority for former slaves. "Their determination to acquire literacy and numeracy generated the energy to build schoolhouses even while they tackled the physical challenges of hunger, disease, and homelessness," writes Heather Andrea Williams.[23] The former slaves' fundamental belief in the value of a literate culture was expressed most clearly in their efforts to secure schooling for themselves and their children. Historians of African American history have unearthed evidence of numerous schools that were started during and immediately after slavery throughout the South.[24] Virtually every account by historians or contemporary observers stresses ex-slaves' demand for universal schooling."[25]

The Freedmen's Bureau

Describing the origins of the Freedmen's Bureau, James Anderson reported,

> The foundation of the freedmen's educational movement was their self-reliance and deep-seated desire to control and sustain schools for themselves and their children. William Channing Gannett, a white American Missionary Association teacher from New England, reported that "they [ex-slaves] have a natural praiseworthy pride in keeping their educational institutions in their own hands. There is a jealousy of the superintendence of the white man in this matter. What they desire is assistance without control."[26]

Thus, the self-determination and self-agency that had been established among enslaved African Americans did not end with Emancipation. Instead, it grew, and former slaves demanded their right to keep the educational institutions they had established on their own. Indeed, the national superintendent of schools for the Freedman's Bureau reported that at least 500 schools had already been established as of 1886, just one year following Emancipation.[27] These included a variety of schools from secular and the Sabbath Schools, which operated during the weekends and in the evenings. By 1889, the Freedman's Bureau superintendent reported that there were "1,512 Sabbath schools with 6,146 teachers and 107,109 pupils."[28] The fervor with which freed black people sought education forced the establishment of universal public education in the South.[29]

Sharecropping and Education

Following Emancipation, another system of oppression formed to keep African Americans tied to serving as cheap farm-based labor. Newly freed people typically did not have farmland of their own and they also needed a place to live, so white landowners established lines of credit to them. In exchange, these sharecroppers would receive a place to live and a portion of the crops they were expected to farm. Newly freed black farmers would also have to rent farming equipment. White landowners manipulated the laws and sharecropping system so that freed black people would typically come up short and remain in debt year after year.[30] As journalist Jared Tetreau explained, that "once up and running, sharecropping itself would deny the formerly enslaved their rights and liberties as free American citizens for nearly one hundred years."[31] Other than portrayals in historical films and books, little is known or taught about the daily life of sharecroppers and their families. However, the photo taken by Russell Lee (1903–1986) provides some insight.[32] Taken in 1939 in Transylvania, Louisiana, the title of the photograph, *Negro Mother Teaching Children Numbers and Alphabet in Home of Sharecropper,* suggests that this is an example of daily life in the homes of black sharecroppers.

Whereas some people might look at this photo and see poverty, based on the condition of the walls and the sparse furnishings, when I look at this photo I see a mother with dignity, self-agency, and a strong sense of purpose who is teaching her children to read. Surprisingly, she is doing so in script! She and her children are dressed in what I imagine would be the best clothing they had. The two children are attentive and focused on their mother's instruction, and their chairs are aligned to form a neat row.

There is intentionality in the mother's stance in the photo, and there is purpose in the way she created this learning space in her home. As a former elementary school teacher, I cannot ignore the calendar hanging

Source: Russell Lee, "Negro mother teaching children numbers and alphabet in home of sharecropper," Transylvania, Louisiana, January 1939, Library of Congress.

in the learning area near the cloth blackboard. Calendars have become a mainstay in modern elementary school classrooms. I imagine this mom using the calendar similarly to today's elementary teachers for reviewing the days of the week and months.

This mother is using the materials and tools she had to ensure that her children learned what she was able to teach them. She appears to have written, "The rain are fallin" on her cloth board, which may indicate that the reason she was able to teach on this day was that it was raining outside and, therefore, they could not work the land. Of course, this is speculation on my part. We do not know if this mother had the time to teach her children in her home daily. We do not know what time of day this learning was taking place. It could be after a long day of working the fields, which would further indicate self-determination.

Even more importantly, from this photo, we know that black mothers taught their children at home even amid their poverty and oppressive living conditions. I confidently generalize the happenings in this photo to other black mothers living in similar conditions during this time because of the deep communal nature of the black community, which has been well-documented. If slaves did not keep their literacy to themselves individually, it is highly likely that this mother shared what she was doing for her children with other mothers in her community. She herself likely learned from someone in the community who had managed to learn to read and count during desperate times. The communal bonds within the black community while under oppressive conditions ensure that this was not the only black mother who taught her children at home.

Jim Crow Education and the Myth of Inferior Segregated Schools

Rosenwald Schools

From 1917 to 1932, close to 5,000 Rosenwald schoolhouses were built in southern rural communities, and they served more than 700,000 black children.[33] Rosenwald Schools were the result of a collaboration between Julius Rosenwald, who was a Jewish German immigrant and the head of the retail company known as Sears, and Booker T. Washington, who was a thought leader of the black community.[34] By 1928, Rosenwald Schools represented 20 percent of the schools that served black children in the South. Andrew Feiler's photo memoir, *A Better Life for Their Children*, presents pictures of a sample of the remaining Rosenwald School buildings and captures the experiences of former students and teachers across each of the 15 Southern states that participated in the Rosenwald School program.

Moreover, numerous black leaders attended Rosenwald Schools as part of their K–12 education. As a Rosenwald alum, the late Congressman John Robert Lewis (1940–2020) wrote an essay in Feiler's book, in which he described his love for his segregated schoolhouse in Alabama, which included a classroom library and field trips.[35] He also wrote about his parents' desire that he go further in his education than they did, but how the farming schedule interrupted his—and most other black children's—education. His description informs us of the richness of his segregated education as we also learn of the limited resources available due to the prevalence of discrimination within the segregated school system. A Google search for other famous African Americans who attended Rosenwald Schools yielded a lengthy list, including Maya Angelou and Medgar Evers. Most importantly, these schools "became beacons of hope" for all black children fortunate enough to attend them.[36]

One Segregated Black School Exemplifies Many Others

In her 1996 seminal work, *Their Highest Potential: An African American School Community in the Segregated South*, Vanessa Siddle Walker offers evidence of the strengths of segregated black schools.[37] Most of us have been taught that segregated black schools were inferior. But, upon reading *Their Highest Potential*, we realize that segregated black schools were provided with inferior resources and yet, due to communal self-agency, self-determination, and resistance, black people persevered and pursued excellence in education, nonetheless. When the Caswell County, North Carolina, school board refused to provide school buses to segregated black schools so children could travel to and from school, community members, even those who did not have children of their own, offered whatever vehicles they had to ensure that children could attend school. When the school board refused to provide land so that new schools could be built for black children, community members donated what land they had so that a school could be built.

Leadership and teaching within segregated schools exemplified excellence as well. Through Vanessa Siddle Walker's account, we learn that N. L. Dillard, the principal of the Caswell County school, led with agency, love, and excellence. Dillard provided his segregated black community with a transparent view of the school finances and what they needed.[38] He insisted that teachers spend time in the community getting to know the families of their students, and even to visit students' homes. He believed, "If you could see the circumstances out of which the children have come, you would understand better how to teach them."[39] Evidence further demonstrated that "Teaching was more than the imparting of subject matter; it was the task of molding children to be successful. Theirs [teachers] was a job of collective racial uplift."[40]

Amazingly, soon after the publication of *Their Highest Potential,* other accounts offering the beneficial perspective of segregated black schools appeared. Having attended Emory University from 1999 to 2004, I observed this phenomenon and had the opportunity to work alongside Vanessa Siddle Walker in collecting data for her continued work to unearth this previously ignored perspective of history. In *Hello Professor: A Black Principal and Professional Leadership in the Segregated South,* Walker unraveled the answer to the question of how so many black segregated schools could have had such similar values and practices.[41] Black educational leaders during Jim Crow not only knew one another, but they also met secretly across state lines to share information and strategies of resistance as part of an intricate system of collaborative educational leadership. Like their enslaved ancestors, racism and oppression led them to collective self-agency, self-determination, and resistance to ensure black children's access to excellence in education.

Civil Rights, Organizational Activism, and Educational Freedom

In the decades leading up to and including the Civil Rights Era, black people in the United States established numerous organizations that engaged in pursuit of educational freedom, either locally or nationally. These organizations included social clubs, such as sororities and fraternities, civic organizations such as the National Association for the Advancement of Colored People (NAACP), and activists such as the Black Panthers. Although civic organizations served as vibrant sites for teaching and learning, they remain understudied.[42] Black organizations and clubs created a public, yet somewhat private and racism-free, space for black communities to meet their needs and to advocate for themselves, including obtaining education.[43]

Black Fraternities and Sororities

The Improved Benevolent and Protective Order of Elks of the World (IBPOEW) represents one example of a black organization that engaged in advocacy, particularly focused on education in the black community. The IBPOEW was established in 1898 and emerged amid another challenging period in history for black people with the rise of the Ku Klux Klan, the threat of lynching, and the onset of Jim Crow. Despite this context, throughout its development, the IBPOEW engaged in education-related programming. The organization's educational philosophy united the perspectives of Booker T. Washington and W. E. B. Du Bois, which were often perceived as being contradictory, by promoting public education for children as well as "home training," which referred to teaching children to work with their hands while also gaining book knowledge.[44] Other programming included black history, fostering literacy among adults, and establishing scholarships for higher education. A brochure exemplified IBPOEW's priorities as ensuring that every child who desired an education should be able to receive one.[45] Additionally, Judge William C. Hueston, who served as the initial head of IBPOEW'S education department, reported,

> The purpose of the Department of Education in our Order is to train thinkers who can match themselves against the great minds of the world. If this race of ours is to still be known among the races of the world, then we must achieve more abundantly; we must build greater buildings; improve transportation; discover great cures; evolve financial systems and make our debtors the human race. And in order to do this, our minds must be trained to the highest possible standards.[46]

Moreover, the organization raised concerns related to inequity of segregated school funding.

The Black Panthers

The Black Panther Party for Self-Defense has been commonly referred to as the Black Panthers and is known for being militant in its push against capitalism in America and its insistence on armed self-defense.[47] Describing the Black Panthers' perspective on traditional American ideas, professor Alex Zamalin wrote, "Action was depicted as a willingness to accept the new and unknown. Freedom became dependent upon a radical notion of self-determination."[48] The Black Panthers were formed in 1966 and emphasized Black Power, which blended African culture with contemporary black culture with the purpose of securing black American's freedom from the constraints of government and capitalism.[49] Although the Voting Rights Act of 1965 and the Civil Rights Act of 1964 had been passed, the Black Panthers represented reluctant believers in these laws' promise of equality. Instead, they sought a better life for people in the poverty-stricken, violence-ridden housing projects.[50] Education fared prominently in their economic goals. They believed in "an educational system that will give to our people a knowledge of self."[51] Of course, knowledge of self referred to an education that valued and featured black history and perspectives.

To accomplish their goals, the Black Panthers initiated numerous community-based programs nationwide in a wide variety of areas, including healthcare, prison reform, and education. The Black Panthers created schools known as Liberation Schools, which focused on developing critical thinking instead of memorization of facts.[52] Interestingly, the Black Panthers' approach to education aligned with John Dewey's concept of experiential learning.[53] While they emphasized black history, they also valued lived experiences. Their approach to teaching and learning "was about creating within black American education three of Dewey's insights: Education was a form of democracy, it was preparation for democracy, and it was an essential condition for democracy."[54] The Black Panthers also established a free breakfast program for children from 1969 to 1980 to ensure they were able to do their best in school.[55] This breakfast program inspired similar programs in dozens of cities and is said to have fostered the federal free breakfast program of today.[56] Overall, the Black Panthers represent a key example of how black organizations blended their activism with education as a pursuit for freedom.

Educational Freedom Among the Black Community Today

Today, while they are not under the horrific circumstances of slavery, black Americans continue to pursue educational freedom for themselves and their children. Black leaders, including Carter G. Woodson at the national level, and Georgia senator Horace Edward Tate at the local level, expressed concern surrounding the concept of desegregation in the schools. In Woodson's 1933 book, *The Mis-Education of the Negro*, he prophetically cautioned that a desegregated, European-based education would cause black children to aspire to whiteness rather than positively embrace their blackness. Today, black parents must guide their children through school conditions such as the discipline disproportionality, limited access to gifted education, teachers' low expectations of their children, and the tendency to over refer black children for special education. These characteristics have effectively pushed black families out of public and private schools as black parents increasingly choose home education to overcome the challenges of persistent racialized schooling experiences.[57] Legal scholar Najarian Peters has posited, "Black parent home-educators protect their children's right to be and become by adhering to a series of practices that include: preserving Black childhood; creating breathing space for Black children to flourish; insulating Black children from distortions; and letting Black children self-author their own lives."[58] Contrary to today's misconception of black parents as not being interested in their children's education, they not only care, they continue to sacrifice and demonstrate self-agency to educational freedom for their children. Today's black home-education movement serves as a contemporary representation of black self-determination, resistance, and self-agency in the pursuit of black educational freedom.

Notes

1. "Teaching About Frederick Douglass: A Resource Guide for Teachers of Cultural Diversity, Part One: Writing, Research, and Literacy, Introduction," *Counterpoints* 406 (2012): 1–4.

2. Jarvis R. Givens, *Fugitive Pedagogy: Carter G. Woodson and the Art of Black Teaching* (Harvard University Press, 2021).

3. Heather Andrea Williams, *Self-Taught: African American Education in Slavery and Freedom* (University of North Carolina Press, 2005), p. 7.

4. H. N. Keskin, "Malcolm X: The Legacy of a Civil Rights Leader," TRT-WORLD: Research Centre (blog), February 21, 2023.

5. "Definitions of Black Agency: The Legacy of Mildred Johnson Edwards," Harlem Education History Project, Humanities New York, February 18, 2020.

6. Allie Igwe, "The Spirit of Juneteenth: The Freedom to Self-Determine," American Society for Microbiology, June 19, 2023.

7. Alex Zamalin, *Struggle on Their Minds: The Political Thought of African American Resistance* (Columbia University Press, 2017).

8. Janel George, "Past Is Prologue: African Americans' Pursuit of Equal Educational Opportunity in the United States," *Human Rights* 44, no. 1 (May 2019): 11–14.

9. See, for example "Born in Slavery: Slave Narratives from the Federal Writers' Project, 1936 to 1938," Library of Congress, manuscript/mixed materials.

10. William L. Andrews, "The Value of Literacy to the Enslaved," in *Harriet Jacobs and Elizabeth Keckly: The Material and Emotional Realities of Childhood in Slavery*, EDSITEment!

11. Amira Dehmani, "Education in Enslaved Communities," Teaching with the Library: Primary Sources and Ideas for Teachers, Library of Congress, August 16, 2022.

12. Williams, *Self-Taught*, p. 19.

13. Williams, *Self-Taught*, p. 19.

14. Williams, *Self-Taught*, p. 21.

15. Lesa Cline-Ransome and James E. Ransome, *Light in the Darkness: A Story about How Slaves Learned in Secret* (Little, Brown Books for Young Readers, 2013).

16. Herbert G. Gutman, *The Black Family in Slavery and Freedom, 1750–1925* (Random House, 1976); and Dehmani, "Education in Enslaved Communities."

17. "The Incredible Story of How Frederick Douglass Learned to Read and Write," Alex & Books, May 10, 2020.

18. Williams, *Self-Taught*, p. 20.

19. Williams, *Self-Taught*, p. 21.

20. Andrews, "The Value of Literacy to the Enslaved."

21. Williams, *Self-Taught*, pp. 23–29.

22. Williams, *Self-Taught*, p. 24.

23. Williams, *Self-Taught*, p. 30.

24. See, for example, Williams, *Self-Taught*.

25. James D. Anderson, *The Education of Blacks in the South, 1860–1935*, (University of North Carolina Press, 1988), p. 5.

26. Anderson, *The Education of Blacks in the South, 1860–1935*, p. 5.

27. Joyce E. King, ed., *Black Education: A Transformative Research and Action Agenda for the New Century* (Lawrence Erlbaum Associates, Inc., 2005), p. 51.

28. Anderson, *The Education of Blacks in the South, 1860–1935*, p. 13.

29. See Anderson, *The Education of Blacks in the South, 1860–1935*; Williams, *Self-Taught*; and King, *Black Education*, pp. 50–57.

30. Jared Tetreau, "Sharecropping: Slavery Rerouted," American Experience, Public Broadcasting System, August 16, 2023.

31. Tetreau, "Sharecropping: Slavery Rerouted."

32. Russell Lee, "Negro Mother Teaching Children Numbers and Alphabet in Home of Sharecropper," Transylvania, Louisiana, January 1939, photograph. Library of Congress, Farm Security Administration/Office of War Information Photograph Collection Lot 1704, call number LC-USF34- 031938-D.

33. Michael J. Solender, "Inside the Rosenwald Schools," *Smithsonian Magazine*, March 30, 2021.

34. Solender, "Inside the Rosenwald Schools."

35. Andrew Feiler, *A Better Life for Their Children: Julius Rosenwald, Booker T. Washington, and the 4978 Schools That Changed America* (University of Georgia Press, 2021).

36. Nicquel Terry Ellis, "Rosenwald Schools Educated Generations of Black Americans. Now, Graduates are Fighting to Preserve Their Legacy," CNN, February 2, 2024.

37. Vanessa Siddle Walker, *Their Highest Potential: An African American School Community in the Segregated South* (University of North Carolina Press, 1996).

38. Walker, *Their Highest Potential*, p. 69.

39. Walker, *Their Highest Potential*, p. 87.

40. Walker, *Their Highest Potential*, p. 149.

41. Vanessa Siddle Walker with Ulysses Byas, *Hello Professor: A Black Principal and Professional Leadership in the Segregated South* (University of North Carolina Press, 2009).

42. Dionne Danns, Michelle A. Purdy, and Christopher M. Span, eds. *Using Past as Prologue: Contemporary Perspectives of African American Educational History* (Information Press Publishing, 2015).

43. Christine Woyshner, "Black Civic Organizations and the Quest for Education: The Improved Benevolent and Protective Order of Elks of the World, 1898–1954," *Journal of African American History* 108 no. 4 (Fall 2023): 578.

44. Woyshner, "Black Civic Organizations and the Quest for Education," p. 585.

45. Woyshner, "Black Civic Organizations and the Quest for Education," p. 587.

46. Woyshner, "Black Civic Organizations and the Quest for Education," pp. 587–88.

47. Zamalin, *Struggle on Their Minds.*

48. Zamalin, *Struggle on Their Minds*, 90.

49. Zamalin, *Struggle on Their Minds*, 88.

50. Zamalin, *Struggle on Their Minds*, 91.

51. Zamalin, *Struggle on Their Minds*, 101.

52. Zamalin, *Struggle on Their Minds*, 113.

53. Zamalin, *Struggle on Their Minds*, 114.

54. Zamalin, *Struggle on Their Minds*, 114.

55. Leah Q. Peoples and Lindsey Foster, "Revisiting and Learning from the Legacy of Black Communities' Education for Liberation Efforts," New York University, Metropolitan Center for Research on Equity and the Transformation of Schools..

56. Peoples and Foster, "Revisiting and Learning from the Legacy of Black Communities' Education for Liberation Efforts."

57. Cheryl Fields-Smith, *Creating Educational Justice: Learning from Black Home Educators* (Harvard Education Press, forthcoming).

58. Najarian R. Peters, "The Right to Be and Become: Black Home-Educators as Child Privacy Protectors," *Michigan Journal of Race and Law* 25 (2020): 43.

Chapter 7

Where Did Choice Go? Pluralism in Education from 1880 to 1955

By Neal P. McCluskey

As discussed in previous chapters, school choice as both an idea and in practice is as old as public schooling itself, but the idea that government should not just fund education but also provide schools is relatively new. School choice evolved from something much more decentralized, a pluralistic system in which numerous providers worked charitably or with freely paying families, though also with some government assistance. The Cato Institute's School Choice Timeline lays out the history of public money following students, or government funding diverse schools, and it is full of events from 1780 to 1878, and from 1955 on.[1] What this chapter seeks to explain is what happened in the intervening hibernation period—basically 1880 to 1955—and what revived the choice movement.

Situating the Hibernation

The timeline starts in 1780, when the Massachusetts Constitution was enacted and called for "legislatures and magistrates . . . to cherish the interests of literature and the sciences, and all seminaries of them."[2] The timeline includes numerous states and other jurisdictions helping to fund education in what would today be called private institutions, but during much of this time people would not have recognized a clear distinction between public and private. It also includes the intellectual supporters of school choice, such as Thomas Paine and John Stuart Mill, and crusades for greater choice, often by Roman Catholics. The timeline is packed up to 1878, when California political leader Zachariah Montgomery called for amending the state's constitution to divide "the school fund on . . . a parental basis."[3]

But then things slow down significantly, with only a few noteworthy happenings. In 1929, Pope Pius XI published the encyclical *Divini Illius Magistri*, condemning funding of only religiously "neutral" state schools and calling for money to go "to the several schools demanded by the families."[4] In 1948, the United Nations published the Universal Declaration of Human Rights, which recognized that "parents have a prior right to choose the kind of education that shall be given to their children."[5] And in 1949, Episcopal priest Bernard Iddings Bell wrote in his book *Crisis in Education* that if public schools are going to eschew religion, "the only decent thing is to permit religious groups to run their own schools, which of course we now do, and to give them tax money to run them with, which we do not."[6]

The battle for school choice picked back up considerably starting in 1955, with Milton Friedman's seminal chapter "The Role of Government in Education," published in the Robert Solo-edited volume *Economics and the Public Interest*.[7] That same year, Minnesota passed a tax deduction for expenses at any school, including private. From that year to today, there have been myriad initiatives to create private school choice programs, and numerous states have passed choice measures after the first modern voucher program was enacted in Milwaukee, Wisconsin, in 1990. As of the end of 2024, more than 1.2 million students were enrolled in private choice programs.[8]

Of course, in 1954, the US Supreme Court declared de jure racial segregation in public schools unconstitutional in *Brown v. Board of Education*, which spurred programs in several Southern states that gave money to families to choose schools, with the intent to remain de facto segregated. This timing has been seized upon by many school choice opponents to brand choice a movement born of segregationist intent.[9] As established, the movement for choice did not start with desegregation—it is as old as public schooling—but the seeming hibernation of the choice movement from roughly 1880 to 1955 can appear to lend credence to the notion that no one cared about choice after 1880, until it was revived by ugly desires to perpetuate racial segregation.

That odious scenario is not the case. What one finds when examining the history is not that the school choice movement went away in the period between 1880 and 1955, but that private education was locked in a more basic, sometimes even existential battle. The period from 1880 to 1955 was a stew of nationalism and industrialization, fear of mass immigration from parts of Europe more socially distant from Anglo-Saxon culture than earlier waves, and two world wars—all of which tended to put private education on its heels.

Nationalism

The Civil War and its aftermath took the United States from being, to a large extent, a collection of states, to a nation, with the national government drafting men into war, creating direct taxation, and more.[10] There had been a nationalist component to the public schooling movement before the Civil War, with Founding generation members such as Benjamin Rush and Noah Webster viewing education as a means to build attachment to the new nation, and common schooling "founder" Horace Mann explicitly pointing to a nation- and citizen-building role for public schools.[11] But especially for Rush and Webster, this was in the context of a newly established federation of colonies-turned-states that had been largely independent before. Meanwhile, as discussed in previous chapters, education had been based on systems of plural options, especially in the mid-Atlantic and Southern states, including diverse religious schools and modes of delivery ranging from tutors and so-called dame schools to private academies.

For much of the early republican period, the education debate was largely whether there would be mass government-provided education, and if there were, whether it would take the form of government schools or government-aided schools founded and run by others. As seen on the School Choice Timeline, families and various types of schools were funded in places such as New York City, Pennsylvania, Virginia, Milwaukee, and New Jersey during this antebellum period.[12] As immigration, especially from Roman Catholic Ireland, started to increase, there were rising worries about a population and educational system that would undermine republican, Anglo-Saxon America.[13] However, until the Civil War, people tended to identify more with states than with a unified nation.[14] States also had varying levels of religious and ethnic diversity and approaches to education.

The Civil War ended much of the decentralized nature of the United States. In part this was because it answered a lingering question: Was the United States a voluntary association that any state could leave if it so chose? Was it essentially a club of states? The answer was no, it was not.

The war also saw, as wars often do, centralization of power, including Union President Abraham Lincoln suspending habeas corpus rights, and, to a lesser degree, the national government of the Confederacy attempting to achieve national control to prosecute its war.[15] Meanwhile, the absence of the more state-centered Southern delegations from Congress enabled that body to take on more national education programs than it could have before, such as the Morrill Act in 1862. This legislation, which provided federal resources to create and fund land-grant colleges in the states, had been defeated, albeit narrowly, prior to the war, suffering a veto by President James Buchanan in 1859.[16] And in an especially significant decision, Congress made the Southern states' readmission into the Union contingent on providing for state public education in their constitutions, even though most Southern states had no such public schooling laws prior to the war.[17] In 1867, the federal government even created a short-lived Department of Education.[18]

In 1864, as the Civil War continued to rage, Pope Pius IX issued the encyclical *Quanta Cura*, which included as an appendix the "Syllabus of Errors." The encyclical was issued largely in opposition to the governments of France and Italy—not primarily for failing to perpetuate Roman Catholicism, as some might assume, but for actively attacking it, including closing its schools.[19] Decrying "Communism and Socialism," the pope objected that "these most deceitful men chiefly aim at this result, viz., that the salutary teaching and influence of the Catholic

Church may be entirely banished from the instruction and education of youth."[20] The syllabus seemed less interested in protecting the right to choose Catholic education than it was in protecting the Church's sphere from civil powers. Focused on other countries, it gave little indication that the Church was seeking to overthrow the United States' republican government, as many who worried about Catholics had at times alleged.[21] But the syllabus did contain some cause for concern, including listing among the common errors, "in the present day it is no longer expedient that the Catholic religion should be held as the only religion of the State, to the exclusion of all other forms of worship."[22]

The syllabus created alarm around the world. It was also cited in debates about a proposed constitutional amendment from Maine Senator James G. Blaine in 1875 that would have barred, nationwide, any public funding supporting the school of any sect, while providing that the amendment could "not be construed to prohibit the reading of the Bible in any school or institution."[23] The amendment would have protected the de facto Protestant public schools while overtly forbidding the kind of sharing of funds with Catholics that had been debated, and sometimes carried out, in many states.

While the federal Blaine amendment failed, Congress passed requirements that territories contain Blaine language in order to be admitted to the union as states.[24] No foreign powers, including the Catholic Church, were to have a say in the newly reunited United States. By 1915, all but three states had Blaine amendments.[25]

Immigration and Assimilation

Intimately connected to nationalism was immigration, especially a desire to shape new immigrants into "proper" Americans, which to many meant living outside of ghettos and other homogeneous groupings and speaking English. This had long been a concern—Benjamin Franklin and other English-speaking Pennsylvanians worried mightily about the colony's large German-speaking population, which they feared would become the majority and turn Pennsylvania from an English colony into a German one.[26] But immigration leapt up around 1880 and continued, with some peaks and valleys, until about 1914, when World War I greatly curtailed it, and dropped further in 1920, when quotas were installed.[27] These immigrants were not the primarily Northern Europeans of earlier waves, but Eastern and Southern Europeans, including many Jews and Italians, who seemed even more foreign and threatening to many Americans than earlier immigrants.

This was considered very much an education problem. Public schools were seen by many as crucial institutions for assimilating newcomers.[28] But despite Catholic schools typically receiving no government assistance, their enrollment was growing markedly in the late 19th and early 20th centuries, and of course those students were *not* attending public schools.[29]

That said, it was German speakers, who tended to be not just Catholic but Lutheran, who were the subjects of the first major divisive attacks on private schooling, though there had been a significant movement to regulate all private schools in various ways.[30] German settlers had long had a separatist bent—some even thought of starting independent lands in North America[31]—and they often insisted on their children learning and speaking German. Two laws in the late 1880s in Wisconsin and Illinois sought to prohibit teaching in foreign languages, both in public and private schools. They also limited private schools that would meet compulsory education requirements to those in the geographic boundaries of a student's public school district.[32] The laws passed, angering ethnic Germans as well as people of Scandinavian and Polish extraction. They were also very unpopular and were soon repealed when the Republicans who had pushed them were voted out of office by an angry populace.

Not surprisingly, World War I put Germans further under the microscope. In 1919, Nebraska passed the Siman Act, which prohibited teaching students in any language other than English until after the eighth grade, with the goal of making students identify as Americans first and foremost. Other states had also debated such laws.[33] This again fell hardest on the German schools, though other, smaller communities were also affected. A teacher at a Lutheran school sued, claiming that the prohibition violated his right to freely contract to provide services, and in 1923 the Supreme Court agreed with him, striking down the law and recognizing that a right to contract to provide a service was more important than engineered unity.[34]

But the war on the mere existence of plural education was not over yet. In 1922, Oregon enacted by referendum the Compulsory Education Act, which stipulated that only attendance at public schools, with a few minor exceptions, would meet compulsory education requirements. Similar efforts had been undertaken, unsuccessfully, in several other states.[35] The result would be the destruction of private schools. The referendum was heavily pushed by the resurgent Ku Klux Klan, which was now more active in parts of the Midwest and Northwest than the previous Southern incarnation, and was more virulently anti-Catholic, anti-immigrant, and antisemitic, as well as resentful of elites.[36] There was also a lot of overlap with the secretive Masons, who were pinpointed as anathema to Catholics in the "Syllabus of Errors."[37] Two groups—the Sisters of the Holy Name and the Hill Military Academy—sued to halt the act, demonstrating that the law threatened all private education with extinction. They prevailed, with the Supreme Court ruling in *Pierce v. Society of Sisters* that while government could regulate private schools, "[t]he child is not the mere creature of the State; those who nurture him and direct his destiny have the right, coupled with the high duty, to recognize and prepare him for additional obligations."[38]

Private schooling had survived, but between the proliferation of Blaine amendments and largely anti-immigrant war on the right to obtain a private education, it is little surprise that school choice—public funding of students or diverse schools—was not an insurgent movement.

Industrialization and Progressivism

Industrialization, and the massive leaps in living standards it created, produced great confidence in the ability of human beings to engineer and improve all aspects of life. It also reduced the importance of religion—and religion in education—to many people.[39] The result was an emphasis on "expert" control of systems, including education, and the application of science to social problems: progressivism.[40] This was seen in powerful efforts to centralize and bureaucratize public school districts, and continued pushes for more regulation of private schools. It also drove forward the idea of the religiously neutral public school. Religion would often remain in the form of basic Protestant Bible reading and prayer, and eventually in some places released time to attend religious education not delivered by district personnel, but the schools would embrace religion no further.[41] The triumph of science and engineering, both intellectually and in public policy, was inconsistent with free choice, especially of largely religious schools.

In this time of industrialization, Roman Catholics were themselves debating how much they could use public schools and how individuals who felt their conscience did not permit their use could be accommodated. In the 1890s, this launched spirited debates among Catholics, with the most progressive view being promulgated by Archbishop John Ireland of the Diocese of Saint Paul, Minnesota. At a speech before the National Education Association in 1890, Ireland extolled the virtues of the "state school," saying, "I would have all schools for the children of the people State schools." He also said, "The right of the state school to exist, I consider, is a matter beyond the stage of discussion. I most fully concede it."[42]

A Catholic bishop celebrating state schooling showed that government control of education, consistent with progressivism, had triumphed. Perhaps the school choice movement had died because the group most marginalized by the public schools—Roman Catholics—had now fully embraced them. At the very least, it showed that the government schooling model had defeated the concept of funding plural options.

But as the number of Catholics increased at a speedy clip due to immigration and high birth rates, they did not give up on parochial schooling. Indeed, the Church struggled mightily to fit all Catholic children into parochial schools.[43] And Archbishop Ireland did not think the state school was sufficient for Catholics. He embraced efforts to accommodate Catholics—efforts that were short of funding students to choose schools or the government directly funding plural institutions. He especially supported the Poughkeepsie Plan—an arrangement in Poughkeepsie, New York, through which the school district leased parochial school buildings for one dollar per year and was responsible for their upkeep; allowed Catholic students to use the schools; and allowed Catholic teachers to teach as long as they met district requirements and no religious instruction occurred during the school day. After school, Catholics could deliver religious education in the building. The plan ran from 1873 to 1898, and similar accommodations short of full choice were tried in several other places.[44] Ireland was also open to government funding schools of all types based on their success in teaching secular subjects.

While the state school was triumphant, even Ireland drew a line on what was unacceptable, a line highlighted by other bishops, popes, and adherents of other religious sects. The religiously neutral school was unacceptable because neutrality itself was a statement on religion, signaling that it did not offer anything important for understanding a student's moral obligations or the world around them. Ireland also invoked conscience rights and decried double taxation—first pay taxes for public schools, pay again for private—as choice supporters had long done.[45] As Ireland said, "Secularists and unbelievers will interpose their rights. I allow them their rights. I will not impose upon them my religion, which is Christianity. But let them not impose upon me and my fellow Christians their religion which is Secularism."[46]

The state-as-organizer could promulgate public schooling. It could also refrain from subsidizing religious education. But expelling religion from education was a bridge too far.

After World War I, the country saw something of a rejection of scientism, human power, and elite leadership, perhaps slowing the progressive impetus to control and standardize society that worked in favor of top-down, expert-controlled public schooling and against private education. Appalled by the human suffering inflicted by industrial-era inventions such as machine guns, tanks, and poison gas, and feeling they had been misled by their leaders' justifications for entering into war—France and England were not that pure, the Central powers not that evil—the country rejected overinflated promises to create utopia, such as President Woodrow Wilson's League of Nations, and embraced more free living during the Roaring Twenties.[47]

On the flip side, in the face of progressive power there was also a battle to make religion—especially conservative Protestantism—dominant in public schools, not merely present. It reached its publicity zenith with the 1925 Scopes "monkey trial," a national sensation in Dayton, Tennessee, about a law that forbade the teaching of evolution in schools. The trial pitted "regular" Americans against urbane progressive elites. Teacher John Scopes openly flouted the law to create the case. He lost but was exonerated on a technicality, and the law remained in effect for many years.[48] This made the public schools more welcoming to conservative Protestants but would likely have made them little more acceptable to Catholics.

The infatuation with engineering society through "scientific" government was waning in the 1920s, to the likely benefit of private education, but a tug-of-war between secularism and fundamentalism was a no-win situation for the biggest private schoolers—Roman Catholics. Meanwhile, progressive efforts to centralize control of, and remove religion from, public schooling would continue, but the latter not prevail until the early 1960s.[49]

Eclipsing Issues: Depression and War

After *Pierce*, efforts emerged to provide some public support for private schools, though there was no major push to get significant public funds to follow children to private schools, or direct funding to make them free for families. Assistance came mainly in the form of textbook or transportation support.[50] Such modest support was provided in part because all schools were hurting financially during the Great Depression, but the demise of parochial schools would pour more students into public institutions. Indeed, that parochial schools relieved public schools of a significant teaching burden had long been a reason even champions of public schooling opposed actions such as the Oregon law later struck down in *Pierce*.[51]

That said, the Great Depression and World War II demanded so much attention, and the war so many resources, that serious efforts to connect funding to students would have almost certainly been ill-timed. Indeed, efforts to provide such minimal support as reimbursements for transportation to parochial schools occurred largely after the war ended.

Sparking Revival: Totalitarianism and Discrimination Against Religion

What brought the school choice effort back? While choice detractors tend to point to efforts to evade integration of public schools that had long been segregated by government, it was actually religion, and fear of totalitarianism such as what the world witnessed in Nazi Germany and the Soviet Union, that spurred much of the choice movement's revival.

As noted earlier, in 1929, Pope Pius XI issued the *Divini Illius Magistri* encyclical, which said that in countries with religiously diverse populations, funding only "neutral or mixed schools" was insufficient.[52] He pointed to several countries with "financial aid granted by the State to the several schools demanded by the families" as examples of what could be done. In 1948, the United Nations' Universal Declaration of Human Rights enshrined the "prior right" of parents "to choose the kind of education that shall be given to their children."[53] It was a controversial provision inserted at the insistence of smaller countries that had seen state education weaponized by the Nazis and that wanted a bulwark of educational pluralism to protect against such domination.[54] And as captured by Episcopal priest Bernard Iddings Bell in 1949, and the group Citizens for Educational Freedom starting in 1959 (see Chapter 9 for more), many religious Americans again recognized that requiring all people to pay once for public schooling, then a second time for religious education, was discrimination against religion.[55]

But what of Milton Friedman's chapter arguing for choice in Solo's *Economics and the Public Interest*, published a year after the 1954 *Brown v. Board* decision? Does that not show that a desire to maintain segregation was the reason choice was revived?

No. First, the chapter, likely written in 1954, included a lengthy note added late in the publishing process discussing and condemning the possible misuse of choice.[56] And Friedman simply had other aims. He argued for choice on the grounds that enabling people to choose diverse schools would spur systemwide improvement and efficiency. The broader impetus was most likely to defend free markets against planned economies, as the intellectual battle between freedom and collectivism was lining up in the early years of the Cold War. In his 1962 book *Capitalism and Freedom*, in which Friedman reproduced much of his 1955 essay, he was explicit about that impetus, writing at the beginning of the first chapter:

> It is widely believed that politics and economics are separate and largely unconnected; that individual freedom is a political problem and material welfare an economic problem; and that any kind of political arrangements can be combined with any kind of economic arrangements. The chief contemporary manifestation of this idea is the advocacy of "democratic socialism" by many who condemn out of hand the restrictions on individual freedom imposed by "totalitarian socialism" in Russia and who are persuaded that it is possible for a country to adopt the essential features of Russian economic arrangements and yet to ensure individual freedom through political arrangements. The thesis of this chapter is that such a view is a delusion, that there is an intimate connection between economics and politics, that only certain combinations of political and economic arrangements are possible, and that in particular, a society which is socialist cannot also be democratic, in the sense of guaranteeing individual freedom.[57]

As shall be seen in subsequent chapters of this book, the modern school choice movement was spurred not primarily by racism—though it was a factor—but by demands for religious equality, diverse options, and overall freedom. It was also driven by a desire to help low-income, often minority children access schools better than their assigned public institutions. Which is at least ironic if you think school choice was born of a desire for racial segregation.

Conclusion

Even as the choice movement seemed to go quiet from 1880 to 1955, the basic rationale remained: Choice was about freedom and equality for a diverse people. What put it into hibernation was not an absence of desire for choice, but concerted efforts to minimize differences among Americans, especially of immigrant stock, and create a new, industrialization-inspired, expertly controlled society. Widespread choice got in the way of such standardization, and choice proponents were to a significant extent fighting for the mere survival of educational freedom.

Notes

1. School Choice Timeline, Cato Institute.

2. Massachusetts Constitution of 1780, ch. V, § 2 ("Fundamental Documents" in *The Founders' Constitution*, University of Chicago Press).

3. Zachariah Montgomery, *Speech on the School Question, Delivered Before the Convention Committee on Education, in the Assembly Chamber at Sacramento City, November 20, 1878* (Oakland, CA: J. J. Montgomery, 1879; Internet Archive, 2010), p. 2.

4. Pope Pius XI, *Divini Illius Magistri*, Encyclical of Pope Pius XI on Christian Education, December 31, 1929 (Vatican Publishing House).

5. Universal Declaration of Human Rights, United Nations, December 10, 1948.

6. Bernard Iddings Bell, *Crisis in Education: A Challenge to American Complacency* (McGraw Hill, 1949), p. 222.

7. Milton Friedman, "The Role of Government in Education," in Robert A. Solo, ed., *Economics and the Public Interest* (Rutgers University Press, 1955), pp. 123–44.

8. *The ABCs of School Choice: The Comprehensive Guide to Every Private School Choice Program in America, 2025 Edition* (EdChoice, 2025), p. 8.

9. See, for instance, Steve Suitts, *Overturning Brown: The Segregationist Legacy of the Modern School Choice Movement* (NewSouth Books, 2020); and Chris Ford, Stephenie Johnson, and Lisette Partelow, "The Racist Origins of Private School Vouchers," Center for American Progress, July 12, 2017.

10. James M. McPherson, "Out of War, a New Nation," *Prologue Magazine* 42, no. 1 (Spring 2010).

11. Frederick Rudolph, ed., *Essays on Education in the Early Republic*, (Belknap Press of Harvard University Press, 1965); and Horace Mann, "Report for 1843," in *Life and Works of Horace Mann*, ed. Mary Mann, vol. 3, *Annual Reports on Education* (Boston: Horace B. Fuller, 1868), p. 242.

12. School Choice Timeline.

13. See, for instance, Lyman Beecher, *A Plea for the West* (Truman and Smith, 1835).

14. Melissa M. Lee et al., "From *Pluribus* to *Unum*? The Civil War and Imagined Sovereignty in Nineteenth-Century America," *American Political Science Review* 118, no. 1 (February 2024): 127–43.

15. Scott Bomboy, "Lincoln and Taney's Great Writ Showdown," National Constitution Center, May 28, 2023; and Paul Escott, "Jefferson Davis as President of the Confederacy," Wake Forest News, Wake Forest University, February 12, 2009.

16. "Roll Call for a Vote on the Morrill Act, US Senate, June 10, 1862, Creating Land-Grant Colleges," US Capitol Visitor Center.

17. Derek W. Black, "The Constitutional Compromise to Guarantee Education," *Stanford Law Review* 70 (March 2018).

18. "Federal Role in Education," US Department of Education.

19. Donald Sullivan, "Pius IX Issues the Syllabus of Errors," EBSCO, 2023.

20. Pope Pius IX, *Quanta Cura*, Encyclical of Pope Pius IX on Condemning Current Errors, 1864, Papal Encyclicals Online.

21. See, for instance, Beecher, *A Plea for the West*; and Samuel F. B. Morse, "Samuel Morse Fears a Catholic Conspiracy, 1835," from his *Foreign Conspiracy Against the Liberties of the United States* (New York: Leavitt, Lord and Co., 1835), excerpted in *American Yawp Reader.*

22. Pope Pius IX, "The Syllabus of Errors," Encyclical of Pope Pius IX, 1864, Papal Encyclicals Online.

23. 4 Congressional Record S5580 (August 14, 1876).

24. "School Choice: The Blaine Amendments & Anti-Catholicism," US Commission on Civil Rights, 2007, p. 33.

25. Timothy Walch, *Parish School: American Catholic Parochial Education from Colonial Times to the Present* (Crossroad Publishing Company, 1996), p. 152.

26. Lawrence A. Cremin, *American Education: The Colonial Experience, 1607–1783* (Harper and Row, 1970), pp. 256–64.

27. Philip Martin, "Trends in Migration to the US," Population Reference Bureau, May 19, 2014.

28. David B. Tyack, *The One Best System: A History of American Urban Education* (Harvard University Press, 1974), pp. 229–55.

29. Robert N. Gross, *Public vs. Private: The Early History of School Choice in America* (Oxford University Press, 2018), pp. 3, 34, 83.

30. Gross, *Public vs. Private*, pp. 83–104.

31. Nathan Glazer, "Ethnic Groups in America: From National Culture to Ideology," in *Freedom and Control in Modern Society*, eds. Morroe Berger et al. (Octagon Books, 1978), p. 161.

32. Lloyd P. Jorgenson, *The State and the Non-Public School: 1825–1925* (University of Missouri Press, 1987), p. 188.

33. Jack W. Rodgers, "The Foreign Language Issue in Nebraska, 1918–1923," *Nebraska History* 39 (1958): 1–22, 5n13.

34. *Meyer v. Nebraska*, 262 U.S. 390 (1923).

35. Gross, *Public vs. Private*, pp. 110–11.

36. David B. Tyack, "The Perils of Pluralism: The Background of the Pierce Case," *American Historical Review* 74, no. 1 (October 1968): 78.

37. Pope Pius IX, "The Syllabus of Errors."

38. *Pierce v. Society of Sisters*, 268 U.S. 510 (1925).

39. Ruth A. Wienclaw, "Religion and Industrialization," EBSCO, 202.

40. Sidney M. Milkis, "Progressivism," *Britannica*, March 20, 2025.

41. B. Edward McClellan, *Moral Education in America: Schools and the Shaping of Character from Colonial Times to the Present* (Teachers College Press, 1999), p. 62; and Jonathan Zimmerman, *Whose America: Culture Wars in Public Schools*, 2nd ed. (University of Chicago Press, 2022), pp. 123-45.

42. John Ireland, speech to the National Education Association, July 1890, reprinted in *The Catholic Telegraph*, July 24, 1890.

43. Walch, *Parish School*, pp. 42, 60; J. David Hacker and Evan Roberts, "Fertility decline in the United States, 1850–1930: New Evidence from Complete-Count Datasets," National Library of Medicine, 2022.

44. Walch, *Parish School*, p. 69.

45. For instance, Archbishop John Hughes of New York decried "the unjust disadvantages of double taxation in 1840. See *The Complete Works of the Most Rev. John Hughes, D.D. Archbishop of New York Comprising His Sermons, Letters, Lectures, Speeches, Etc.*, Lawrence Kehoe, ed., (Lawrence Kehoe, 1866), p. 64.

46. Ireland, speech to the National Education Association.

47. Douglas Brinkley, *American Heritage History of the United States* (Viking Press, 1998), pp. 358–61.

48. Adam Laats, *Fundamentalism and Education in the Scopes Era: God, Darwin, and the Roots of America's Culture Wars* (Palgrave Macmillan, 2012).

49. See *Engel v. Vitale*, 370 U.S. 421 (1962) and *Abington School District v. Schempp*, 374 U.S. 203 (1963).

50. Walch, *Parish School*, pp. 159–68.

51. Gross, *Public v. Private*, p. 64.

52. Pope Pius XI, *Divini Illius Magistri*.

53. United Nations, "Universal Declaration of Human Rights."

54. James Stanfield, "Parental Choice and the Right to Education: Revisiting Article 26 of the Universal Declaration of Human Rights," UNESCO, 2021.

55. James Shuls, "Papists and Pluralists: The Founding of America's First Grassroots School Choice Organization," *Journal of School Choice* 16, no. 3 (1968): 416–32.

56. Friedman, "The Role of Government in Education," 131n.

57. Milton Friedman, *Capitalism and Freedom* (University of Chicago Press, 1962), pp. 7–8.

Chapter 8

From Common Schools to Parental School Choice: Protestants, Catholics, and the Growing School Choice Movement in the Early 20th Century

By Matthew H. Lee

In his 1954 book, *The Churches and the Schools*, Francis Xavier Curran declared, "American Protestantism has relinquished the age-old claim of the Christian Church to control the formal elementary education of its children."[1] Whatever Protestants may have conceded, as Protestant education historian Edwin Rian wrote in 1949, the consequences have been "detrimental to the youth, religiously and morally."[2] Why did Protestants largely abandon church-based schools for government-run schools? And what caused the return to parental school choice in the early 20th century?

Protestants initially cast their lot with government-run schools not only because of concern of Catholic influence in education but also because Protestant political thought allowed for education to remain under the state's sphere of influence. Early common schools, while situated in the state's sphere, were Protestant in culture and largely remained under the control of parents and the local community. However, as government-run schools began to slip away from local control toward more centralized bureaucracies, Protestants ultimately shifted their support back to parental school choice.

Protestants and Catholics alike were part of a growing movement for parental school choice in the early 1900s. Protestant support for parental school choice expanded in the 1930s and 1940s for three reasons: (a) the triumph of natural philosophy, (b) the failure of Protestant education systems, and (c) the weakening of parental oversight of education as power shifted from local to state to federal control. Catholic support for parental school choice also grew during this time as the Catholic Church affirmed more strongly the right of parents to exercise choice, despite initially compelling attendance at parochial schools.

Protestant Public Schools

Many have contended that Protestant opposition to Catholic influence in education was merely motivated by anti-Catholic bigotry.[3] However, Protestant resistance to a Catholic system of education also had historical, theological, and political grounds. Historically, Catholic persecution of Protestants (such as the reign of Mary Tudor in England, the St. Bartholomew's Day massacre in France, and the Penal Laws in Ireland) was a recent memory to American Protestants. Theologically, the rejection of the doctrine of justification by faith alone in the Council of Trent was odious to Protestants. Politically, the Catholic Church operated as a hierarchical and centralized system, which was incompatible with the decentralized Protestant polity of the early American republic. Beyond simple bigotry, Protestants worried that a Catholic education system would promulgate anti-Protestant sentiment, contradict the fundamental teachings of Protestantism, and challenge the political system of a Protestant society.

Furthermore, distinctions between Catholic and Protestant political thought make clear why American Protestants trusted the state to run a system of public schools. According to Catholic canon law, the Catholic Church maintains a position of supremacy over other institutions like the state or the family. As Rian explains, "The Church occupies this position of superiority because its prime purpose is to teach. The Church has been granted infallibility by God so that she has freedom in teaching. In this capacity the Church has the right to evaluate the social heritage and to determine what part of it is true and good and worthy of perpetuation by education."[4]

In contrast, Protestant political thought often divides these institutions into spheres with distinct responsibilities. Dutch political leader and Calvinist Abraham Kuyper's theory of sphere sovereignty, for example, differentiated responsibility among separate institutional spheres.[5] Applied to education, three spheres—the state, the church, and the family—take an interest in education and should respect the discrete responsibilities of the other institutions. As prime minister of the Netherlands from 1901–1905, Kuyper advocated for policies in which the state funded education, but schools were operated by churches and families.

This separation of church and state allowed American Protestants to support government-run common schools. The spiritual mission of the church included only the preaching of the Bible, administration of the sacraments, and propagation of the gospel.[6] This understanding of the secular-sacred distinction meant that secular institutions could assume a religious identity or serve religious purposes.[7] Indeed, public life in the early republic drew heavily from its ecclesial counterparts, even fashioning the republican system after Protestant church polity.[8]

There is much evidence of how the secular (that is, non-churchly) work of education extended from and promoted a Protestant worldview in colonial America. The oldest provision for public education in the colonies was the Massachusetts Old Deluder Satan Law,[9] passed in 1647, which stated that the purpose of education was to promote learning and knowledge of the Scriptures. The close integration of religion and education continued through the American Revolution when the delegates of the Second Continental Congress in 1778, on the basis that "true religion and good morals are the only solid foundations of public liberty and happiness," resolved that each state would "take the most effectual measure for the encouragement thereof."[10] National policies like the Northwest Ordinance as well as various state statutes made public provisions for religious public schools.[11]

Though these writings and laws predate the signing of the US Constitution, the idea that civic virtue could be germinated only in religious soil persisted with the formation of the new republic. In his 1796 Farewell Address, George Washington declared religion and morality to be "indisputable supports" for "all the dispositions and habits which lead to political prosperity."[12] Washington's successor, John Adams, expressed in a 1798 letter to the Massachusetts militia, "Our constitution was made only for a moral and religious people."[13] Benjamin Rush, one of the signers of the Constitution, wrote that same year, "The only foundation for a useful education in a republic is to be laid in religion."[14]

These early common schools were nonsectarian in the sense that they did not prefer any Protestant sect, but they were Protestant in culture and character. The schools governed by the Public School Society were "Protestant in teaching staff, in textbooks, in Bible and in the general atmosphere of the classroom."[15] Even by the time Horace Mann implemented his reforms in Massachusetts, the Bible "was regarded in practically every instance as a non-sectarian book" that was intended to "speak for itself without comment."[16]

The Triumph of Natural Philosophy

In the years after the American Revolution, the humanistic and naturalistic philosophy of Jean-Jacques Rousseau began to take hold in education. In the opening line of his 1762 work *The Social Contract*, Rousseau contended, "Man is born free; and everywhere he is in chains."[17] Rousseau extended his naturalistic philosophy to education in his 1762 book *Emile*, arguing that education had the effect of enslaving natural man. According to Rian, "Perhaps more than any other book, *Emile* undermined the foundations of the religious theory of education" by challenging the Protestant notion that man's natural inclination is toward evil.[18]

The triumph of naturalistic philosophy in state education was completed by the mid-20th century with the 1938 publication of John Dewey's *Experience and Education* and the 1947 publication of the self-guided teacher training textbook *Preface to Philosophy* by William Ernest Hocking (Harvard), Brand Blanshard (Yale), Charles William Hendel (Yale), and John Herman Randall (Columbia). Dewey argued that personal experience was authoritative, and thus, against "imposition from above"; he advocated for "expression and cultivation of individuality."[19] Similarly, Hocking, Blanshard, Hendel, and Randall exchanged absolute truth and morality for relativism, arguing that moral rules "may be regarded as experimental and variable."[20]

Thus, natural philosophy in education was one reason for the growing concern for public education and the growing support for parental school choice, particularly among Protestants. Princeton professor J. Gresham Machen expressed such concern at a 1926 address to the Sentinels of the Republic, a national political organization opposed to federal overreach, in which he critiqued Deweyan morality codes in public schools, which based "morality upon experience, instead of upon an absolute distinction between right and wrong."[21] Rian, Machen's student, wrote that the consequence of shifting the "fundamental source of truth and of right . . . from God to man and the world" has resulted in a rejection of the Christian philosophy of truth and morality as the foundation for education.[22] According to Rian,

> What has naturalism done to the realm of truth? Here the most destructive effects are evident. In modern education the idea of absolute truth in any field of knowledge is ridiculed as obsolete. Truth is relative the same as morals are relative. What is true for one is not necessarily true for another. Human reason, experience and investigation determine the validity of any proposition in every field of human endeavor.[23]

Protestants erred in believing the state to be capable of promoting a Protestant worldview. Instead, a system antithetical to Protestantism became the prevailing philosophy in education.

The Failure of Protestant Education Systems

The second reason that Protestant support for parental school choice grew was because of various failed efforts to create Protestant education systems. Initially, many Protestant denominations sought to create their own educational institutions. In 1838, the Episcopalians "called for the training of

Christian teachers, declared it to be the duty of Episcopalians to maintain church schools, and insisted that these schools be established immediately."[24] Similarly, "In 1847 the conservative or old-school faction [of Reformed Presbyterians] initiated a drive for a system of parochial schools" and "founded about three hundred ephemeral schools."[25] The minutes of the annual Quaker meetings in the early 1800s "manifested Quaker determination to keep the control of the education of their children out of the hands of the state, and firmly in the grip of their denomination."[26]

These efforts quickly diminished. Efforts to create Episcopalian schools were "postponed until after the Civil War."[27] Similarly for Presbyterians, momentum for a Reformed system of schools "had been lost by the time of the Civil War, when a sectional schism broke the [old-school/new-school] halves of the church into quarters [Northern and Southern churches]."[28] Industrialization, which introduced "new social problems of pauperism, housing, suffrage for all groups, intemperance and juvenile delinquency," and the mass immigration of Catholics in the 1820s melted away Protestant desire for denominational schools and accelerated support for the secularization of education.[29] Ultimately, Protestant denominational efforts largely failed for lack of teachers, money, and pupils.[30]

Unable to create entire denominational systems, many Protestants made attempts to supplement common schools with religious instruction through Sunday schools and weekday church schools. Sunday schools, or Sabbath schools as they were sometimes called, were intended to provide explicit religious instruction to children in the context of a local church. The earliest recorded example of a Sunday school was in 1740, but these efforts were organized nationally about a century later when the American Sunday School Union was founded in 1824 and held its first national convention in 1832.[31] However, these efforts saw little fruit, and by the early 20th century, Rian estimates that total Sunday school enrollment was only about 15 percent of all children in America and decreasing.[32]

Weekday church schools were church-operated programs in which students were pulled out of regular academic courses for midweek religious instruction. These schools "carried on under the direction of the local churches or councils and convened in church buildings, in public buildings rented by churches or even in public schoolrooms whenever possible" and were intended "to supplement the public school and to guide the pupil in a knowledge of the Christian faith."[33] By 1940, 38 states had school districts cooperating with weekday church schools, but at its peak, "the total attendance of these classes did not aggregate more than 200,000 students."[34] Ultimately, these efforts failed not only for lack of time (typically one hour per week) and resources, but also because the practice bifurcated religion and education, implying "that one can study all subjects apart from religion and even part from God. Religion is something which can be attached to the learning process or left off at the discretion of the educand or his parents."[35]

It was clear that these efforts were insufficient for promoting the Protestant faith to the American youth. Just as Protestants erred by believing that the state could effectively promote the Protestant faith, they erred in believing that these supplemental and peripheral efforts were enough to combat the growing influence of natural philosophy in public schools.

The Centralization of Power over Education

Finally, Protestant support for parental school choice grew because the progressive centralization of education oversight from local to state to federal power reduced the control that parents exercised over their children's education. It should be noted that American Protestants, even while supporting common schools, maintained that parents had the right and responsibility of overseeing their children's education (and many continue to hold this view today[36]). Although support of common schools ultimately yielded control of education to the state, Protestants believed that common schools required enough cooperation of parents to be satisfied with the arrangement. The Episcopal Church, for example, "urged that parents should keep a careful eye on the common schools, and directed ministers to visit the schools and make their presence felt."[37]

In colonial America, common schools operated "under the control of the town" and, further evidence of the close relationship between civic and religious life, "the affairs of the town, both civil and religious, were conducted in the Meeting House, which served as church, town hall, and school."[38] Control gradually shifted "away from family and community toward more centralized institutions under the control of a professional class."[39]

Even while support for systems of parochial schools along denominational lines declined, many Protestants emphasized the right of the parent or the parent-society to govern education. When the National Union of Christian Schools was established in 1920, it published a pamphlet, *The Organization of the Local Parent-Society Christian School Plan*, which identified four guiding principles:

1. According to the Scripture, God holds parents responsible for the training of their offspring. (Deut. 6:6–7; Eph. 6:4)
2. True to the principle of the Reformation and of democracy, personal responsibility should be met personally (or in union with other persons having like responsibility) with no intermediaries, be it church or state.
3. Neither the state nor the church is qualified to give all-around instruction to the youth. The state—especially in this country—must maintain a hands-off policy regarding matters religious; and the church—being a spiritual commonwealth—is not called to prepare the youth for "secular" pursuits. The institution of the home embraces both religion and "secular" interests.
4. The parent-society controlled school may have the aid and interest of the church but not be at its mercy. A school board elected for the sole purpose of managing a school has many advantages.[40]

By the early 20th century, Congress had drafted several bills to establish a federal department of education or to reorganize the federal departments to allow for greater oversight of education. Though local communities had already conceded great control over education to state governments, for many Protestants, federal oversight of education was a bridge too far. Machen argued in his 1926 Sentinels address that a federal department of education "would be the very worst calamity into which this country could fall," in part because it would produce "not something that is uniformly high, but something that is uniformly low."[41] He continued,

> The reason why I am opposed to this proposal is that it represents a very ancient principle in the field of education, which, it seems to me, has been one of the chief enemies of human liberty for several thousand years—the principle, namely, that education is an affair essentially of the State, that education must be standardized for the welfare of the whole people and put under the control of government, that personal idiosyncrasies should be avoided.[42]

Machen provided expert testimony on behalf of the Sentinels against the proposed department of education before the House and Senate committees, expressing his doubts that "the personal, free, individual character of education can be preserved when you have a Federal department laying down standards of education which become more or less mandatory to the whole country."[43]

The Protestant confidence that common schools would continue to operate with the permission and approval of parents failed to prove true.

Catholic Subsidiarity and Parental School Choice

Alongside growing Protestant support for parental school choice, Catholic support for choice grew around the 1930s. Historically, American Catholics supported parental school choice de jure, but not necessarily parental school choice de facto. As a policy, they embraced school choice because it allowed parents to opt their children out of the Protestant public schools and enroll them in parochial schools overseen and operated by the Catholic Church.

But Catholic ecclesial policy did not embrace full parental choice. The Code of Canon Law of the Catholic Church states, "The duty and right of educating belongs in a special way to the Church, to which has been divinely entrusted the mission of assisting persons so that they are able to reach the fullness of the Christian life."[44] Similarly, the Third Plenary Council of Baltimore in 1884 concluded, "All Catholic parents are bound to send their children to the parochial schools."[45] The Protestants created a system of common schools to which they compelled the attendance of all children, but the Catholics created a system of parochial schools to which they compelled the attendance of all Catholic children.

With common schools closed off and public funding largely unavailable for their school system, Catholics went to great lengths to develop their own education system, free from the purview of the state. Bishop John Hughes launched a campaign in the mid-1800s for Catholic Churches to start their own schools, and his success "was evident almost immediately. Academies, schools and colleges began to spring up with more frequency in many parts of the country."[46] Here in private, unchallenged by other sects of Christianity, "Catholic leaders of education have laboriously worked out a complete system of thought and principles of education, taking into account the whole man with all his powers of soul and body. They have constructed a philosophy of education which is completed, and, from their point of view, the only Christian philosophy of education."[47]

In the early 20th century, Catholic attitudes shifted in favor of a more robust parental school choice. In 1929, Pope Pius XI's encyclical *Divini Illius Magistri* (*The Divine Teacher*) emphasized the right of parents to oversee their children's education, over and even against the state.[48] These principles were consistent with the idea of subsidiarity, first declared in Pope Pius XI's 1931 encyclical *Quadragesimo Anno*.[49] Whereas canon law and the Third Plenary Council had previously declared the supreme position of the Catholic Church over other "societies" or institutions, subsidiarity argued that decisions should be made at the most local level possible.[50] According to subsidiarity, decisions about a child's education should be made by the parent.

Catholic legal scholar John E. Coons has written extensively to develop a Catholic case for parental school choice. He names four reasons why parents should have the freedom to choose, including: (1) parents' self-interest in developing the child's independence, (2) parents' care for the child, (3) parents' knowledge of the child, and (4) parents' own liberty and political dignity.[51] Parents' unique position in society makes them ideal choosers of schools: "*Qua* parent, one seeks transmission of one's beliefs to the child. *Qua* citizen, one chooses a school that puts one's particular beliefs into the ideological market."[52]

Concluding Thoughts

On closer examination of Curran's critique of American Protestantism, it is unclear whether the systems of parochial schools developed by European Protestants or by American Catholics enjoy an advantage in intergenerational transmission of faith compared with schools developed by American Protestants. Most European parochial schools have succumbed to a rigid arrangement of strict oversight by the state and religious adherence among its citizens has consequently lessened.[53] One descriptive study of private school administrators finds that Protestant school principals are more likely than Catholic school principals to view themselves as spiritual role models to students.[54] Descriptive studies of private school student outcomes suggest that Protestant schools are more likely to inculcate Christian values and that Catholic school graduates are similar to secular school graduates with respect to marriage and family outcomes, charitable giving and engagement in religious practices, and civic engagement.[55] At the same time, some scholars have expressed concerns of declining Catholic school enrollment.[56] While the National Catholic Educational Association continues to serve the greatest number of schools and the largest number of students, it is followed by a number of Protestant organizations, including the Association of Christian Schools International, Accelerated Christian Education, and the American Association of Christian Schools.[57]

We should avoid oversimplifying both Protestant and Catholic educational thought. Not all Protestants favored common schools. Charles Hodge, an old-school presbyterian, "appealed to the example of the Roman Catholic churches and to the parochial schools of the Calvinists in Holland and Scotland"[58] in advocating for a Protestant parochial system of schools. Not all Protestants were zealously opposed to Catholics exercising freedom of religion when it came to education. The fifth annual session of the Baptist Congress in 1886 expressed a range of views, including advocating for religious liberty and immunity from taxation for Catholics, necessity of church control of secondary schools, critiques of state schools, and arguments for religion to be taught in state schools.[59] J. Gresham Machen serves as one notable example of a prominent Protestant academic who praised the Supreme Court's decision in *Pierce v. Society of Sisters* for protecting Catholics' right to religious liberty in education.[60] Not all Catholics yielded absolute control to the Catholic Church over the family in matters of education. Rian noted that "in some dioceses the prelates punished the parents of children who went to public school by excluding them from the sacraments. In other parishes the parents were given free choice, so that there was much discussion and confusion among both parents and clergy."[61]

By the 1930s, Protestants and Catholics both contributed to a broad and growing movement for parental school choice. In 1948, the United Nations ratified the Universal Declaration of Rights, which affirmed parents' "prior right to choose the kind of education that shall be given to their children,"[62] echoing the writings of Machen and Rian, as well as the *Divini Illius Magistri*. By the time Milton Friedman penned his words that the "separation of a child from a parent who cannot pay for the minimum required education is clearly inconsistent with our reliance on the family as the basic social unit and our belief in the freedom of the individual,"[63] Protestants and Catholics had declared their staunch support for the parental right to oversee their children's education.

In recent years, Protestant thought, Catholic thought, and natural evidence have converged upon the conclusion that the proper locus of educational control is with the parent. The failed Protestant experiment with common schools led to the conclusion that parents, not the government, are best positioned to hold schools accountable for both academic and religious outcomes. Protestant parents are members of both church and state societies, and research shows that parents of children enrolled in private Protestant schools strongly desire both high-quality spiritual formation and academics.[64] The arc of Catholic reason is bending toward parental choice as well.[65] And the weight of empirical evidence thoroughly demonstrates that parents are efficient choosers of schools, as school choice produces positive academic, civic, and other outcomes.[66]

The Protestant Machen testified before Congress, "The proper tendency, it seems to me, would be to diminish rather than to increase the function of the public school, and to place the responsibility for the moral and religious training of children exactly where it belongs, upon the individual parents."[67] The Catholic Coons argued, "As responsible moral beings, parents have by nature the best reason to wage social peace through choice, even as they conscientiously (and properly) wage cultural war through words."[68] Despite historical differences in educational thought, Protestants and Catholics find themselves agreeing at this moment in time on the principle that parents ought to have the great right of freely choosing the school that best meets the needs of their children.

Notes

1. Francis X. Curran, *The Churches and the Schools: American Protestantism and Popular Elementary Education* (Loyola University Press, 1954), p. 2.

2. Edwin H. Rian, *Christianity and American Education* (The Naylor Company, 1949), p. 232.

3. See, for example, John E. Coons, *The Case for Parental Choice: God, Family, and Educational Liberty*, ed. Nicole S. Garnett, Richard W. Garnett, and Ernest Morrell (University of Notre Dame Press, 2023); Curran, *Churches and the Schools.*

4. Rian, *Christianity and American Education*, p. 145.

5. Abraham Kuyper, *On Education*, ed. Wendy Naylor, trans. Harry Van Dyke (Lexham Press, 2019).

6. Alan D. Strange, *Empowered Witness: Politics, Culture, and the Spiritual Mission of the Church* (Crossway, 2024).

7. Miles Smith, *Religion and Republic: Christian America from the Founding to the Civil War* (Davenant Press, 2024).

8. Mark D. Hall, *Did America Have a Christian Founding? Separating Modern Myth from Historical Truth* (Nelson Books, 2019).

9. Old Deluder Satan Law of 1647.

10. Charles Thompson, "Resolution by the Continental Congress Concerning Moral Behavior," *North Carolina Gazette*, November 20, 1778.

11. "Ordinance for the Government of the Territory of the United States North-West of the River Ohio," July 13, 1787, papers of the Continental Congress,

National Archives; and Mark D. Hall, "A Connecticut Yankee in Georgia: Abraham Baldwin and the Establishment Clause," *Law & Liberty*, October 18, 2018.

12. George Washington, "Washington's Farewell Address to the People of the United States," 1796, US Senate Historical Office.

13. John Adams to Massachusetts Militia, October 11, 1798, "Founders Online," National Archives.

14. Benjamin Rush, "Of the Mode of Education Proper in a Republic," in *The Selected Writings of Benjamin Rush,* ed. Dagobert D. Runes (Philosophical Library, 1947), pp. 87–89.

15. Rian, *Christianity and American Education*, p. 124.

16. Rian, *Christianity and American Education*, pp. 41, 51.

17. Jean-Jacques Rousseau, *The Social Contract and Other Later Political Writings*, ed. and trans. Victor Gourevitch (Cambridge University Press, 1997), p. 41.

18. Rian, *Christianity and American Education*, p. 59.

19. John Dewey, *Experience and Education*, 1st ed. (The Macmillan Company, 1938), pp. 19–20.

20. William Ernest Hocking et al., *Preface to Philosophy: Textbook* (The Macmillan Company, 1947).

21. J. Gresham Machen, *Education, Christianity, and the State,* ed. John W. Robbins (Trinity Foundation, 1987), p. 93.

22. Rian, *Christianity and American Education*, p. 96.

23. Rian, *Christianity and American Education*, p. 116.

24. Curran, *Churches and the Schools*, p. 18.

25. Curran, *Churches and the Schools*, p. 59.

26. Curran, *Churches and the Schools*, p. 72.

27. Curran, *Churches and the Schools*, p. 26.

28. Curran, *Churches and the Schools*, p. 59

29. Rian, *Christianity and American Education*, pp. 62, 64.

30. Curran, *Churches and the Schools*, p. 128.

31. Rian, *Christianity and American Education*, pp. 216–18.

32. Rian, *Christianity and American Education*, p. 218.

33. Rian, *Christianity and American Education*, p. 220.

34. Rian, *Christianity and American Education*, p. 220.

35. Rian, *Christianity and American Education*, p. 222.

36. Alison Johnson and Matthew H. Lee, *Learning to Lead: An Analysis of the Administrator Pipeline in Christian Schools* (Association of Christian Schools International, 2023); Alison Johnson and Matthew H. Lee, *Tending the Teacher Pipeline: An Analysis of the Teacher Pipeline in Christian Schools* (Association of Christian Schools International, 2023); Matthew H. Lee et al., "How Do Parents Choose Schools for

Their Children? Experimental Evidence from the Private Christian School Sector," *Journal for the Scientific Study of Religion* 63, no. 3 (2024): 579–95.

37. Curran, *Churches and the Schools*, p. 22.

38. Rian, *Christianity and American Education*, p. 14.

39. Paul E. Peterson, *Saving Schools: From Horace Mann to Virtual Learning* (The Belknap Press, 2011), p. 16.

40. Rian, *Christianity and American Education*, pp. 207–208.

41. Machen, *Education, Christianity, and the State,* pp. 86, 91.

42. Machen, *Education, Christianity, and the State,* p. 87.

43. J. Gresham Machen, Testimony Before the House and Senate Committees on the Proposed Department of Education, February 25, 1926, available at "Christian Family," Reformed.org.

44. Code of Canon Law, Book III, Title III, 794 §1.

45. Peter Meyer, "The Real 'Crisis' in Catholic Education?," *Education Next* (blog), October 20, 2009; Rian, *Christianity and American Education*, p. 136.

46. Rian, *Christianity and American Education*, p. 129.

47. Rian, *Christianity and American Education*, pp. 140–41.

48. Pope Pius XI, *Divini Illius Magistri: On Christian Education*, 1929.

49. Pope Pius XI, *Quadragesimo Anno*, 1931.

50. Michelle Evans, "The Principle of Subsidiarity as a Social and Political Principle in Catholic Social Teaching," *Solidarity: The Journal of Catholic Social Thought and Secular Ethics* 3, no. 1 (2013): 44–60; Michelle Evans and Augusto Zimmermann, *Global Perspectives on Subsidiarity* (Springer Netherlands, 2014); Robert P. George, "Ruling to Serve," *First Things*, April 2013, pp. 39–44.

51. Coons, *Case for Parental Choice*, pp. 12–15.

52. Coons, *Case for Parental Choice*, p. 59.

53. Charles L. Glenn, "Challenges to Educational Freedom in Europe," in *Religious Liberty and Education: A Case Study of Yeshivas vs. New York,* ed. Jason Bedrick, Jay P. Greene, and Matthew H. Lee (Rowman & Littlefield Publishers, 2020), pp. 75–87; and Benjamin W. Arold et al., "Can Schools Change Religious Attitudes? Evidence from German State Reforms of Compulsory Religious Education," CESifo Working Paper no. 9504, January 2022.

54. David Sikkink, "Religious School Differences in School Climate and Academic Mission: A Descriptive Overview of School Organization and Student Outcomes," *Journal of School Choice* 6, no. 1 (2012): 20–39.

55. Patrick J. Wolf et al., "The School to Family Pipeline: What Do Religious, Private, and Public Schooling Have to Do with Family Formation?," *Journal of Catholic Education* 25, no. 1 (2022): 206–33; Beth Green et al., *Cardus Education Survey 2016: Educating to Love Your Neighbour* (Cardus, 2016); Lynn E. Swaner et al.,

School-Sector Influence on Graduate Outcomes and Flourishing: Findings from the 2023 Cardus Education Survey (Cardus, 2024); and Cardus, *Cardus Education Survey 2018: Involved and Engaged* (Cardus, 2019).

56. Meyer, "The Real 'Crisis' in Catholic Education?"

57. Stephen P. Broughman et al., "Characteristics of Private Schools in the United States: Results from the 2019–20 Private School Universe Survey," First Look Report NCES 2021-061, National Center for Education Statistics, September 2021.

58. Rian, *Christianity and American Education*, p. 31.

59. Rian, *Christianity and American Education*, p. 114.

60. Machen, *Education, Christianity, and the State.*

61. Rian, *Christianity and American Education*, p. 135.

62. United Nations, "Universal Declaration of Human Rights," adopted December 10, 1948.

63. Milton Friedman, "The Role of Government in Education," in *Economics and the Public Interest*, ed. Robert A. Solo (Rutgers University Press, 1955), pp. 123–44.

64. Lee et al., "How Do Parents Choose Schools for Their Children?"

65. Coons, *Case for Parental Choice.*

66. M. Danish Shakeel et al., "The Participant Effects of Private School Vouchers Around the Globe: A Meta-Analytic and Systematic Review," *School Effectiveness and School Improvement* 32, no. 4 (2021): 509–42; M. Danish Shakeel et al., "The Public Purposes of Private Education: A Civic Outcomes Meta-Analysis," *Educational Psychology Review* 36, no. 40 (2024); Diether W. Beuermann and C. Kirabo Jackson, "The Short- and Long-Run Effects of Attending the Schools That Parents Prefer," *Journal of Human Resources* 57, no. 3 (2022): 725–46; Diether W. Beuermann et al., "What Is a Good School, and Can Parents Tell? Evidence on the Multidimensionality of School Output," *The Review of Economic Studies* 90, no. 1 (2023): 65–101; and Marco Ovidi, "Parents Know Better: Primary School Choice and Student Achievement in London," Working Paper no. 919, Queen Mary University of London, School of Economics and Finance, 2021.

67. Machen, "Testimony Before the House and Senate Committees."

68. Coons, *Case for Parental Choice*, p. 140.

Chapter 9

Educational Freedom: A Civil Rights Issue of Their Time

By James V. Shuls

Introduction

In recent years, advocates have taken to calling school choice the civil rights issue of our time. The title of Denisha Allen's 2024 piece in *The Hill* says it explicitly, "School choice really is the civil rights issue of our time." Allen, a senior fellow at the American Federation for Children, argues, "there is no more central issue to the modern civil rights movement than education." School choice, she believes, is key to helping black Americans "exit a cycle of poverty and systemic racism."[1]

Allen is not alone. Reince Priebus, then the chairman of the Republican National Committee, marked the 60th anniversary of the *Brown v. Board of Education* ruling in 2014 by arguing that school choice was a continuation of the civil rights movement. "We uphold the legacy of *Brown* best when we continue the work of tearing down barriers to educational opportunity," he wrote.[2]

Critics, meanwhile, suggest this use of civil rights language is ironic, since school choice policies, such as vouchers, were the "primary tools for segregationists to preserve unequal education for African American and Hispanic children" following *Brown*.[3] These arguments have gained much purchase among those on the political left who oppose school choice. They decry the "racist history of 'school choice'"[4] or the "racist origins of private school vouchers."[5] Led by polemic scholars and writers such as Jack Schneider and Jennifer Berkshire, these critics argue that school choice policies, particularly vouchers, emerged as a direct response to desegregation efforts, allowing white families to circumvent integration mandates by enrolling their children in private or newly formed academies.[6] They believe that school choice policies have historically been wielded to uphold educational stratification rather than to dismantle it, thus positioning modern advocates as unwitting or deliberate heirs to a legacy of segregationist resistance.

In this chapter, I offer a different way to view the school choice movement—not as the civil rights issue of our time, nor as an obstacle to the civil rights movement of the 1950s and 1960s, but as an extension of that movement. In other words, educational freedom has long been seen by advocates as a civil rights issue. And rather than springing from opposition to desegregation efforts, the sustained and prolonged movement to promote educational opportunities for all children both predated *Brown* and was inspired by the advancement of civil rights for black Americans.

This is not an attempt to whitewash segregationists' efforts to use private school tuition payments as part of massive resistance to federal integration rulings, but to properly situate that part of school choice history within the broader narrative. After all, private schools were the segregationists' fallback position when they were no longer able to maintain their historic segregation of public schools. Their attempt to use private school tuition payments or scholarships to maintain segregated schools was equally as flawed as the separate but equal public schools, and ultimately it was also found to be unconstitutional. In other words, when we consider the long struggle for educational freedom, the segregationists' voucher push was a flash in the pan. It was not the movement's origin, nor a boon. It was an obstacle that had to be wrestled with.

This chapter draws heavily from the archival records of Citizens for Educational Freedom (CEF) housed at the University of Missouri—St. Louis' Mercantile Library and the Virgil Blum papers at Marquette University. Using firsthand accounts, letters, and other primary source documents, we see that Blum and the individuals involved with Citizens for Educational Freedom often presented their arguments using civil rights language. Whereas Southern segregationists were fighting to maintain a segregated, publicly funded education system, Blum and the CEF advocated for the free exercise of religion via educational freedom. Seeing the success of black Americans during the civil rights movement, they borrowed tactics and language from the movement to advocate for educational freedom. Not only did they worry that segregationists hurt the movement to expand educational opportunities for students, but many also argued that school choice was a better mechanism to bring about integration. In short, Blum and the CEF saw educational freedom as an important civil rights issue of their time.

More Than a Century of Advocacy

On July 1, 1970, William Ball spoke to the United States Catholic Conference.[7] Ball, an attorney who would go on to argue before the United States Supreme Court in the famous precedent-setting religious liberty cases *Lemon v. Kurtzman* and *Wisconsin v. Yoder*, spoke on the matter of freedom of choice in education. He opened his remarks with the following:

> We are probably now coming to the final answer to an historic question. For at least 140 years (taking as a starting date the emergence of Archbishop Hughes in New York) there has been a struggle in this country for freedom of choice in education. Not a decade nor a year since the high tide of the Know-nothing Party in 1853 has been without manifestations of a searing controversy over whether public funds may be used in aid of education taking place in parochial schools.[8]

Ball was referring to the vigorous battle over funding for Catholic schools led by Archbishop John Hughes from 1839 to 1842.[9]

New York City had a history of providing public funding for church-related schools until the suspension of this policy in 1825. When Hughes arrived in New York in 1838, the Catholic diocese in New York had roughly 5,000 students registered to attend one of the "eight makeshift parochial schools, meeting in church basements or rented halls."

Another 7,000 Catholic children "either lacked accommodation or made no effort to go to school." At the time, there was no public school system in the city. Rather, the Public School Society of the City of New York, which was funded by public dollars and operated by "a Quaker-oriented philanthropy," ran schools that "leaned heavily toward evangelistic Protestantism."[10] The Public School Society denied funds to Catholic schools, instead attempting to educate Catholic children in Protestant-oriented schools. Despite vigorous advocacy, New York City administrators and school officials denied appeals from Hughes and other Catholics to provide funding for their parochial schools.

Catholics were, however, successful in getting the Maclay Act passed in April 1842. The act essentially created the secular public school system of New York. It established New York City's first elected board of education, which would "have general jurisdiction over, the schools of the School Society, the orphan and half-orphan asylums, the Mechanics' School, and other stated institutions."[11] The state did not take over the Catholic schools, thus helping to create the separate, unfunded Catholic school system.

As Ball alluded, Catholics continued to advocate for the next century and a half. Examples of this continual advocacy abound. In 1937, legislation was introduced in Ohio to pay for textbooks and transportation to students not enrolled in public schools.[12] Similar efforts were led by Catholics in New York in 1940.[13] On November 20, 1940, *The Christian Century*, a Protestant publication that was regularly opposed to aid for Catholic schools, noted, "It is a long continued story, this record of the Roman Catholic demand for subvention from public taxation for the parochial schools, but new chapters of it are constantly being written." The periodical was reporting on a release from the National Catholic Educational Association, which advocated that Catholics continue to fight for "a just share of funds."[14] Similarly, on June 5, 1946, the periodical reported, "The century-old and continuing campaign to get public money for Catholic schools is a matter of common knowledge."[15]

This common knowledge seems to have been forgotten by modern-day opponents of school choice, who argue that vouchers and tuition programs found their origin in Southern segregationists' attempts to avoid school integration.[16] While it is true that private school tuition programs were a part of the resistance to integration, this appears to be a case of revisionist history that ignores the long-standing efforts of Catholic and other religious groups to secure funding for private education. Advocacy for school choice predates the civil rights movement by over a century and was rooted in the struggle for religious and educational freedom.

Moreover, even the story of vouchers in the South is not quite what critics make it out to be. Vouchers, or private school tuition payments, were not the "primary tools" that were used to fight integration. They were a last-ditch effort when all efforts to maintain segregated public schools had failed. And it was an effort that was doomed to fail as well.

The South's Massive Resistance

On May 17, 1954, the United States Supreme Court overturned the long-standing doctrine of "separate but equal," with a unanimous 9–0 ruling in *Brown v. Board of Education*. Prior to *Brown*, states could establish separate school systems for students of different races. Following *Brown*, separate school systems were considered inherently unequal. The following year, in *Brown II*, the Court declared that states must advance desegregation plans "with all deliberate speed."[17] However, it left those plans to school districts and federal district courts to work out. By and large, initial orders to integrate schools were met with outright refusal.

In 1956, Harry Byrd, Sr., the longtime Democratic senator from Virginia, declared, "If we can organize the Southern States for massive resistance to this order, I think that in time the rest of the country will realize that racial integration is not going to be accepted in the South."[18] In a special session of the Virginia legislature that year, 23 acts were passed as part of the state's massive resistance efforts. The bills proved that the state was willing to do just about anything—including closing public schools—to avoid integrating schools. Generally, public school officials would refuse to integrate until they received a court order mandating the admission of a black student who had been denied admission and who had filed suit. If a public school integrated, even at the behest of a court order, Virginia legislation stated, "such school is closed and removed from the public school system."[19] Students in these closed schools would be provided with financial support to attend private schools.[20]

It is clear that the goal of Southern legislators, especially those in Virginia, was not educational freedom. They were not making a positive case for school choice or educational freedom as advocates had done previously or have done since. They wanted to maintain a segregated public school system. Byrd made this point at his annual Labor Day picnic in 1958, "We Virginians seek only to preserve our school system. The right to run it, and to preserve the sovereignty of our Commonwealth which is our most sacred heritage. This is the objective of our massive resistance to the Warren court decision."[21] They were fighting against integration and what they saw as federal overreach. And they were fighting at all costs. In his 1961 book, *Virginia's Massive Resistance*, Benjamin Muse noted, "Above all, a sacrifice of public education, extremists believed, would show to the world the depth of Virginia's resentment of the Supreme Court's 'intrusion.'"[22]

Notably, it was not Catholics, the historic champions of funding for parochial education, who were leading the charge for what we now call "vouchers." Just before the ruling in *Brown*, "the Catholic Bishop of Richmond had announced that Catholic parochial schools would be desegregated the following September."[23] The progressive periodical, *The Christian Century*, long opposed the funding of parochial schools. They also opposed segregation. When Georgia passed a bill supporting tuition in private schools, the magazine noted, "Under other circumstances, the Roman Catholics, who seldom worry much about the dangers of seeking public funds, might be involved. But in the south Catholic Parochial schools are committed to ending segregation."[24]

The narrative of school choice critics today suggests that private "segregation academies" sprung up throughout the South as parents left public schools. While there is certainly some truth to that claim, Muse's contemporary account suggests another way to view this phenomenon. "The resort to private schools was not actually an escape from integrated public schools," he wrote, "it was an escape from no schools at all."[25] School boards and school leaders were forced to close their schools when federal court orders made them integrate, which then triggered the state law that removed funding from integrated schools. In 1961, Muse wrote, "It is worthy of note that no new private schools were set up in Virginia except in districts where public schools were actually closed."[26]

As court rulings and segregationist state laws forced individual schools to close, parents scrambled to find educational outlets. Nevertheless, the use of private school scholarships was not widespread. The *Richmond News Leader* reported in 1959 that just 1,820 scholarships had been awarded. Reminiscent of arguments against school choice today, Muse noted, "Much of the state's 'scholarship' money was being distributed among private school pupils not immediately concerned with the matter of race segregation. Many parents whose children had long attended private schools were glad to accept this contribution from public funds toward the cost of their children's education."[27] While no scholarships were awarded in Prince Edward County, the first area to close public schools, 263 scholarships were awarded in Fairfax County, a wealthier community where there were no integrated schools.

Although it is not deniable that extreme segregationists would rather close public schools and fund private school scholarships than integrate schools, there are two key facts left out of modern discussions of this issue. First, integrating public schools and allowing students to use scholarships to attend private schools was often seen as the moderate position. It was a way to comply with federal law while not using force to compel students to attend integrated schools. And, if adopted, this path may have averted the disastrous closing of public schools. While this thought may still shock our modern senses, it was about the best we could expect from Southern politicians of the time. Once again, Muse sums up the situation quite well:

> Disappointment is sometimes expressed because no Southern leader on a high pedestal has called boldly for an end to flouting the law and an end to the shame of race discrimination. That kind of miracle is not to be expected. The politician anywhere is helpless unless he holds office or has a following; and in most of the South today a politician who advocated school integration out of hand would soon have neither.[28]

Another important omission from modern discussions of this time period is that some advocates saw private school scholarships or vouchers as a tool to aid integration. I do not mean just as a release valve by allowing segregationist pupils to attend segregated academies. I mean as a positive influence, encouraging integration. Milton Friedman, often referred to as the father of the modern voucher movement,[29] makes this case in a 1973 opinion piece. Looking back on the period of "massive resistance," he wrote, "Voucher plans were adopted for a time by a number of Southern states as a device to avoid integration. They were ruled unconstitutional. Discrimination under such a plan can be easily prevented by permitting vouchers to be used only in schools that do not discriminate."[30] While some argued that vouchers made segregation worse, Friedman contended, "I believe that it would have precisely the opposite effect—that nothing could do more to moderate racial conflict and to promote a society in which black and white co-operate in joint objectives, while respecting each other's' separate rights and interests." He went on to say, "Integration has been most successful when it has been a matter of choice—not coercion. . . . Let schools specialize, as private schools would, and the pull of common interest will overcome the pull of color—leading, I believe, to far more rapid integration than is now in process."[31]

Far from being the origin of vouchers or private school choice programs, the attempt by Southern legislators to utilize private schools to further their segregationist aims is seen as a stain upon the educational freedom movement. As George Kizer wrote in his 1965 doctoral dissertation, "The movement among Southern segregationists to establish private, racially segregated schools contributes to a situation giving negative support to the private-parochial school movement in general."[32] Of course if segregation is a stain on vouchers, it must also be a stain on public education. Public schools were segregated from the first, and a segregated public system was the goal of massive resistance.

Today, we recognize that discrimination has no place in education, especially public education. Nevertheless, we can wonder whether racial integration may have developed at a faster pace had Southern states been able to integrate public schools while allowing for private school choice. Or whether Southern states would have even contemplated private school options if they were allowed to desegregate at a slower pace. While we cannot know the answer to those questions, we do know this: When federal courts forced integration with all deliberate speed, it led to a disastrous implementation of desegregation policies, especially in the South. As an unintended consequence, *Brown* had a tremendous negative effect on black school communities.[33] In many cases, black schools, staffed with highly trained and capable black educators, were closed. As civil rights leader Samuel DeWitt Proctor wrote in his 1995 memoir, "These segregated schools were ours. Black teachers, principals, choir directors, and coaches made their schools a refuge from an ugly world that constantly looked down on their pupils."[34] Often, those black teachers were fired, and black students were forced into white schools that were hostile to their presence.

Virgil Blum and Citizens for Educational Freedom

The same year that the *Brown* decision was handed down, Father Virgil Blum completed his doctoral dissertation, *Legal Aspects of Equality and Religious Liberty*, at Saint Louis University. As the title suggests, his work focused on the free exercise of religion. Although his dissertation did not specifically deal with tuition grants or vouchers, Blum made the legal argument that public funds could be provided to religious schools. He would later make this point more clearly in his 1959 book, *Freedom of Choice in Education*. Unlike the segregationists in Virginia and elsewhere, Blum did not make the case for private school funding as a fallback position. He made the positive case for educational freedom. He argued that educational freedom was a civil right.

In his 1960 pamphlet, "No Bus Rides for Nonconformists," he clearly situated the issue in the realm of civil rights:

> Protestant, Catholic and Jewish parents who send their children to church-related schools are nonconformists. As nonconformists, their children are denied most of the civil rights enjoyed by those children who conform to the established religion. This denial of civil rights because of religious beliefs is a violation of the First and Fourteenth

> Amendments. These amendments guarantee religious freedom against federal and state violations.
>
> If parents exercise their religion in the choice of a church-related school, they are penalized. And their children are penalized. They must walk to school. Or their parents must drive them. This is a penalty on the exercise of religion. . . .
>
> In no other democracy in the world are children so discriminated against because of their religious beliefs.[35]

In the 1950s and 1960s, Blum's advocacy was just getting started. He would go on to be a political science professor at Marquette University, where he served until his death in 1990. That same year, the nation's first modern voucher program was created in Blum's hometown.

As Blum was writing about educational freedom as a civil rights cause, another major education issue was occurring, aside from desegregation. The federal government was considering massive new funding for education. Traditional education groups, such as the National Education Association, supported federal funding but wanted those funds restricted to only public schools. In St. Louis, Martin Duggan, an editor of the *St. Louis Globe-Democrat*, and his wife Mae read Blum's work with great interest. They were concerned about the possibility of federal aid discriminating against parents who sent their children to private and parochial schools. Blum connected the Duggans to other like-minded individuals, such as Vincent Corley, and encouraged them to form a group dedicated to the cause of educational freedom. That group would eventually be called Citizens for Educational Freedom.

While modern-day critics of school choice paint the mid-20th-century school choice movement as inherently racist, that is simply not a fair characterization. As a Catholic, Blum opposed segregation, as did most of the officials who represented Citizens for Educational Freedom. Nevertheless, they remained focused on their primary goal—educational freedom. In his book *Freedom of Choice: Vouchers in American Education*, Jim Carl writes, "Blum's writings and activism helped break the association of school vouchers with massive resistance to school desegregation in the South."[36]

Due, in part, to Blum, the CEF grew quickly. An internal document detailing CEF membership as of July 15, 1964, reported 22,445 members and 542 chapters in 49 states and the District of Columbia. Membership in Southern states was minimal, with Alabama, Arkansas, Florida, Georgia, Mississippi, North Carolina, South Carolina, and Virginia contributing just 89 members.

Far from being a movement of the South, educational freedom was gaining adherents throughout the country. The majority of members tended to come from Northern states with strong Catholic populations: Michigan (10,073); Ohio (2,763); Pennsylvania (2,288); Minnesota (1,387); Wisconsin (1,247); New York (1,199); and Missouri (955). In a 1962 letter to Mae Duggan, Blum noted that the "fight" was "raging and progressing . . . particularly in such states as Michigan and New York and Wisconsin." He went on to say, "Hardly a week passes but that the *New York Times* does not carry an article on the CEF."[37]

The CEF appealed to people on the basis of their rights as citizens. An early recruitment flyer from the organization stated, "You are an American citizen. You pay taxes. Perhaps you, your husband or brother fought in Europe or Asia in defense of freedom and America. As Americans, you and your children deserve to be treated as first-class citizens." It went on to state, "Congress should not discriminate against you because of your religion." Tapping into the angst about federal education funding, the flyer declared, "Many pressure groups are urging Congress to discriminate against your children in a federal aid to education bill. Will Congress do so? Will it violate your civil rights?" It offered a call to action: "What can you do about it? You can join other Protestants, Catholics, and Jews in defense of your civil rights in the education of your children. . . . The CITIZENS FOR EDUCATIONAL FREEDOM is a non-profit organization of citizens who are dedicated to securing the civil rights of independent school children and their parents."[38]

In the 1960s, the CEF was fighting the battle for educational freedom on all fronts. In a document noting its achievements, it listed actions the organization had taken at the national and state level (Table 9. 1). Twenty-two states were listed. The activities ranged from advocating

TABLE 9.1

Summary of Citizens for Educational Freedom Achievements, as of 1970

Textbooks—Legislation that would subsidize or support materials for nonpublic schools	**Supported drives or legislation in**: Colorado, Kentucky, Missouri, New York **Legislation passed in**: Indiana (1969)
Purchase Services—Legislation that subsidized the purchase of services or teacher salaries	**Supported drives or legislation in**: Illinois, Louisiana, Maryland, Missouri, New York, **Legislation passed in**: Connecticut (1969); Michigan (1965); Ohio (1969); Pennsylvania (1968); Rhode Island (1969)
Tuition Grants or Reimbursements—Legislation that assisted in the payment of private school tuition	**Supported drives or legislation in**: Connecticut, Michigan, Missouri, Nebraska, New Jersey, New Mexico, New York, Texas, Wisconsin
College Scholarship Program—Legislation that included K–12 private school graduates	**Supported drives or legislation in**: Michigan, Missouri, Washington **Legislation passed in**: Illinois (1965); Indiana (1965); Iowa (1969); New York (1965); Wisconsin (1965)
Busing—Legislation that allowed private school students to receive transportation to school	**Supported drives or legislation in**: Indiana, Iowa, Missouri **Legislation passed in**: Michigan (1963); Minnesota (1969); New Jersey (1967); Pennsylvania (1965); Wisconsin (1967)
Tax Credit or Deductions—Legislation that supported gifts to nonpublic schools	**Supported drives or legislation in**: Indiana (1969 vetoed); Missouri
Constitutional Changes—Efforts to change constitutions to allow public funds to flow to nonpublic schools	**Supported drives or legislation in**: Nebraska, New Mexico, New York, Oregon, Wisconsin

for funding for bus services in states including Michigan, Minnesota, and New Jersey, to advocating for constitutional changes in New York and New Mexico, among other states.

In addition to robust engagement at the state level, the CEF was active on federal issues as well. Today we take it for granted that nonpublic school students are eligible for aid via the Elementary and Secondary

Education Act. This, however, was not a foregone conclusion. Tireless advocacy from the CEF was a critical factor in nonpublic schools being included in the massive federal legislation.

The CEF was also active in the courts. In 1968, it submitted an amicus curia brief in the New York textbook case, *Board of Education v. Allen* and in the private school tuition case, *Griffin v. Prince Edward County School, VA*. The CEF argued the state's tuition bill was unconstitutional because it prohibited religious schools from participating. While the tuition bill was ultimately ruled unconstitutional because it was part of the state's massive resistance efforts, the argument of the CEF would ultimately prevail. In *Espinoza v. Montana Department of Revenue*, 52 years later, the Supreme Court ruled that Montana could not prevent religious schools from participating in the state's private school choice program.

The End of Citizens for Educational Freedom

Just as it seemed the CEF was gaining ground, disastrous court rulings ground the organization and the movement almost to a halt. In the late 1960s, Pennsylvania and Rhode Island passed laws that allowed private funds to be spent on religious schools. The laws were challenged in *Lemon v. Kurtzman*, which overruled the laws and established the three-pronged *Lemon* test for assessing whether a law violated the establishment clause. Later, after New York passed a private education aid law in 1972, the *Lemon* test was applied to assess the law in *The Committee for Public Education and Religious Liberty v. Nyquist*. As in *Lemon*, the Supreme Court ruled that the law was unconstitutional.[39]

In a letter dated April 11, 1974, to Eugene Haggerty, the president of Public Choice in Education, Blum explained the deleterious effect recent court rulings had on the movement:

> Due to the serious demoralization that set in after the adverse decision of the Supreme Court in the Nyquist case, CEF has hit upon hard days. The pessimism that exists among our Catholic school leaders and, to a certain extent, among our Catholic school parents, has made it increasingly difficult to raise the money and to get the kind

> of cooperation that is necessary if CEF is to be effective in playing its role in American democracy.[40]

He repeated this sentiment a year later, May 16, 1975, in a letter to Eugene Bleck, "After the decision of the Supreme Court in the Nyquist case, it became increasingly difficult to raise the money to keep the organization active."[41]

The CEF continued to exist well into the 2000s, but never with the same level of engagement or enthusiasm that the organization had gained prior to *Nyquist*. In 2004, the Heritage Foundation, the Institute for Justice, and the Educational Freedom Foundation hosted a 45th anniversary event for the CEF and the Duggans. The event was sponsored by the Milton and Rose Friedman Foundation (now EdChoice), the Alliance for School Choice, the Cato Institute, the Heartland Institute, and the National Catholic Educational Association. Many of these organizations continue to carry on the legacy of Blum and the CEF, advocating for educational freedom.

Conclusion

While *Brown v. Board of Education* spurred the South's massive resistance movement, it also inspired the renewed push for educational freedom as a civil right. Noting the success of black Americans in securing their rights by appealing to the United States Constitution, Virgil Blum and the Citizens for Educational Freedom followed suit, arguing that the denial of educational benefits based on the parents' desire to send their child to a religious school that upholds their family's values was a denial of fundamental religious rights. Today's school choice movement is built upon this legacy.

Notes

1. Denisha Allen, "School Choice Really Is the Civil Rights Issue of Our Time," *The Hill*, February 14, 2024.

2. Reince Priebus, "Why School Choice Is a Civil Rights Issue," CNN, May 17, 2014.

3. Steve Suitts, *Overturning Brown: The Segregationist Legacy of the Modern School Choice Movement* (NewSouth Books, 2020), p. 8.

4. Raymond Pierce, "The Racist History of 'School Choice,'" *Forbes*, May 6, 2021.

5. Chris Ford et al., "The Racist Origins of Private School Vouchers," Center for American Progress, July 12, 2017.

6. Jack Schneider and Jennifer Berkshire, *A Wolf at the Schoolhouse Door: The Dismantling of Public Education and the Future of School* (The New Press, 2020).

7. Ball's remarks were included in a July 8, 1970, letter to Father Virgil Blum, Marquette University Archives.

8. Letter to Father Virgil Blum, July 8, 1970.

9. Joseph J. McCadden, "Bishop Hughes Versus the Public School Society of New York," *Catholic Historical Review* 50, no. 2 (July 1964): 188–207.

10. McCadden, "Bishop Hughes," pp. 188–207.

11. McCadden, "Bishop Hughes," pp. 188–207.

12. "Churchmen Oppose New Efforts for Parochial School Aid," *Christian Century* 54, no. 12 (March 24, 1937): 397.

13. "Bishop Campaigns for Amendment," *Christian Century* 55, no. 46 (November 16, 1938): 1,409.

14. "Demand for Tax Money for Catholic Schools," *Christian Century* 57, no. 47 (November 20, 1940): 1,438.

15. "Federal Aid for Schools," *Christian Century* 63, no. 23 (June 5, 1946): 711.

16. Schneider and Berkshire, *A Wolf at the Schoolhouse Door*; and Suitts, *Overturning Brown*.

17. *Brown v. Board of Education of Topeka*. 349 U.S. 294 (1955).

18. Benjamin Muse, *Virginia's Massive Resistance* (Indiana University Press, 1961), p. 22.

19. As quoted in Muse, *Virginia's Massive Resistance*, p. 31.

20. Muse, *Virginia's Massive Resistance*, p. 31.

21. Virgil Blum, letter to The Most Reverend Joseph E. Ritter, September 16, 1953, Marquette University Archives.

22. Muse, *Virginia's Massive Resistance*, p. 53.

23. Muse, *Virginia's Massive Resistance*, p. 3.

24. "Georgia Adopts Private School Amendment," *Christian Century* 71, no. 46 (November 17, 1954): 1,388.

25. Muse, *Virginia's Massive Resistance*, p. 76.

26. Muse, *Virginia's Massive Resistance*, p. 157.

27. Muse, *Virginia's Massive Resistance*, pp. 158–59.

28. Muse, *Virginia's Massive Resistance*, p. 174.

29. James V. Shuls, "The Father of the School Choice Movement," *Journal of School Choice* 18, no. 3 (2024): 334–50.

30. Milton Friedman, "Voucher Plan for Pupils," *St. Louis Post-Dispatch*, October 22, 1973.

31. Milton Friedman, "Voucher Plan for Pupils," *St. Louis Post-Dispatch*, October 22, 1973.

32. George Alvis Kizer, "An Analysis of the Drive for Public Funds for Parochial Schools: 1945–1963," (PhD thesis, University of Oklahoma, 1965), p. 69.

33. Stuart Buck, *Acting White: The Ironic Legacy of Desegregation* (Yale University Press, 2010).

34. Samuel DeWitt Proctor, *The Substance of Things Hoped For: A Memoir of African-American Faith* (G. P. Putnam's Sons, 1995), p. 67.

35. Virgil Blum, "No Bus Rides for Nonconformists," *Citizens for Educational Freedom*, 1960, University of Missouri, St. Louis Archives, p. 5.

36. Jim Carl, *Freedom of Choice: Vouchers in American Education* (Praeger, 2011), p. 88.

37. Virgil Blum, letter to Mae Duggan, October 30, 1962, Marquette University Archives.

38. Parents' Civil Rights in Education (ND), Citizens for Educational Freedom, University of Missouri, St. Louis Archives, pp. 1–2.

39. George A. Clowes, "'Never Give Up!' An Exclusive Interview with Mae and Martin Duggan," Heartland Institute, December 1, 2004.

40. Virgil Blum, letter to Eugene Haggerty, April 11, 1974, Marquette University Archives.

41. Virgil Blum, letter to Eugene Bleck, May 16, 1975, Marquette University Archives.

Chapter 10

The Progressive Case for School Choice

By Ron Matus

Leo Ryan is a name lost to school choice history.[1] In 1978, the popular Democratic congressman and former public school teacher from San Francisco liked what he read in a well-received new book about education reform.[2] Written by Berkeley law professors John E. "Jack" Coons and Stephen D. Sugarman, *Education by Choice: The Case for Family Control* made a passionate claim for expanding educational opportunity to low-income families. It also detailed a grand plan for getting there: a universal system of state-funded education choice that included not only traditional public schools but also private school vouchers, charter schools, and education savings accounts, with variable funding pegged to family income.[3]

Ryan thought this Berkeley blueprint should go on the California ballot. He huddled with Coons and others. He pledged to be the face of the effort. Coons, a school choice supporter since the 1960s, felt as if the sea had parted. All they needed to do was wait for Ryan to get back from the jungles of Guyana, where a crisis involving some of his constituents had improbably migrated.[4]

Alas, Ryan never returned. The crisis was the Peoples Temple. Cult leader Jim Jones ordered his followers to commit suicide. His thugs killed Ryan. Back home, Coons and Sugarman soldiered on, heartened, at least, by polls showing solid support among voters.[5] But without

Ryan's leadership, they couldn't secure enough signatures. A remarkable opportunity to plant the flag for universal choice—four decades before Arizona would in 2022—fizzled in a tragic twist of fate.[6]

Rainbow Coalition

What could have been in disco-era California seems even more unbelievable because the full, rich history of education freedom in America is so forgotten, buried, and distorted.

Constituencies on the political left have long sought alternatives to traditional government schools. Yet for decades, critics, news media, and even many choice supporters themselves have perpetuated the myth that school choice is "conservative." According to the dominant narrative, school choice begins with Milton Friedman, who conceptualized vouchers in 1955.[7] The concept quickly became actualized with Southern states funneling taxpayer funding to private segregation academies to evade *Brown v. Board of Education* and has been propelled by a vast, right-wing conspiracy ever since. Now the movement is represented by Donald Trump, Betsy DeVos, and the architects of Project 2025, a nefarious (to progressives) cast aiming to "radically redefine public education in America,"[8] if not destroy it for something more private, conservative, Christian, and segregated.[9] This narrative is often boilerplate in news stories.[10]

And yet, it is wildly misleading.

When Howard Fuller, for decades one of America's most influential choice supporters, embraced vouchers in the late 1980s, he had never heard of Milton Friedman. He and Wisconsin state Rep. Polly Williams, a Democrat later dubbed "the mother of school choice" for her role in establishing the nation's first voucher program, were simply trying to find a way to support black families after efforts to establish "community control" over public schools in black neighborhoods failed. "To me," Fuller wrote, "vouchers just seemed like the next step in a logical progression of the struggle."[11]

Nobody has better corrected the record on choice and the left than James Forman Jr., son of civil rights leader James Forman and now a Pulitzer Prize–winning law professor at Yale. The title of his 2005 article,

"The Secret History of School Choice: How Progressives Got There First," says it all.[12] Among other building blocks for choice, Forman pointed to the black-led community control movement of the 1960s, and to the Mississippi Freedom Schools that his father, as head of the intrepid Student Nonviolent Coordinating Committee, helped establish in 1964. On a parallel track, scholar and choice advocate Gerard Robinson argued in 2004 that it is easy to distinguish today's "freedom-based" choice movement from the "fear-based" movement post-*Brown*. But choice opponents conflate them to create the impression that the racist vouchers of the "massive resistance" are, today, just "clothed in a corporate blue suit rather than a pearly white sheet."[13] More recently, Michael Bindas, senior attorney with the Institute for Justice, meticulously differentiated the segregationist vouchers that flared post-*Brown* from the myriad vehicles for education choice that have surfaced throughout American history. The former, he concluded, "were an aberration, a bastardization of the very concept of choice as it has existed for two and a half centuries." For choice opponents to argue choice is "rooted in bigotry" is a "slap in the face" to its diverse lot of supporters, including black and progressive advocates.[14]

All these scholars offer a clear-eyed take on the big picture. Throughout American history, people from all walks of life have sought educational options for a variety of pressing reasons, most of them rooted in freedom. The roots on the left are deep and fascinating: They are found in the centuries-old struggle for educational opportunity in the black experience, in the liberal academics who saw vouchers as a tool in the War on Poverty, in the counterculture dissidents who sparked the "free schools" and homeschooling movements, and even, for 20 years, in the Democratic Party's national platform.

Rosa Parks is in this mix.[15] So is Cesar Chavez.[16] And Steve Jobs.[17] And James Baldwin.[18] And Mary McLeod Bethune.[19] And Martin Luther King III.[20] So are many other influential figures on the left who do not have iconic names.[21] Adding them to the historic ledger for education freedom recasts the political bent of the movement. It rights the disconnect between the dark narrative peddled by choice opponents; the polling that shows broad popular support; and now, in states where education choice is becoming mainstream, the colorful continuum of families and communities flocking to it.

The progressive roots of choice yielded especially vibrant shoots in the 1960s and 1970s, which are the focus of this chapter. This growth put fresh cracks in the facade of the "common school." By the late 19th century, Horace Mann and his devotees had so stemmed the rise of a pluralistic school system that the common school became "something like an established religion, one of the dominating myths of American public life."[22] Subsequent waves of top-down reformers continued to concentrate power in the hands of "professionals." As schools became institutions "run for the people but not by the people," visions of factory efficiency produced classrooms where children sat "as regular as rows of machine-planted corn."[23]

Some of the power-to-the-people progressives of the 1960s and 1970s were sick of it. They wanted agency and diversity, power and pluralism. Their counterparts on the right did too. But those on the left were especially concerned about low-income families and communities of color. And they were buoyed by the anti-establishment currents of the time, particularly the civil rights movement. "There was a lot of people in those days who were very unhappy about how many inner city families, low-income families, had their kids trapped in very poor schools," Sugarman told the Berkeley Oral History Center in 2016. "We saw (school choice) as a way for families to have a chance. And we weren't the only ones."[24]

The individuals, groups, events, and documents highlighted in this chapter are not disconnected anomalies (as they are sometimes depicted, if acknowledged). They're part of a strand. The left wing of the education freedom movement has long been catalyzed by social justice, parental authority, civil rights, human dignity, robust pluralism, and teacher empowerment. At the same time, its motivations have been symbiotically intertwined with compelling rationales advanced more fervently by the political right, including free markets and religious liberty. At times, these choice camps have been at odds. Some on the left continue to bemoan the fact that most private school choice programs do not vary voucher amounts on a progressive scale; many on the right, meanwhile, have long chafed at the left's generally more favorable disposition toward program regulations.[25] More often than not, however, their motivations have been complementary.

This drive for education freedom from the left did not emerge from the fringe. Private school choice in the form of tuition tax credits was mainstream enough—*on the left*—to constitute a plank in the Democratic Party platform from 1964 to 1984. There are significant connections between those platform positions, the liberal academics who framed a social justice rationale for choice, and the free schools and freedom schools associated with more radical reformers.

The Democratic Party eventually purged choice from its platform, but core Democratic constituencies never let go.[26] In choice-rich Florida alone, one million students are now enrolled in options outside of school districts, including at least 140,000 black students and 310,000 Hispanic students.[27] As choice in Florida accelerated to "escape velocity" ahead of other states over the past decade, hundreds of new schools and other learning options emerged, benefiting students, families, and educators of all stripes, including many who would define themselves as pedagogically or politically left.[28]

That diversity and dynamism syncs with the full history of education freedom in America. It also points to a more precise description of the factions that have pursued it. Then and now, the education freedom movement isn't a right-wing cabal. It's a rainbow coalition.

The Voucher Left

Published in 1968, "A Proposal for a Poor Children's Bill of Rights" begins by condemning America for failing to provide equal opportunity in education and ends with a knock on the war in Vietnam.[29] In between, it pitches a $15 billion a year federal voucher program that would serve half the students in the country and "frankly discriminate in favor of poor children." This school choice manifesto was cowritten by Theodore "Ted" Sizer, then dean of the Harvard Graduate School of Education and an influential education reformer for the next four decades.[30]

To get a sense of scale, $15 billion in 1968 would be $135 billion in 2024, adjusted for inflation. That dwarfs the $79 billion Congress allocated to the US Department of Education for its 2023–2024 budget.[31] It makes current Republican proposals for a $5 billion federal private school choice program look skimpy.[32] Sizer's proposal is all the more striking because it was but one of several ambitious bids for choice in the 1960s and 1970s from the left. In 1999, a journalist for *The Atlantic* bestowed a fitting moniker on this forgotten collective: the "voucher left."[33]

This group included an influential cluster of public intellectuals—Sizer, Coons and Sugarman, Christopher Jencks, and Sen. Daniel Patrick Moynihan, in particular—who floated state-funded choice proposals that encompassed private schools. Others orbiting education freedom on this end of the spectrum embraced more radical alternatives, like free schools and freedom schools; or options within the government-run system, like charter schools and magnet schools;[34] or features that have become core to choice schools, like community control and school-based autonomy. Coons and Sugarman may have even been the first to begin to sketch out what we now call ESAs (education savings accounts), which they described as "divisible" vouchers.[35]

Whatever the delivery vehicle, the shared objective was urgent: Make public education in America more diverse, responsive, and effective, particularly for low-income and minority students, by shifting power to families, teachers, and communities.

In 1966, Jencks asked, "Is the public school obsolete?" The Harvard sociologist and education researcher slammed inequitable funding for high-poverty schools and the "organizational sclerosis" that made them ineffective. "Were it not for their monopoly on educational opportunities for the poor," he wrote, "most big city school systems would probably go out of business."[36] As a remedy, Jencks suggested private school vouchers for low-income families as well as public schools managed by groups of teachers or parents, similar to today's charter schools.

This was not just a thought exercise. A few years later, Jencks led a large, multiyear experiment funded by the US Office of Equal Opportunity—the agency executing the War on Poverty—to introduce public school choice into the school district of Alum Rock, California. The original plan included private school vouchers, but the researchers couldn't find a district willing to participate, and the final project ended up being "so bobtailed that it demonstrated very little."[37] Still, the thought counts, especially given its pedigree.

In 1970, Coons and Sugarman entered the debate. They briefly embraced the idea of private school choice in *Private Wealth and Public Education*, cowritten with University of Wisconsin professor William H. Clune III.[38] The book detailed their theories about education finance reform, which they channeled into *Serrano v. Priest*, a monumental series of lawsuits that led to more equitable public school funding in California and beyond.[39] But the Berkeley law professors also made clear that, in their view, the most equitable approach was giving families themselves control over education funding, a concept they called "family power equalizing."[40] They fleshed out their ideas for choice in a 1971 *California Law Review* article,[41] then crystallized them in the 1978 book that captivated Representative Ryan.

Coons has since become one of the most relentless and prolific supporters for choice in American history.[42] For a half century, his arguments have been rooted in human dignity and parental authority—and in a belief that educational pluralism is a path to civic peace. Long before the Moms for Liberty and other, more recent expressions of "parent power" from the right, Coons was all in for working-class families, and in deeper, more inclusive terms than the demonizing rhetoric that characterizes today's culture wars.[43] "This society could do nothing better for the battered and beleaguered American family than to give it the capacity to decide for its own children," he wrote in 1981. "Therein lies sanity and a stabler social order."[44] Families should be given wide latitude in what they decide, he and Sugarman wrote, because cultural and ideological diversity in education signals strength and beauty in the social order: "Society needs variety in its institutions as a composer needs variety in the tones of his music."[45]

The Berkeley professors and others on the Voucher Left did not shy from criticizing government schools. They distrusted bureaucracy. They did not deny public schools had become monopolies, with all the problems monopolies manifest.[46] They were quick to highlight the exclusionary, elitist outcomes of student assignment by zip code.[47] "Those who would argue that our proposal would destroy the public schools raise a false issue," Sizer wrote of his voucher plan. "A system of public schools which destroys rather than develops positive human potential now exists."[48] Jencks likened some public schools serving minority students to jails, "ruled by fear, not love, infected by boredom, not curiosity." Better to close such schools, he continued, than to give them more money.[49]

The Voucher Left accentuated other common rationales for choice as much if not more than their counterparts on the right. They extolled diversity and decentralization. They stood in solidarity with the broad aims of the community control movement. While the latter battle was playing out in New York City, Jencks wrote in the *New York Times* that black-led schools created by private school choice would benefit their constituents just as Catholic schools had done for theirs. "For those who value a pluralistic society," he wrote, "the fact that such a solution would, for the first time, give large numbers of non-Catholics a choice about where to send their children to school, ought, I think, to outweigh all other objections."[50] A decade later, Moynihan bemoaned the demise of Catholic schools as better-funded public schools squeezed them out of the market. Their slow fade is tragic, he argued, because Americans want a healthy pluralism where "inherited distinctiveness" is not submerged into a "homogenous whole."[51] "We cherish these values," he continued, "and I do not believe it excessive to ask that they be embodied in our national policies for American education."[52]

The Voucher Left was perhaps most distinctive in underscoring the benefits of choice to teachers.[53] Public school choice advocate Mario Fantini argued in 1973 that expanding learning options would liberate "the imprisoned teacher"[54] by giving teachers power to create their own alternatives.[55] The Jencks-led team behind the Alum Rock project wrote that with freedom and funding, "educators might create large numbers of schools that are significantly different from those now operated by local boards of education."[56]

In *Education by Choice*, Coons and Sugarman spotlighted teacher empowerment from the start, by describing a hypothetical student and teacher in the first few pages. The student has a penchant for art, but no place to hone those passions because her working-class parents can't afford private school. The art teacher, meanwhile, has created an innovative arts immersion curriculum, but can't actualize it. His public school district rejected it; he can't afford to start his own private school; and even if he could, he couldn't serve the low-income students he wants most to help. The solution, for both, is state-supported choice.[57] Coons later predicted choice would yield smaller schools, better-paid teachers, and teacher entrepreneurs. "Who in his right mind would offer risk capital to finance a school today?" he wrote. "But given a system of scholarships there would be every reason to invest in good teaching."[58]

Decades later, teacher empowerment is not high on the list of rationales typically advanced by choice advocates. The oversight is odd, especially given historic levels of dissatisfaction among public school teachers. There are notable exceptions.[59] Thankfully, too, there is a growing body of work[60]—and philanthropy—focused on the fast-growing numbers of choice-enabled education entrepreneurs. Many of them are former public school teachers[61]—and, as the motley history of choice would predict, many are proud progressives.[62]

The Free Schoolers

By the end of the 1960s, one of the best-known schools on the planet was an offbeat little boarding school in England. Educator A. S. Neill founded Summerhill in 1921 and told the world about it in 1960, in a book by the same name.[63] Over the next 10 years, *Summerhill* sold three million copies. By 1970, it was required reading in 600 university courses. For many in this era, Neill's vision "defined the education rebellion."[64]

Neill and other "education dissidents" may not have explicitly supported private school choice. But they sought alternatives to government schools, pushed the envelope on what those options could be, and opened the door to a wider debate about the ever-expanding possibilities with state funding.

Summerhill synced with the radical sensibilities of the time. Students pursued their own education at their own pace. They were rarely disciplined. They rarely took tests. And they exercised a remarkable degree of self-governance. Every student had the same power as the adults at the school to bring up issues for debate—and to vote on them. The result of this atmosphere, Neill wrote, was "possibly the happiest school in the world." He described multiple graduates who went on to fulfilling jobs and healthy families. They grew into good citizens, he said, because they were given control over their own destinies, free from the neurotic hang-ups of a smothering mainstream culture he called "anti-life."[65]

Neill exercised incredible patience with students at Summerhill. He was not so forgiving of the traditional schools he believed psychologically harmed them. Factory schooling, he wrote, is producing "a generation of robots."[66] Paul Goodman, John Holt, Ivan Illich, and other anti-authoritarian education theorists of the 1960s and 1970s offered similarly negative views. They collectively portrayed modern schools as "grim, joyless places" that led to "the mutilation of a child's spirit."[67] In response, they pushed the concept of agency, so core to school choice rationales, to another level. Mainstream choice advocates preached education freedom for parents, teachers, communities, and markets.

The radicals wanted students to be free, too.

They struck a chord. By the early 1970s, hundreds of communities across America had created their own little schools, deploying "libertarian pedagogy" to spur "social change through the development of happy free children."[68] They became known as "free schools." Allen Graubard likened their do-it-yourself spirit to the *Whole Earth Catalog*, that classic tome of 1960s-era self-reliance.[69] He estimated about 600 free schools blossomed between 1967 and 1972, with an average enrollment of 33 students.[70]

It is not a stretch to see the free schools as forerunners of today's microschools: nimbly and organically created in response to local needs; led by resourceful parents and teachers; diverse in terms of structure, pedagogy, and communities served. The McKinney School in San Mateo, California, was representative of many free schools, with no homework, tests, grades, or report cards. The New School in rural Plainfield, Vermont, started in a garage. The Second Foundation School in Minneapolis opened in 1970, founded by public school teachers "tired of taking the garbage we had to take from the administration."[71]

Like their mainstream counterparts in the Voucher Left, the free schoolers were motivated by the civil rights movement. The latter inspired them to challenge a system they found oppressive and immoral, and offered an invaluable template in the form of freedom schools. Without the civil rights movement, wrote free schools historian Ron Miller, "the free school movement might not have been conceivable."[72]

Other ideological currents fueled the free schoolers, too. Their worldview reflected "the New Left's romantic, utopian vision of participatory democracy," but also meshed with free-market theorists who wanted to limit the government's role in education.[73] This cross-pollination is not surprising: Throughout American history, the varied roots of education freedom have tangled and merged. The free schoolers pursued their own ideals about education, but also echoed parent power positions advanced by voices as varied as Jack Coons, libertarian Leonard Read, and the Catholic-led Citizens for Educational Freedom.[74] "If there is any idea that holds us together," said one free school teacher, "it is that it is the right and duty of parents to provide for their children the kind of education that they believe in."[75]

The free schools movement faded quickly, but it never disappeared. The Alternative Education Resource Organization, founded in 1989, counts nearly 120 "democratic schools" in the United States as members.[76] Other alternative schools with special appeal to progressive-minded families have continued to gain traction, including Montessori, Waldorf, and Sudbury schools, and, more recently, post-pandemic, an explosion of microschools. Homeschooling, too—which traces its modern origins at least in part to the views of John Holt[77]—has continued to flourish and diversify.[78] In some states, homeschool families are eligible for state-supported education savings accounts, and in Florida, at least 60,000 students not enrolled in either public or private schools are using them.[79]

It is difficult to sum up where the free schoolers and the thinkers who inspired them came down on state support for learning options. Some were excited by the possibility.[80] Some feared regulatory creep. But debates about choice a half century ago were based on hypotheticals. Those who desire options today, including the modern equivalents of free schools, can make better-informed decisions based on actual policies and impacts.

Ten years ago, that's what a free school in Florida did.[81] The late Pat Seery founded Grassroots Free School in Tallahassee in 1972, after meeting A. S. Neill. Seery wanted to work at Summerhill, but Neill told him it would be more productive for the movement if he started his own school. So he did.[82] In 2015, Grassroots voted on whether it should participate in Florida's private school choice program. Some members of the community worried about accompanying regulations, including a requirement for low-stakes standardized testing.[83] Others, however, wanted the school to be even more accessible to low-income families. The yes votes won.[84]

Pro-Choice Democrats

Jimmy Carter supported private school vouchers.[85] Running for president in 1976, he praised Catholic schools, referred to the right of low- and middle-income Americans to choose a religious education for their children, and argued for school choice in Voucher Left terms. Carter told *Today's Catholic Teacher* he was committed to finding "constitutionally acceptable" ways to provide financial assistance to parents whose children attend private schools. As governor of Georgia, he supported state-funded scholarships for private colleges. Similar scholarships are needed for K–12, he said, "if we are to maintain a healthy diversity of educational opportunity for all our children."[86]

Carter's position was, for that era, relatively unremarkable. For two decades, the Democratic Party also supported public funding for private schools.

Between 1964 and 1984, there was little daylight between the Democratic and Republican Party platforms on this issue. Both were in favor. In 1964, the Democratic Party platform said, "New methods of financial aid must be explored, including the channeling of federally collected revenues to all levels of education, and, to the extent permitted by the Constitution, to all schools." In 1976, the Democratic Party supported a "constitutionally acceptable method" of providing tax aid to students in nonsegregated, private schools to "insure parental freedom in choosing the best education for their children." In 1980, the platform said much the same, but added "private schools, particularly parochial schools" are important to "our diverse educational system."[87]

Moynihan undoubtedly had a hand in creating that last bit. Just three years prior, his bill to establish a federal tax credit for private school tuition drew 50 cosponsors—26 Republicans and 24 Democrats. The latter included Sen. Hubert Humphrey, the Democratic candidate for president in 1968, and Sen. George McGovern, the Democratic candidate for president in 1972.[88]

It's no mystery why the Democratic Party reversed course.[89] The National Education Association (NEA) and the American Federation of Teachers (AFT) flexed new muscle after the 1968 strikes in New York City that crushed the community control movement. That showdown pitted the predominantly white New York teachers' union, led by future AFT president Al Shanker, against black and Hispanic parents.[90] Eight years later, the NEA bestowed its first-ever presidential endorsement on Carter. In return, it asked Carter to make the federal Department of Education a Cabinet position—and to retreat on private school choice.[91]

The Republican Party platform in 1980 referenced what happened. It listed support for tuition tax credits, co-opting language from the Voucher Left. It called the policy "a matter of fairness, especially for low-income families, most of whom would be free for the first time to choose for their children those schools which best correspond to their own cultural and moral values." The Carter administration, it continued, "cruelly reneged" on campaign promises: "Next year, a Republican White House will assist, not sabotage, Congressional efforts to enact tuition tax relief into law."[92]

By 1988, the Democratic Party platform no longer mentioned private school choice.[93] Today, it is hostile. Such programs, the 2024 platform says, "divert taxpayer-funded resources away from public education."[94] The 2024 GOP platform, by contrast, proclaims support for universal choice in every state in America.[95]

The Democratic Party's official stance belies deep, abiding support for choice among core constituencies. For some Democratic lawmakers, the result has been a kind of political identity disorder.[96] In recent decades, it has not been hard to find, here and there, influential Democrats offering support for choice beyond traditional government schools.[97] But waffling, triangulating, and flip-flopping are common story lines, too.[98]

In 1990, Arkansas Gov. Bill Clinton wrote Wisconsin state Rep. Polly Williams, saying he was "fascinated" by the Milwaukee voucher program and "concerned" the Democratic Party establishment was not more encouraging. "The visionary is rarely embraced by the status quo," he concluded.[99] Shortly afterward, candidate and then President Clinton became an opponent of vouchers but a leading supporter of charter schools. In 1997, he praised Rosa Parks at the NAACP national convention for her efforts to establish a charter school. In 2012, he praised the highly regarded charter school network KIPP (Knowledge is Power Program) as the keynote speaker at its summit: "I wish there were 10 times or 100 times as many KIPP schools," Clinton said, "because you have proved that you have solved the No. 1 challenge in American education."[100]

Before he was elected president, US Sen. Joe Biden also expressed sympathy for vouchers. In a 1997 speech, he referenced "abysmal or dysfunctional" public schools, then asked whether competition through private school choice would help. "Is it not possible," he said, "that giving poor kids a way out will force the public schools to improve and result in more people coming back?"[101] Today, officially, Biden is opposed to private school vouchers.

It's unlikely so many Democratic lawmakers would oppose choice sans hostility from teachers' unions. A final Florida example is instructive. In 2014, the Republican-dominated Florida legislature created the state's first ESA program, for students with special needs. Leaders of the teachers' union said it would "blow the doors off public education"—and promptly filed a lawsuit to kill it.[102] After two unfavorable court rulings, though, the union dropped the suit.[103] Since then, the program has been expanded multiple times, with near unanimous support from Republicans *and* Democrats.[104] It's now one of America's biggest ESA programs, serving more than 100,000 students with roughly $1 billion in state funding.

Conclusion

There is no denying the importance of Milton Friedman in laying the conceptual foundation for the modern school choice movement. Or the pivotal role conservative advocates have played in recent decades. Or the stain some Southerners left by founding segregation academies with state help. But the epic story of education freedom in America spans centuries. These are hardly the only acts in the drama. And truth be told, many of the key actors have entered from stage left.

Black churches, black school founders, and the black-led community control movement are part of this story. So is the War on Poverty, the Poor Children's Bill of Rights, and the forgotten little freedom school that Cesar Chavez held up as a model for the future of education. So are Democrats like Senator Moynihan, Representative Ryan, and Polly Williams. So are Voucher Left stalwarts like Jack Coons and Stephen Sugarman. So are the radical thinkers who inspired free schools. The values that led them to conclude all parents deserve the power to control the educational destinies of their children—as a matter of equal opportunity, human dignity, and common decency—continue to pulse through the choice movement today.

School choice isn't the only policy realm to suffer from false advertising. But in the case of vouchers, tax credit scholarships, education savings accounts, and related options, the myths are particularly egregious. Telling the more textured, multidimensional story is vital. As education researcher Ashley Rogers Berner put it, "Illuminating cultural blind spots can be the first, important step in legitimizing diverse kinds of schools."[105]

It could also mean more vigorous debates about policy designs the left once promoted, such as sliding scales for choice funding, hinged to family income. Or, in Berner's view, a central role for a high-quality, content-rich curriculum alongside that broad array of state-supported options.[106] The possibility of such debates seems remote as leadership of the choice movement has tilted right. But there's no reason it must remain that way.

The reformers of the 1960s and 1970s who saw education choice in terms of social justice routinely rejected the arguments that opponents still use today. They did not believe choice would yield an unconstitutional establishment of religion.[107] They did not think it would lead to increased racial segregation or a new push for segregation academies.[108]

They did not buy the claim that regulations would exact accountability better than parents.[109] They also rejected the notion that choice is "conservative."[110] Moynihan, in fact, called educational pluralism "essentially liberal" and said it would be a "great failure of American liberalism" if liberals don't recognize it.[111]

Is it possible for more of today's progressive leaders to return to those roots—to *their* roots—on choice?

The late economist and education theorist Herbert Gintis may have best summed up the core problem.[112] In 2004, he wrote in the foreword to *The Emancipatory Promise of Charter Schools: Toward a Progressive Politics of School Choice* that he, like his progressive friends, once opposed choice. They knew it was a right-wing plot aimed at defunding public schools and throttling social justice. "Not that I had ever really thought about the matter," he continued. "I just knew that if Milton Friedman (the conservative University of Chicago economist) was for it, and if the teachers union were against it, I must be against it, too."

"Well, we were all very wrong."[113]

Notes

1. Ron Matus, "Remember This School Choice Democrat," *Next Steps* (blog), May 24, 2018.

2. Ron Matus, "California Dreamin': How the Left Almost Pulled Off a School Choice Revolution," *Next Steps* (blog), December 16, 2015.

3. John E. Coons and Stephen D. Sugarman, *Education by Choice: The Case for Family Control* (University of California Press, 1978), pp. 225–30.

4. Ron Matus, "California Dreamin'."

5. Dale Lane, "School Voucher Plan Resurfaces—to Stormy Welcome," *San Jose Mercury News*, February 16, 1979.

6. Ron Matus, "California Dreamin'."

7. Milton Friedman, "The Role of Government in Education," in *Economics and the Public Interest*, ed. Robert A. Solo (Rutgers University Press, 1955), pp. 123–44.

8. Cara Fitzpatrick, *The Death of Public School: How Conservatives Won the War Over Education in America* (Basic Books, 2023), p. 2.

9. Jon King, "A 'Religious Separatist Movement in American Education': MSU Professor's New Book Deconstructs the School Voucher Movement," *Michigan Advance*, September 26, 2024.

10. Kiara Alfonseca and Jennifer Vilcarino, "Where Harris, Trump Stand on School Choice, Voucher Programs," *ABC News*, October 4, 2024.

11. Howard Fuller and Lisa Frazier Page, *No Struggle No Progress: A Warrior's Life from Black Power to Education Reform* (Marquette University Press, 2014), pp. 204–5.

12. James Forman Jr., "The Secret History of School Choice: How Progressives Got There First," *Georgetown Law Journal* 93 (2005): 1287–319.

13. Gerard Robinson, "Freedom of Choice: *Brown*, Vouchers, and the Philosophy of Language," in *Educational Freedom in Urban America: Brown v. Board after Half a Century*, ed. David Salisbury and Casey Lartigue Jr. (Cato Institute, 2004), p. 14.

14. Michael Bindas, "School Choice Is Racist (& Other Myths)," *Syracuse Law Review* 74 (2024): 938, 959.

15. Ron Matus, "Rosa Parks, School Choice Supporter," *Next Steps* (blog), March 1, 2016.

16. Ron Matus, "School Choice? Si, Se Puede," *Next Steps* (blog), March 31, 2017.

17. Ron Matus, "Steve Jobs, the Unsung Champion of School Choice," The 74, April 18, 2016.

18. Ron Matus, "James Baldwin on Education Alternatives," *Next Steps* (blog), August 29, 2018.

19. Ron Matus, "Mary McLeod Bethune Fitting Florida Pick to Grace US Capitol," *Orlando Sentinel*, June 20, 2018.

20. Ron Matus, "School Choice & Civil Rights," *Next Steps* (blog), January 16, 2017.

21. Ron Matus, "From MLK's 'Field General' to Charter School Champion," *Next Steps* (blog), August 3, 2016.

22. Charles L. Glenn, *The Myth of the Common School* (University of Massachusetts Press, 1987), p. 14.

23. David B. Tyack, *The One Best System: A History of American Urban Education* (Harvard University Press, 1974), pp. 54, 77.

24. Ron Matus, "What Drives a School Choice Stalwart," *Next Steps* (blog), June 22, 2016.

25. Ron Matus, "California Dreamin'." As but one example, the proposed 1970s ballot initiative in California included a list of requirements on participating private schools for transportation, discipline policy, enrollment, etc. The proposed regulations alarmed libertarian choice supporters in California and spurred them to create a competing ballot initiative. Milton Friedman also opposed the Coons-Sugarman blueprint.

26. According to the 2024 Schooling in America Survey from the research and advocacy group EdChoice, 83 percent of Hispanic respondents, 78 percent

of black respondents, and 73 percent of white, non-Hispanic respondents support education savings accounts.

27. In the 2022–2023 school year, 981,723 Florida students were enrolled in private schools, charter schools, and home education, according to data available on the Florida Department of Education website and compiled by the author. Given the trend lines, it's all but certain that Florida surpassed one million students enrolled in nondistrict options in 2023–2024. But as of the time of this writing, the official 2023–2024 enrollment numbers for private schools and home education were not available. There were 142,384 black students and 314,242 Hispanic students enrolled in charter schools or using state-supported choice scholarships in 2023–2024, according to calculations based on data available from the state and from Step Up for Students, the nonprofit scholarship-funding organization that employs the author. The figure does not include home education students and students attending private schools but not using state scholarships, because the state does not track enrollment in those sectors by race. The figure also does not include a small number of scholarship students served by another scholarship funding organization.

28. Michael McShane, "School Choice's Undeniable Momentum," *Forbes*, March 22, 2023. A September 18, 2024, article in the *Free Press* offers one example: The Colossal Academy microschool in Fort Lauderdale. "School choice, to me, means freedom to be able to have an LGBTQ+ classroom and inclusive classroom," said the founder, former public school teacher Shiren Rattigan. "What can happen with school choice is you can actually create those affirming spaces." Francesca Block, "The Return of the One-Room Schoolhouse," *Free Press*, September 18, 2024.

29. Theodore Sizer and Phillip Witten, "A Proposal for a Poor Children's Bill of Rights," *Psychology Today*, August 1968, pp. 59–63.

30. Margalit Fox, "Theodore R. Sizer, Leading Education-Reform Advocate, Dies at 77," *New York Times*, October 22, 2009.

31. Department of Education Fiscal Year 2024 Congressional Action.

32. Educational Choice for Children Act, H.R. 9462, 118th Cong. (2024).

33. Matthew Miller, "A Bold Experiment to Fix City Schools," *The Atlantic*, July 1999.

34. Ted Kolderie, "Ray Budde and the Origins of the 'Charter Concept,'" *Education Evolving*, June 2005. Former public school teacher Ray Budde is often credited with first surfacing the idea of charter schools in 1974. Jencks touched on a similar idea in 1966, and Coons and Sugarman wrote at length about what were essentially charter schools (they called them "independent public schools") in 1978.

35. Coons and Sugarman, *Education by Choice*, p. 198. Coons and Sugarman described scenarios involving multiple teachers and tutors operating indepen-

dently of each other but serving the same child. They also described "living-room schools," "mini schools," and "personally tailored education," foreshadowing learning pods, microschools, and a la carte education.

36. Christopher Jencks, "Is the Public School Obsolete?," *Public Interest* (Winter 1966): 18–27.

37. Adam Emerson, "From Sargent Shriver to School Choice," *Next Steps* (blog), January 19, 2011.

38. John E. Coons et al., *Private Wealth and Public Education* (Harvard University Press, 1970).

39. Stanford University, "Landmark US Cases Related to Equality of Opportunity in K–12 Education."

40. Coons et al., *Private Wealth and Public Education*, p. 259.

41. John E. Coons and Stephen D. Sugarman, "Family Choice in Education: A Model State System for Vouchers," *California Law Review* 59, 2 (1971): 323–438.

42. As of this writing, Jack Coons is 95 years old. He continues to write, to inspire compilations of his work, and to influence a new generation of thinkers. Ashley Rogers Berner, a leading advocate for educational pluralism, credits Coons and Sugarman with first articulating "the civil rights argument for school choice and academic accountability." John E. Coons, *School Choice and Human Good: Why All Parents Must Be Empowered to Choose* (Balboa Press, 2021); John E. Coons, *The Case for Parental Choice: God, Family, and Educational Liberty*, ed. Nicole Stelle Garnett et al. (University of Notre Dame Press, 2023); and Ashley Berner, "The Progressive Case for Educational Pluralism," Cardus, May 14, 2024, p. 10.

43. Choice enthusiasts on the left like Coons weren't the only ones advocating for parental rights decades ago. So were choice pioneers like Father Virgil Blum, longtime professor of political science at Marquette University, and Leonard Read, founder of the Foundation for Economic Education.

44. John E. Coons, "Making Schools Public," in *Private Schools and the Public Good: Policy Alternatives for the Eighties*, ed. Edward McGlynn Gaffney Jr. (University of Notre Dame Press, 1981), p. 101.

45. Coons and Sugarman, *Education by Choice*, p. 97.

46. Daniel Patrick Moynihan, "Government and the Ruin of Private Education: An Argument for Tuition Tax Credits as a Way to Sustain Nongovernment Schools," *Harper's*, April 1978, p. 28. Moynihan did not believe the decline of faith-based schools was an accident—and he opposed creation of the US Department of Education in 1980 because he thought it would further empower those seeking to end them. "Government," he wrote, "has got to stop choking the life out of institutions that could be seen to compete with it."

47. Coons and Sugarman, "Family Choice in Education," p. 323. In the foreword, Berkeley education professor Charles S. Benson writes: "If a set of families

enters a state park to go hiking, that group would be shocked indeed to discover that the scenic trails were reserved for its richer members and that only barren and rocky paths were held open for the poor. Nevertheless, our public schools operate in such a discriminatory way."

48. Sizer and Witten, "A Proposal for a Poor Children's Bill of Rights," p. 62.

49. Jencks, "Is the Public School Obsolete?," p. 22.

50. Christopher Jencks, "Private Schools for Black Children," *New York Times*, November 3, 1968.

51. Moynihan, "Government and the Ruin of Private Education," p. 38.

52. Moynihan, "Government and the Ruin of Private Education," p. 38.

53. Choice supporters on the left are not the only ones who have noted the benefits of education freedom for teachers. In *Market Education: The Unknown History*, Andrew Coulson highlighted societies, from ancient Greece to modern Japan, where innovative teachers thrived. In patriarchal Athens, the feminist Aspasia set up a school that many wealthy Athenians appreciated for their daughters. "Crusty conservatives" condemned it, Coulson wrote, but the market rewarded it. "One great virtue of this system was that as long as there were enough people interested in what a teacher had to say, it did not matter if the rest of the public was actively hostile to his work, he could still carry on." Andrew Coulson, *Market Education: The Unknown History* (Routledge, 1999), p. 44.

54. Mario Fantini, *Public Schools of Choice: A Plan for the Reform of American Education* (Simon and Schuster, 1973), p. 12.

55. Fantini, *Public Schools of Choice*, p. 248.

56. Center for the Study of Public Policy, *Education Vouchers: A Report on Financing Elementary Education by Grants to Parents*, for the US Office of Economic Opportunity, December 1970, p. 121.

57. Coons and Sugarman, *Education by Choice*, pp. 8–10.

58. Coons, "Making Schools Public," p. 99.

59. Doug Tuthill, "School Choice Is Good for Teachers, Too," *Education Week*, August 4, 2015.

60. Nobody has put a bigger spotlight on education entrepreneurs than Kerry McDonald, senior fellow at the Foundation for Economic Education and host of the popular LiberatED podcast. For example: Kerry McDonald, "Education Entrepreneurship and Innovation Across the US: A Case Study of Unconventional Learning Models in 5 Cities," Foundation for Economic Education, May 2023.

61. Ronda Dry et al., "How Can I Stay In It But Not Stay In It? Leaving a Classroom but Starting a School," *Next Steps* (blog), August 23, 2022.

62. Ron Matus, "From Public School Teacher to Rebel for Educational Choice," *Next Steps* (blog), September 11, 2019.

63. A. S. Neill, *Summerhill: A Radical Approach to Child Rearing* (Hart Publishing Company, 1960).

64. Ron Miller, *Free Schools, Free People: Education and Democracy After the 1960s* (State University of New York Press, 2002), p. 51.

65. Neill, *Summerhill*, pp. 8, 103.

66. Neill, *Summerhill*, p. 12.

67. Allen Graubard, *Free the Children: Radical Reform and the Free School Movement* (Pantheon Books, 1972), pp. 15–16.

68. Graubard, *Free the Children*, p. 11.

69. The reference offers an interesting connection to Steve Jobs, who grew up in a hotspot for free schools, became an education choice supporter, and cited the *Whole Earth Catalog* to conclude one of the most viewed college commencements addresses ever.

70. Graubard, *Free the Children*, pp. 39, 41.

71. Graubard, *Free the Children*, pp. 39, 46, 50.

72. Miller, *Free Schools, Free People*, p. 22.

73. Miller, *Free Schools, Free People*, p. 5.

74. Leonard E. Read, "The Case for the Free Market in Education," Foundation for Economic Education, September 1, 1964; and James Shuls, "Papists and Pluralists: The Founding of America's First Grassroots School Choice Organization," *Journal of School Choice* 16, no. 3 (2002): 416–32.

75. Graubard, *Free the Children*, p. 141.

76. Alternative Education Resource Organization, "Member Schools and Organizations," accessed October 1, 2024.

77. Milton Gaither, "Homeschooling in the USA: Past, Present, and Future," *Theory and Research in Education* 7, no. 3 (2009): 337.

78. Laura Meckler et al., "Home Schooling Today Is Less Religious and More Diverse, Poll Finds," *Washington Post*, September 26, 2023.

79. The Personalized Education Program (PEP) scholarship is a state-supported education savings account in Florida that was first offered in the 2023–2024 school year. The students who use it are legally distinct from home education students, but they cannot be enrolled full-time in public or private schools. The state-imposed cap on the number of PEP scholarships is set at 60,000 in 2024–2025 and is likely to be met. There are also thousands of official home education students who are using another ESA in Florida for students with special needs.

80. Graubard, *Free the Children*, p. 287.

81. Ron Matus, "'Hippie School' Votes for School Choice," *Next Steps* (blog), May 18, 2016.

82. Grassroots Free School, "About Us," accessed October 1, 2024.

83. The test results do not impact a student's or school's status, but by law they are annually analyzed by a state-hired researcher, and the average learning gains by school are posted on a state website.

84. Matus, "'Hippie School' Votes for School Choice."

85. Ron Matus, "Betsy DeVos, Jimmy Carter and Democratic Retreats on School Choice," *Next Steps* (blog), February 13, 2017.

86. Matus, "Betsy DeVos, Jimmy Carter and Democratic Retreats on School Choice."

87. "1980 Democratic Party Platform," American Presidency Project, August 11, 1980.

88. A bill to amend the Internal Revenue Code of 1954 to permit a taxpayer to claim a credit for amounts paid as tuition to provide education for himself, for his spouse, or for his dependents, and to provide that such credit is refundable, S. 2142, 95th Cong. (1977).

89. Doug Tuthill, "Teachers Unions, School Choice and the Democratic Party's Retreat," *Next Steps* (blog), October 20, 2015.

90. Gerald Podair, *The Strike That Changed New York: Blacks, Whites, and the Ocean Hill-Brownsville Crisis* (Yale University Press, 2002).

91. Tuthill, "Teachers Unions, School Choice and the Democratic Party's Retreat."

92. "Republican Party Platform of 1980," American Presidency Project, July 15, 1980.

93. Tuthill, "Teachers Unions, School Choice and the Democratic Party's Retreat."

94. "2024 Democratic Party Platform," American Presidency Project, August 19, 2024.

95. "2024 Republican Party Platform," American Presidency Project, July 8, 2024.

96. Matt Barnum, "Cory Booker Now Says He Opposes School Vouchers. But He Backed DC's Voucher Program Just Months Ago," *Chalkbeat*, September 23, 2019.

97. Ron Matus, "Joe Trippi: It's Time to Put All School Choice Options on the Table," *Next Steps* (blog), February 18, 2014.

98. Elizabeth Warren and Amelia Warren Tyagi, *The Two-Income Trap: Why Middle-Class Parents Are Going Broke*, (Basic Books, 2003). Before she was elected, US Sen. Elizabeth Warren offered a powerful case for decoupling public school assignment from zip codes, both to level the educational playing field for low-income families and to drive educational diversity and quality from the bottom up. "An all-voucher system would be a shock to the educational system," she wrote in this book, "but the shakeout might be just what the system needs." Barely a decade later,

Senator Warren opposed a statewide referendum to expand charter schools in Massachusetts, even though those schools do not limit enrollment by zip code and are, according to highly regarded analyses, among the highest performing in America.

99. Ron Matus, "Bill Clinton, Voucher Guy?," *Next Steps* (blog), November 9, 2015.

100. Ron Matus, "Bill Clinton: KIPP Charter Schools Have 'Solved the No. 1 Challenge in American Education,'" *Next Steps* (blog), August 5, 2012.

101. Laura Meckler, "Democrats Abandon Charter Schools as 'Reform' Agenda Falls from Favor," *Washington Post*, June 25, 2019.

102. Jon East, "Union Lawsuit: It's About Winning, Not How the Game Is Played," *Next Steps* (blog), August 6, 2014.

103. Lynn Hatter, "Judge Dismisses FEA Lawsuit over Vouchers, Disabled Student Learning Accounts," *WFSU*, December 30, 2014.

104. Travis Pillow, "Florida Special Needs Scholarship Expansion Headed to Gov. Rick Scott," *Next Steps* (blog), January 14, 2016.

105. Berner, "Progressive Case for Educational Pluralism," p. 27.

106. Berner, "Progressive Case for Educational Pluralism," pp. 16–18.

107. Moynihan, "Government and the Ruin of Private Education," pp. 31–36. Much of Moynihan's essay is devoted to a dismantling of that argument.

108. Jencks, "Private Schools for Black Children"; and Coons and Sugarman, "Family Choice in Education," p. 340. Jencks suggested the courts had put that possibility to rest. Coons and Sugarman agreed, and suggested Southern states may steer clear as a result: "If that is so, however, the model cannot be faulted as a threat to integration."

109. "A Proposed Experiment in Education Vouchers: An OEO Pamphlet," US Office of Economic Opportunity, January 1971, p. 2. As but one example, the pamphlet says the experiment seeks to "introduce greater accountability" into schools by giving low-income parents a wider range of choices.

110. Sizer and Witten, "A Proposal for a Poor Children's Bill of Rights," p. 62. They pointed to Tom Paine's proposal, from 1790, to offer government funding to low-income families for schooling so "ignorance will be banished from the rising generation."

111. Daniel Patrick Moynihan, "What the Congress Can Do When the Court Is Wrong," in *Private Schools and the Public Good: Policy Alternatives for the Eighties*, ed. Edward McGlynn Gaffney Jr. (University of Notre Dame Press, 1981), p. 84.

112. Ron Matus, "No, School Choice Isn't a Conservative Plot," *Next Steps* (blog), January 11, 2017.

113. Herbert Gintis, "Foreword," in *The Emancipatory Promise of Charter Schools: Toward a Progressive Politics of School Choice*, ed. Eric Rofes and Lisa M. Stulberg (State University of New York Press, 2004), p. viii.

Chapter 11

The Legal Arc of School Choice

By Nicole Stelle Garnett

Introduction

June 2022 was a monumental month for religious liberty and parental choice advocates. On June 21, 2022, the US Supreme Court held, in *Carson v. Makin*,[1] that the First Amendment's Free Exercise Clause prohibits states both from excluding religious schools from participating in private school choice programs and from requiring them to secularize their curricula as a condition of participation. Less than a week later, in *Kennedy v. Bremerton School District*, the Court announced the final interment of the much-maligned "*Lemon* test," which opponents had frequently wielded to block the extension of public funds to religious institutions, especially schools.[2]

In important ways, these decisions represent the culmination of more than a century and a half of legal battles over the public funding of educational options other than government schools. This chapter tells—in a nutshell—the story of those battles. The necessarily oversimplified version of the story told in this chapter proceeds as follows: Section one situates the origins of the legal battle for parental choice in 19th-century disputes over the pervasive Protestant ethos of fledgling public schools, Catholics' responses to them, and the backlash that these responses have provoked both politically and legally. Section two traces the Supreme

Court's Establishment Clause doctrine from its inception, through the "strict separation" phase to the 2002 decision upholding school vouchers. Section three discusses the Court's subsequent free exercise decisions clarifying that the First Amendment prohibits the government from discriminating against religious organizations or conduct in public programs. Section four contains a few reflections on unresolved questions and legal battles to come in the fight for parental choice in education.

From Voice to Exit

Legal battles over parental choice in education commenced in the first half of the 19th century when Catholic parents' demands for religious accommodation within public schools fell on deaf ears. Then, to borrow from Albert Hirschman, the failure of Catholic parents' efforts to exercise "voice" led them to "exit,"[3] to build a separate system of private Catholic schools, and to demand public funding for the education of the children that those schools served.

During the first half of the 19th century, the development and rapid expansion of public schools (or "common schools," as they were then known) coincided with a dramatic increase in Catholic immigration. The story of the common school movement has been covered deeply in this volume, so I will dispense with retelling it again, save to say that the battle for parental choice in education arguably began when Catholics objected to the pervasive Protestant ethos of early common schools. Catholic parents, and Catholic leaders, frequently sought accommodations from curricular practices that they found objectionable on religious grounds, especially mandatory recitations from the King James Bible. While accommodation undoubtedly occurred in some places, elsewhere, Catholic children were punished when they refused to participate in these recitations.

Some of these disputes wound up in court. *Donahoe v. Richards* is illustrative of what happened when they did.[4] In 1853, 16 students were expelled from a public school in Ellsworth, Maine, for refusing—at their priest's direction—to recite from the King James Bible. One of the children—Bridget Donahoe—challenged her expulsion in Maine state court on religious liberty grounds. But the Maine Supreme Court rejected her claims, reasoning,

> Large masses of foreign population are among us, weak in the midst of our strength. Mere citizenship is of no avail, unless they imbibe the liberal spirit of our laws and institutions, unless they become citizens in fact as well as in name. In no other way can the process of assimilation be so readily and thoroughly accomplished as through the medium of the public schools.[5]

Donahoe v. Richards was not an outlier. During the 19th century, state courts routinely rejected challenges, rooted in both state free exercise and establishment clauses, to the inclusion of the King James Bible and other Protestant texts and practices in the public school curriculum. Typically, these decisions simply summarily rejected the claims out of deference to public school administrators, holding that the reading of the King James Bible was not "sectarian" instruction and deferring to school authorities. Some courts praised the practice as supporting the development of morals and good discipline, taking care to emphasize the foundational role of "nonsectarian" Christianity in American society. One court characterized the argument that the King James Bible could not be constitutionally included in the public school curriculum as "absurd."[6]

As Joseph Viteritti has observed, Catholic schools began "in a spirit of protest."[7] When Catholic efforts to exercise "voice" failed, they turned to "exit." In 1852, when the US Catholic bishops met for the first time as a "Plenary Council," they issued a decree urging all Catholic parishes to establish schools.[8] As the fiery bishop of New York, "Dagger John" Hughes, explained at the time, the common school practice of putting Protestant material "into the hands of our own children, and that in part at our expense, was . . . unjust, unnatural, and at all events to us intolerable. Accordingly, through very great additional sacrifices, we have been obliged to provide schools . . . in which to educate our children as our conscientious duty required."[9] Early on, Hughes and others likely were optimistic that they could secure public funding for Catholic schools on equality grounds. After all, early public schools were, for all practical purposes, Protestant schools. As early as 1840, Bishop Hughes clashed with New York school officials, demanding that Catholic schools be awarded a per-pupil share of public education funds for the students that they enrolled. The state legislature responded by passing legislation prohibiting the public funding of "sectarian" schools and mandating King James Bible recitations in all public schools.[10]

In the years that followed, demands for the public funding of Catholic schools increased; these demands also fueled new waves of nativism and conspiracy theories that Catholics were engaged in a concerted effort to destroy American democracy. In 1875, James G. Blaine, then-speaker of the US House of Representatives, proposed an amendment to the US Constitution prohibiting any public funds from flowing to "sectarian" schools. That anti-Catholic animus fueled this effort is widely accepted. Expressing support for the Blaine amendment, President Grant referred to the "Romish Church" as a source of "superstition, ambition and ignorance" and charged that it was seeking to overthrow the common school system. Although the federal Blaine amendment narrowly failed to secure approval—passing overwhelmingly (180–7) in the House, but failing by four votes in the Senate—Congress thereafter required new states to adopt similar language in their state constitutions as a condition of statehood. Other states voluntarily amended their own constitutions to include one. Eventually, 37 states' constitutions would include "Baby Blaine" amendments that prohibited the funding of "sectarian" schools. During this same period, most states also ratified constitutional provisions requiring the maintenance of public school systems, often at the same time as the Baby Blaine amendments were ratified. At least some states were required to do so as a condition of statehood.[11]

While these provisions—state public education mandates and Blaine amendments—had the effect of encouraging students to attend public schools, nativist organizations, including the Ku Klux Klan, wanted to go further and require all students to attend them. The Klan and allied organizations, including the Masons, joined movements for obligatory public schooling in various states, including Alabama, Arkansas, California, Michigan, Nebraska, Ohio, Oklahoma, Oregon, Texas, Washington, and Wyoming.[12] These efforts were ultimately successful in Oregon, which enacted a law (by ballot initiative) mandating instruction in public schools in 1922. Three years later, in *Pierce v. Society of Sisters*, the US Supreme Court held that the law violated the due process rights of both parents and private schools.[13] "The fundamental theory of liberty upon which all governments in this Union repose excludes any general power of the state to standardize its children by forcing them to accept instruction from public teachers only."[14]

From Separation to Neutrality

The *Pierce* decision made clear that the US Constitution protects the right of parents to send their children to private schools, but it left unanswered many other questions. Important among them was whether the Constitution had anything to say about the government providing financial or other assistance enabling parents to do so. Despite the battles over the public funding of Catholic schools in the 19th century, it is clear that local governments, states, and the federal government had, from the time of the Founding, financially supported private religious schools for a variety of reasons, including—in the case of the federal government—the education of Native Americans and freed slaves.[15] And, as Sarah Barringer Gordon has detailed, urban and rural school districts had responded to state and federal education mandates by turning to Catholic and other religious schools to operate as sites of "public education."[16]

For decades, these practices by and large flew under the federal constitutional radar. The Supreme Court had never suggested that the federal Establishment Clause was enforceable against states. That changed in 1947 with the Supreme Court's decision in *Everson v. Board of Education*.[17] In *Everson*, the Court considered a federal Establishment Clause challenge to a New Jersey law that authorized school boards to reimburse parents for the cost of transporting their children to private schools, including religious ones. In an opinion upholding the law, the Court made two significant moves that would shape future litigation challenging parental choice programs. First, the Court "incorporated" the Establishment Clause, holding that it applied to state and local laws as well as federal ones.[18] Second, employing the familiar "wall of separation" metaphor, it held that the clause requires government neutrality toward religion, observing, "The 'establishment of religion' clause . . . means at least this: Neither a state nor the Federal Government can . . . pass laws which aid one religion, aid all religions, or prefer one religion over another . . . [the] Amendment requires the state to be a neutral in its relations with groups of religious believers and non-believers; it does not require the state to be their adversary. State power is no more to be used to handicap religions, than it is to favor them."[19] Two decades later, in *Board of Education v. Allen*, the Court relied on the neutrality principle to uphold a New York program that lent textbooks to students attending religious schools, reasoning that the beneficiaries of the program were students, with religious schools benefiting only incidentally.[20]

While *Everson* and *Allen* took a relatively accommodationist approach to programs providing public benefits to children attending religious schools, the Supreme Court's Establishment Clause doctrine took a strong "separationist" turn in the early 1970s. Importantly, in *Lemon v. Kurtzman*, the Court established a three-part test to determine whether a law violated the Establishment Clause, which dominated its jurisprudence for decades.[21] In *Lemon*, the Court concluded that the programs at issue violated the Establishment Clause due to the potential for excessive entanglement and found that monitoring the secular content of instruction would require substantial, ongoing state oversight.[22]

Two years later, in 1973, in *Committee for Public Education & Religious Liberty v. Nyquist*, the Court deployed the *Lemon* test to invalidate a New York tuition reimbursement and tax benefit program for parents of private school students.[23] Although finding the programs were nominally neutral, the Court concluded that the financial aid would "advance religion" in violation of the Establishment Clause.[24] Thereafter, the Court repeatedly held that a variety of public benefit programs violated the *Lemon* test. For example, in *Meek v. Pittenger*,[25] the Court struck down a Pennsylvania program that provided instructional materials and equipment to religious schools while upholding only loaned textbooks. The Court reasoned that items like maps, films, and projectors could be diverted to religious instruction, making state aid impermissible.[26] The incongruence of the books-but-not-maps reasoning led the late

Sen. Daniel Patrick Moynihan to quip, "But what about atlases?"[27] In *Wolman v. Walters*, the Court relied on *Lemon* to partially invalidate an Ohio program that provided standardized tests and diagnostic services to religious schools, permitting aid for health, diagnostic, and guidance services but forbidding aid involving instructional materials.[28] And in *Aguilar v. Felton*, the Court held that the *Lemon* test prohibited states from using federal education funds to pay teachers in religious schools to provide supplemental tutoring to disadvantaged students.[29]

Beginning in the 1980s, the Court gradually began to soften this position, returning to the neutrality benchmark established in *Everson*, especially when government aid reached religious schools indirectly through individual choice. In *Mueller v. Allen*, the Court upheld a Minnesota tax deduction for educational expenses that benefited both public and private (including religious) school students.[30] In *Witters v. Washington Department of Services for the Blind*, the Court held that the Establishment Clause did not prohibit a state from permitting a blind student to use public funds to pursue a degree in ministry.[31] In 1993, in *Zobrest v. Catalina Foothills School District*, it reached the same conclusion about a publicly funded sign language interpreter for a deaf child attending a Catholic school.[32] And in the 1997 case *Agostini v. Felton*, it allowed public school teachers to provide remedial instruction in religious schools under a federally funded program.[33]

In 1995, two important things happened in the history of the parental choice movement. First, Wisconsin expanded eligibility to participate in the Wisconsin Parental Choice Program—the nation's first modern voucher program—to include religious schools.[34] Second, Ohio enacted the Cleveland Pilot Scholarship Program, a modest means-tested program that also enabled participants to attend religious schools.[35] Both of these programs were challenged on Establishment Clause grounds, and the Court ultimately granted certiorari in the Cleveland case. In 2002, in *Zelman v. Simmons-Harris*, the Court upheld the Cleveland program, rejecting an establishment for two reasons: The program was both neutral toward religion and of "true private choice," with public funds ultimately flowing to religious schools only as the result of parents' independent choices.[36]

Neutrality Runs Both Ways

Although *Zelman* was a monumental victory because it cleared the federal constitutional path to the expansion of private school choice, it left important questions unanswered. Key among them was whether states would embrace a greater degree of church-state separation than required by the Establishment Clause and *exclude* religious schools from the options available to children participating in choice programs. This question was a critical one because, as discussed previously, many state Blaine amendments explicitly prohibit government funding of religious schools. After *Zelman*, litigation over the legality of parental choice programs shifted to state courts, with opponents wielding Blaine amendments as the weapon of choice, and many commentators predicted that they would represent a major roadblock to school choice expansion.[37] By and large, this prediction proved wrong; only a few states' supreme courts held that Blaine amendments preclude private school choice.[38]

Most importantly, in recent years, the US Supreme Court has rendered Blaine amendments a dead letter in a series of decisions making clear that the First Amendment's neutrality principle runs both ways: The Establishment Clause prohibits the government from favoring religion, but the Free Exercise Clause prohibits it from disfavoring it.

The first decision to address the question of whether states could exclude religious options from choice programs, however, seemed to signal that the opposite was true. In *Locke v. Davey*, the Court held, 7–2, that Washington State could rely on its Blaine amendment to exclude a student pursuing a theology degree from a state-funded scholarship program. Emphasizing the "play in the joints" between the Establishment and Free Exercise Clauses, Chief Justice Rehnquist's majority opinion suggested that while the First Amendment did not mandate this exclusion, it permitted it because of Washington's "historic and substantial state interest" in "not funding the pursuit of devotional degrees" due to the state's interest in avoiding direct funding of religious training.[39]

More recent cases, however, have effectively confined *Locke v. Davey*'s holding to its facts, emphasizing that the First Amendment prohibits states from excluding religious institutions from generally available public benefit programs, including parental choice programs. In *Trinity Lutheran Church of Columbia v. Comer*,[40] the Court held that Missouri violated the Free Exercise Clause by excluding a preschool from participating in a program that provides recycled tires for playground resurfacing because it was religious. Writing for the majority, Chief Justice Roberts wrote that this policy put Trinity Lutheran to an unconstitutional test: "It may participate in an otherwise available benefit program or remain a religious institution."[41] The Court explicitly rejected Missouri's argument that its discriminatory policy could be justified by the demands of its Blaine amendment.[42] Three years later, in *Espinoza v. Montana Department of Revenue*, the Court held that the Montana Supreme Court violated the Free Exercise Clause by invalidating—on Blaine amendment grounds—a modest private school choice program because it included religious schools. Again writing for the majority, Chief Justice Roberts observed, "A State need not subsidize private education. But once a State decides to do so, it cannot disqualify some private schools solely because they are religious."[43]

Carson v. Makin, decided in 2022, rejected the final hook on which the government might hang its discriminatory-funding hat: Maine's argument that it wasn't discriminating against faith-based schools because they were religious but rather because they taught religion. This argument was made possible by the fact that both *Trinity Lutheran* and *Espinoza* held that the laws at issue discriminated on the basis of religious status, leaving open the question of whether the government might choose not to fund religious "uses" of money. *Carson* makes clear that the so-called "status-use" distinction is a distinction without a difference. As Chief Justice Roberts, again writing for the majority, observed, the prior "decisions never suggested that use-based discrimination is any less offensive to the Free Exercise Clause. This case illustrates why. '[E]ducating young people in their faith, inculcating its teachings, and training them to live their faith are responsibilities that lie at the very core of the mission of a private religious school.'"[44] This is self-evidently true. For schools in many faith traditions, the integration of faith and reason—the imbuing of secular instruction with religious content—is central to what it means to be a religious school.

To ask Catholic schools to stop teaching Catholicism, Islamic schools to stop teaching Islam, or Jewish schools to stop teaching Judaism is tantamount to requiring them to make the choice that the Supreme Court has made clear is unconstitutional: "You may participate in this program, or you may remain a religious school." And in *Carson*, while the Court chose not to overrule *Locke v. Davey*, it effectively limited it to its facts. The chief justice observed, "*Locke*'s reasoning expressly turned on what it identified as the 'historic and substantial state interest' against using 'taxpayer funds to support church leaders.' But . . . *Locke* cannot be read beyond its narrow focus on vocational religious degrees to generally authorize the State to exclude religious persons from the enjoyment of public benefits on the basis of their anticipated religious use of the benefits."[45]

The cases culminating in *Carson* make the following clear: If the government creates a private school choice program, it not only may give parents the option of sending their kids to religious schools, but it must also give them that option. The government cannot exclude schools in a private school choice program either because they are religious or because they do religious things. And it cannot require them to secularize, or to spend choice funds only on secular activities and instruction, as a condition of participating. The fight for the equal treatment of faith-based schools and the students whom they serve, which began more than a century and a half ago, has—at long last—triumphed in the Supreme Court of the United States.

The Legal Battles to Come

Carson v. Makin was a decisive victory, but it did not spell the end of legal battles over parental choice. Questions remain about the scope of the Court's recent religious liberty precedents. These include whether the *Carson* nondiscrimination principle applies to laws prohibiting religious charter schools, as well as how the Court's abandonment of the *Lemon* test in favor of an Establishment Clause standard rooted in history and tradition will play out in the lower courts.[46]

Additionally, most new programs—and even some long-standing ones—are and will continue to be challenged on state constitutional grounds. With Blaine amendments off the table, opponents now seek to convince state courts that private school choice violates state constitutional provisions related to public education. There are two basic versions of these arguments: The first—that state constitutional provisions requiring public schools preclude the state from providing for education by other means—is the cornerstone of ongoing litigation, as of this writing, challenging new education savings account (ESA) programs in Utah and Ohio.[47] The second—that parental choice programs are unconstitutional because they drain money away from, and undermine the effectiveness of, public schools—features prominently in current litigation challenging Ohio's long-standing voucher programs.[48] There is not much to be said about these arguments except that they are wrong, and most, if not all, state supreme courts will ultimately reject them.

Other battles will be fought defensively when opponents inevitably seek to impose regulations on participating schools and families that may deter participation and undermine program effectiveness. Of particular concern are regulations that burden religious liberty. After the Supreme Court held in *Carson* that Maine's exclusion of religious schools from its town tuitioning program violated the Free Exercise Clause, the state imposed new regulations that prohibited participating schools from discriminating on the basis of (among other things) *religion* in both admissions and employment. The new regulations also—remarkably—require participating religious schools to accommodate religious dissent in the classroom.[49] And perhaps more remarkably, two federal judges have recently rejected the argument that these regulations violate the free exercise or free speech rights of religious schools, reasoning that the burden on expression and religious exercise is minimal and insufficiently weighty to overcome the state's interest in nondiscrimination.[50] Two federal judges in Colorado, however, have recently reached the opposite conclusion about similar regulations imposed on religious providers seeking to participate in the state's new universal pre-K program. These regulations, among other things, prohibit in most cases participants from preferring coreligionists and restrict their ability to convey certain beliefs about, among other things, human sexuality. Both judges enjoined these regulations, reasoning that they discriminated against religious providers and unconstitutionally restricted their free exercise and free speech rights.[51] Thankfully, these examples, however concerning, are outliers. Thus far, the regulation of providers participating in parental choice regulations has been relatively light-touch and respectful of participants' autonomy and religious liberty.

Conclusion

Legal battles over parental choice span more than a century and a half. And in recent years, the arguments of parental choice proponents have largely prevailed in the courts. Parental choice proponents have the legal wind in their sails, and the fight for parental choice has, in important respects, now shifted to the courts of public opinion. The momentum there also favors an expansion of educational options for parents. But court battles over both the legality of new programs and the rights of educational providers in them undoubtedly will persist. Attending to these legal battles remains essential to a secure and stable future for educational liberty.

Notes

1. *Carson v. Makin*, 596 US 767 (2022).
2. *Kennedy v. Bremerton School District*, 597 US 507 (2022).
3. Albert O. Hirschman, *Exit, Voice, and Loyalty: Responses to Decline in Firms, Organizations, and States* (Harvard University Press, 1972).
4. *Donahoe v. Richards*, 38 Me. 379 (1854).
5. *Donahoe*, 38 Me. at 413.
6. *Spiller v. Inhabitants of Woburn*, 94 Mass. (12 Allen) 127, 128–29 (1866) (noting, with respect to mandatory Bible recitation, that "[n]o more appropriate method could be adopted of keeping in the minds of both teachers and scholars that one of the chief objects of education, as declared by the statutes of this commonwealth, and which teachers are especially enjoined to carry into effect, is 'to impress on the minds of children and youth committed to their care and instruction the principles of piety and justice, and a sacred regard for truth.'") (citation

omitted); *Stevenson v. Hanyon*, 7 Pa. D. 585, 590 (Ct. Com. Pl. of Pa. 1898) (rejecting request for an injunction preventing reading of King James Bible in public schools as "absurd[]" because Christianity was part of the law of Pennsylvania and observing that "[w]e do not understand how the reading of the Bible in the public schools can be termed sectarian instruction."); *Pfeiffer v. Bd. of Educ. of City of Detroit*, 77 N.W. 250 (Mich. 1898); *Moore v. Monroe*, 20 N.W. 475 (Iowa 1884); *Nessle v. Hum*, 2 Ohio Dec. 60 (Ct. of Com. Pl. 1894).

7. Joseph P. Viteritti, "Framing the Issue: Liberty, Equality, and Opportunity in Historical Perspective," Proceedings, White House Summit on Inner-City Children and Faith-Based Schools, in *Preserving a Critical National Asset: America's Disadvantaged Students and the Crisis in Faith-Based Urban Schools* (White House Domestic Policy Council, 2008), p. 76.

8. Margaret F. Brinig and Nicole Stelle Garnett, *Lost Classroom, Lost Community: Catholic Schools' Importance in Urban America* (University of Chicago Press 2014), p. 15.

9. The bishops reiterated this plea in 1866, and converted it to a command in 1884. Brinig and Garnett, *Lost Classroom, Lost Community*, p. 16.

10. Brinig and Garnett, *Lost Classroom, Lost Community*, p. 15.

11. Derek W. Black, "The Constitutional Compromise to Guarantee Education," *Stanford Law Review* 70, no. 3 (2018): 735, 779–80.

12. Philip Hamburger, *Separation of Church and State* (Harvard University Press 2002), pp. 414–15.

13. *Pierce v. Society of the Sisters of the Holy Names of Jesus and Mary*, 268 US 510 (1925).

14. *Pierce*, 268 US at 535.

15. See *Espinoza v. Montana Department of Revenue*, 591 US 464, 480–81 (2020) (citing examples).

16. Sarah Barringer Gordon, "'Free' Religion and 'Captive' Schools: Protestants, Catholics and Education, 1945–1965," *DePaul Law Review* 56, no. 4 (2007): 1177, 1201–3.

17. *Everson v. Board of Education*, 330 US 1 (1947).

18. *Everson*, 330 US at 14–15.

19. *Everson*, 330 US at 15–18.

20. *Board of Education of Central School District No. 1 v. Allen*, 392 US 236, 243–44 (1968).

21. *Lemon v. Kurtzman*, 403 US 602, 612–13 (1971).

22. *Lemon*, 403 US at 615.

23. *Committee for Public Education & Religious Liberty (PERL) v. Nyquist*, 413 US 756 (1973).

24. *PERL*, 413 US at 774–80.

25. *Meek v. Pittenger*, 421 US 349 (1975).

26. *Meek*, 421 US at 365–66.

27. George F. Will, "When the Separation of Church and State Leads to Children with Scraped Knees," *Washington Post*, April 14, 2017.

28. *Wolman v. Walters*, 433 US 229, 255 (1977).

29. *Aguilar v. Felton*, 473 US 402, 414 (1984).

30. *Mueller v. Allen*, 463 US 388, 391 (1983).

31. *Witters v. Washington Department of Services for the Blind*, 474 US 481, 482–83 (1986).

32. *Zobrest v. Catalina Foothills School District*, 509 US 1, 3 (1996).

33. *Agostini v. Felton*, 521 US 203, 208–9 (1997).

34. "Milwaukee Parental Choice Program," Wisconsin Legislative Fiscal Bureau Informational Paper 29, January 2003 (noting that initially, "only nonsectarian private schools could participate," but the program was expanded in 1995 "to include sectarian schools").

35. Drew Lindsay, "Ohio House Approves Voucher Bill Targeting Cleveland Schools," *Education Week*, April 12, 1995.

36. *Zelman v. Simmons-Harris*, 536 US 639, 653 (2002).

37. See, for example, Thomas C. Berg, "Vouchers and Religious Schools: The New Constitutional Questions," *University of Cincinnati Law Review* 72 (2003): 151; Richard W. Garnett, "The Theology of the Blaine Amendments," *First Amendment Law Review* 2 (2004): 45; Ira C. Lupu and Robert W. Tuttle, "Zelman's Future: Vouchers, Sectarian Providers, and the Next Round of Constitutional Battles," *Notre Dame Law Review* 78, no. 4 (2003): 917.

38. Nicole Stelle Garnett, "Sector Agnosticism and the Coming Transformation of Education Law," *Vanderbilt Law Review* 70, no. 1 (2017): 24 (discussing cases).

39. *Locke v. Davey*, 540 US 712 (2004).

40. *Trinity Lutheran Church of Columbia v. Comer*, 582 US 449 (2017).

41. *Trinity Lutheran*, 582 US at 462.

42. *Trinity Lutheran*, 582 US at 462–63.

43. *Espinoza v. Montana Department of Revenue*, 591 US 464, 487 (2020).

44. *Carson*, 596 US at 767, 787.

45. *Carson*, 596 US at 770 (citations omitted).

46. Troy Closson, "Supreme Court to Hear Oklahoma Religious Charter School Case," *New York Times*, January 24, 2025.

47. See Complaint, *Labresh v. Cox*, No. 240904193 (May 29, 2024).

48. *Columbus City School District, et al. v. Christopher Boggs, et al.*, No. 22-cv-000067 (2022).

49. Aaron Tang, "There's a Way to Outmaneuver the Supreme Court, and Maine Has Found It," *New York Times*, June 23, 2022; David Sharp, "Maine Law Thwarts Impact of School Choice Decision, Lawsuit Says," Associated Press, September 5, 2024.

50. Christina Grube, "Maine Court Upholds Law Excluding Religious Schools from State Tuition Program," *WORLD*, August 12, 2024.

51. Ann Schimke, "After Decision in Catholic Preschool Lawsuit, Colorado Moves to Repeal Religious Preschool Rule," *Chalkbeat Colorado*, October 10, 2024.

Chapter 12

The Universal Choice Explosion

By Jason Bedrick

Introduction

America's education system is undergoing a fundamental transformation.

In the past 35 years, the concept of universal education choice has gone from fringe to mainstream to practically inevitable. For three decades, the choice movement made incremental progress, passing small programs with limited eligibility. But over the past four years, from 2021 through early 2025, the movement has achieved a series of stunning victories, passing universal education choice policies in more than a dozen states. The idea of education choice for all finally appears to be hitting escape velocity. By the time this book is published, it is likely that more than one-half of America's K–12 students will be eligible for some form of private education choice policy.

Some have attributed the school choice movement's recent successes to the COVID-19 pandemic. When district schools remained closed far longer than parents would tolerate, parents began searching for other schooling options, first in "pandemic pods" or microschools, and then more permanently via school choice policies. Yet although the district school system's response to COVID-19 was certainly a key factor, it was far from determinative. The pandemic does not explain why all the recent school choice successes were concentrated in "red states" with

Republican trifectas. Indeed, if COVID-19 were the primary cause, then Democratic-run "blue states" where the school shutdowns were longest, and where mask mandates and social distancing requirements were the harshest, should have seen more school choice progress.

The driving force in the sudden success of school choice is the adoption of a new strategy that highlights the gap between the values that parents espouse and the values expressed in public schools. Previously, the school choice movement pursued a bipartisan strategy that, in practice, often meant taking Republican support for granted while using liberal messaging in an attempt to appeal to Democrats. However, the strength of the teachers' unions within the Democratic coalition, among other factors, limited the success of this strategy to relatively incremental progress.

Although the bipartisan strategy ultimately failed, it is important to understand its widespread and lasting appeal.

The Appeal of the Bipartisan Strategy

For decades, the school choice movement employed a bipartisan strategy, attempting to appeal to both Republicans and Democrats. The school choice movement's bipartisan strategy tended to focus its resources on winning over Democrats because Republicans were already considerably more sympathetic to policies that were market-based, family centric, and that fostered traditional values. Moreover, the main opponents of school choice (i.e., the teachers' unions) formed an important part of the Democratic Party's coalition. Indeed, even though Republican lawmakers were much more likely to vote for school choice legislation, a 2019 study of the political giving among staff at major education reform organizations found that nearly 90 percent of their political contributions went to Democrats.[1]

It's easy to understand why such bipartisan strategy was so appealing. Having strong support within both major parties in a two-party system is clearly better than having support in only one. Tying the success of a given policy to the political fortunes of only one party comes at a significant cost.

For example, a one-party strategy could foreclose the opportunity to make progress in states governed by the other party. In the early 2000s, political scientists began talking about red states and blue states, and political trends pointed to a "political sorting" that was making the Republicans more conservative and Democrats more liberal.[2] Regional political sorting combined with gerrymandering also meant that red states were getting redder and blue states were getting bluer.[3] Advocates who dreamed of enacting school choice policies in all 50 states were understandably unwilling to give up on the children living in a dozen or more states.

Tying the issue to one party could also make policy successes vulnerable to repeal if the other party takes over. Even though such gains might be relatively safe in a state that is likely to see one-party control for the foreseeable future, any gains made in "purple" states might be undone if the opposing party takes over. A bipartisan coalition would therefore appear to provide greater political sustainability.

There were also practical considerations that made a bipartisan strategy so appealing. In the early days of the school choice movement, the coalition was small and considered somewhat fringe. They could not afford to be so particular about their allies and were happy to accept support from nearly anywhere it came, whether libertarians like Milton Friedman, conservatives like Bill Bennett, or liberals like Jack Coons and Stephen Sugarman. Although there were significant differences in each camp's motivations and policy preferences, necessity kept the coalition together.[4] For example, liberals were skeptical of the universal eligibility proposals that conservatives and libertarians supported, believing that, as a matter of justice, school choice policies should be targeted to those most in need. Conservatives and libertarians, for their part, were willing to support programs that were smaller and more targeted than their ideal, seeing such policies as incremental progress. And although they supported school choice for all, many conservatives and libertarians were sympathetic to the argument that, when political or financial constraints meant that a school choice policy could only serve a limited number of students, justice and fairness demanded that those most in need take priority.

Political dynamics also appeared to warrant a bipartisan strategy that focused on winning over the Democrats. Although historically the Democratic Party was less supportive of school choice than the Republican Party, there was reason to believe that could be changed. Polls consistently showed that black and Hispanic Americans—long considered core Democratic constituencies—supported school choice policies even more strongly than the average American.[5] In the first *Education Next* survey in 2007, 68 percent of black Americans and 61 percent of Hispanic Americans said they favored school choice, compared with 45 percent of respondents generally.[6] By 2022, one-half of the general public supported universal school choice, as did 72 percent of black Americans and 58 percent of Hispanic Americans.[7] If Democratic politicians listened to those core constituents, then they would be more supportive of school choice policies—hence the school choice movement's messaging focused heavily on the benefits of school choice policies for low-income minorities.

Given the political and coalitional dynamics, the school choice movement tended to make a liberal or libertarian case for school choice, while avoiding conservative messaging.[8] Liberals focused on how school choice policies expanded educational opportunities for low-income families and minorities who would otherwise be trapped in failing district schools. Libertarians focused on how school choice policies expanded freedom, fostered greater competition, and led to better outcomes. Although the appeal of each argument varied based on the audience, most members of the school choice coalition were sympathetic to both arguments, and few were repulsed by either. The conservative case, however, focused on how school choice policies empowered families to choose schools that aligned with their values—inevitably entailing a discussion of *which* values. Appeals based on conservative values were met with strong objections from liberals and even many libertarians, so school choice advocates tended to avoid them. In general, even conservative school choice advocates made their appeals on libertarian or liberal grounds.

The bipartisan strategy showed early promise. The first modern private school choice program was a school voucher for low-income students in Milwaukee sponsored by a black Democrat state legislator, Rep. Annette "Polly" Williams, and it was signed into law in 1990 by the Republican governor of Wisconsin, Tommy Thompson.

However, progress was slow. A decade later, only a handful of other states had followed suit, in addition to states like Maine and Vermont, which had enacted school choice policies in the mid-1800s. By 2015, 25 years after enacting the Milwaukee voucher, there were 59 school choice programs in 28 states—but nearly all of them were limited to a very small number of students.[9] According to EdChoice, in 2015, there was not a single state with at least 5 percent of K–12 students participating in a private school choice program, and only a dozen states had more than 1 percent participation.[10] Barely 0.7 percent of K–12 students nationwide were participating in a private school choice program.[11]

Despite its appeal, the bipartisan strategy failed to deliver more than incremental gains.

The Shortcomings of a Bipartisan Strategy

Although the school choice movement tailored its policies and messaging to appeal to Democrats, it never succeeded in winning over a critical mass of Democratic state legislators. Black and Hispanic voters might comprise a significant bloc of Democratic voters, but the teachers' unions—with their formidable fundraising and grassroots organization—proved the more powerful constituency.[12] As a 2020 article in the *Harvard Political Review* observed, the teachers' unions' "capacity to donate immense sums of money and engage their membership in campaign activities have historically contributed to the success of Democratic candidates in conservative states or the downfall of moderate Democrats in areas more hospitable to progressive agendas."[13] Nearly all the extant school choice policies were enacted by Republican majorities with little to no Democratic support. "Bipartisan" in the context of school choice legislation was generally a euphemism for "most of the Republicans and a few token Democrats."

A 2021 analysis by Jay P. Greene of the Heritage Foundation and James D. Paul of the Education Freedom Institute showed that school choice policies were overwhelmingly passed by Republican legislative majorities with very little Democratic support. Between 1990 and 2020, in 70 votes held on final passage for stand-alone legislation to create a private school choice program, all were passed with majority-Republican support, and 40 percent of the time they passed without a single Democratic vote.[14] On average, the school choice bills received the support of 85 percent of the Republican caucuses versus only 24 percent of the Democratic caucuses.

Moreover, Democratic support was very rarely decisive. Out of 70 votes, "there were only three instances when Republicans needed any Democratic votes to reach the 50 percent threshold (Louisiana in both chambers in 2008 and the Utah Senate in 2020)."[15] This likely indicates that Democratic Party leadership was willing to allow some party members leeway to vote for school choice bills that were going to pass anyway, but exercised party discipline to block defections when it mattered.

The bipartisan strategy not only failed to deliver Democratic votes, but it also came at significant costs, both seen and unseen. To win over a handful of Democratic votes, conservatives often had to add regulations to the school choice legislation and scale back the eligibility criteria. For example, Louisiana was the one state where Democrats provided the necessary votes to pass a school choice proposal in both legislative chambers. The school choice movement would almost certainly be better off today had the Louisiana measure failed.

Unfortunately, the Louisiana bill created the nation's most over-regulated school voucher program, which mandated the state test, required participating private schools to replace their admissions criteria with a lottery, and imposed price controls by requiring private schools to accept the voucher as the full value of tuition. Two-thirds of Louisiana's private schools opted not to accept voucher students. Evidence suggests that those schools were the higher-performing ones, as they had increasing enrollment, on average, before the voucher program was implemented, whereas the participating schools had declining enrollment.[16] Although previous random-assignment studies of school choice policies all found neutral to positive effects on academic performance, the studies of Louisiana's voucher program found large negative effects.[17]

These studies were then hung like an albatross around the neck of the school choice movement by the teachers' unions and their media allies, which conveniently ignored all the prior positive research.

The bipartisan strategy's compromises on eligibility also held back the school choice movement. Limited programs not only help fewer people, but they also have more limited appeal. Universal programs are more politically sustainable than targeted ones because they have broader appeal. Polls have consistently shown that universal school choice policies are considerably more popular than ones targeted to low-income families.[18] Moreover, universal programs benefit higher-income families that have more political capital than lower-income families. When state legislatures amended universal school choice bills to limit the eligibility, the school choice movement often saw some of its most engaged grassroots activists disappear.[19]

The bipartisan strategy failed even to protect a school choice program for low-income children in a blue state. The only school choice program ever to be repealed after being implemented was in Illinois, which enacted a tax-credit scholarship program for low-income families in 2017 as a part of a budget compromise between the Republican governor and Democratic legislature. The program included a five-year sunset provision, which the Democratic legislature extended once for an additional year before allowing it to expire in 2023. Democratic legislators were not swayed by the advocacy of the low-income families of the nearly 10,000 children who benefited from it, nor were they swayed by the moral arguments regarding the justice of aiding low-income families.

The focus on appealing to Democrats also came at the cost of appealing to parts of the Republican coalition that were skeptical of school choice, particularly rural conservatives. It was assumed by many at legacy school choice organizations that rural conservatives would never come on board because district schools were often the largest employers in rural areas. By 2020, some of the reddest states—including Idaho, Kentucky, Missouri, North Dakota, Texas, West Virginia, and Wyoming—still lacked any private school choice policy.[20]

Making significant gains in those states would require an entirely new strategy.

The Red State Strategy

Recognizing the shortcomings of the bipartisan strategy, a small group of school choice supporters at conservative think tanks and school choice advocacy organizations began devising a new strategy in the late 2010s. In their view, red states were the "low-hanging fruit." Although education reformers had failed to persuade Democrats to vote *against* powerful core constituencies, winning over recalcitrant Republicans in rural areas would necessitate persuading them to vote *with* their core constituencies. Not only was that an easier lift politically, but it would also make it easier to pursue more robust education choice policies. By cutting the Democrats out of the negotiations over bill design, the school choice movement could advance policies that made all K–12 students eligible and took a free-market approach to regulations.

This new strategy to win in red states would require, among other things, a shift in messaging. An open secret among school choice advocates was that their best messaging lost in a head-to-head matchup against their opponents' best messaging. In focus groups, people tended to respond positively to various messages promoting school choice on liberal or libertarian grounds. Liberal messaging focused on how school choice helps the disadvantaged and provides the less fortunate with greater educational opportunities. "Your future should not be determined by your zip code." Libertarian messaging focused on freedom. School choice policies give families the freedom to choose the schools that work best for their children. However, when paired with the strongest message from school choice opponents—that school choice takes money out of the public schools that serve 90 percent of children, thereby harming the education of most children—the opponents' messaging consistently won.[21] In voters' minds, the promise of theoretical benefits—choice, freedom, equality—could not overcome the prospect of concrete harms.

This problem was particularly acute in rural areas. The "bipartisan" messaging focused on helping minorities that were assigned to failing schools in urban areas did nothing to appeal to families living in rural areas. Meanwhile, opponents of choice told rural families that their small public schools were especially threatened by school choice, as even a small number of students leaving would have major financial ramifications. "Help those kids there at the expense of your kids here" is not a winning message.

Choice advocates needed a new message that appealed to rural conservatives on their own terms, aligned with their values, and offered concrete solutions to challenges they were facing. Left-wing overreach in schools provided just such an opportunity. Although the school choice movement worked hard to avoid alienating liberals, left-of-center groups took little care to avoid alienating either conservatives or the typical parent. As Jay P. Greene—then a professor at the University of Arkansas—and Frederick Hess of the American Enterprise Institute observed in 2019,

> In seeking to win the intramural fight on the left, both union and reform Democrats have taken to one-upping each other by staking out positions farther and farther left on hot-button cultural issues. As they've done so, reformers have seemingly gone out of their way to alienate Republicans. Indeed, today's reformers have been engaged in noteworthy efforts to soften school discipline, conscript schools into progressive battles over sexual orientation and gender identity, and enlist schools as outspoken advocates for [liberalizing immigration policy].[22]

Conservative education reformers developed a four-step plan, which they called the "Red State Strategy," to advance universal school choice in Republican-controlled states.[23] The first step was a shift in messaging to appeal to conservatives on "culture war" issues. Instead of appeals to abstract principles, we would show how school choice solved concrete problems they were facing as their public schools moved far to the left on issues like school discipline, gender identity, and critical race theory. Not only did a school choice policy provide frustrated families with an exit option, but also it gave them additional leverage in negotiations with the school administration and school board. Having a choice enhanced their voice.

Once frustrated parents and the conservative base of the Republican Party viewed school choice as a solution to the challenges they faced in schools, the next step entailed directing their energy toward recalcitrant Republican legislators. For too long, those legislators had only been hearing from a small number of school choice activists and think tankers on one side, and an army of union members, public school employees, and a host of lobbyists representing various interest groups on the other. Winning them over would require hearing from a host of their constituents.

The third step was to make school choice a litmus test issue in Republican primaries. If GOP legislators refused to listen to their base when voting on school choice legislation, then their constituents would vote them out of office. That would require some school choice organizations to take a more active role in GOP primaries to knock out school choice opponents. Others in the movement would highlight the victories in the press and on social media to ensure that legislators understood the price of crossing their base on school choice.[24]

Once recalcitrant Republicans came on board or were replaced by primary voters with supporters of school choice, the fourth and final step was to translate those electoral victories into legislative victories. As state lawmakers adopted robust school choice policies, advocates would shower them with praise to induce healthy competition among other states—such as via the Heritage Foundation's Education Freedom Report Card.[25] The celebrated successes would then generate momentum to spread school choice in other red states.

Some in the school choice movement feared that such a "hyper-partisan" strategy would foreclose the opportunity to pass school choice in blue states in the long run. But blue states were not passing school choice policies anyway. Widespread adoption of school choice in the red states was the surest path to normalize school choice and eventually make significant gains in the purple and blue states.

As conservative education reformers prepared to put their plan into action, a major development put their plans on hold—but soon provided the perfect opportunity to test their theory of change.

COVID-19 and Its Aftermath: Implementing the Red State Strategy

When the COVID-19 pandemic hit in early 2020, leading to near-universal school closures, not a single state had a publicly funded universal school choice policy. Just a few years later, a dozen did. Many attributed the rapid adoption of robust school choice policies to the prolonged school closures and "social distancing" mandates that interfered with students' learning and emotional well-being long after the public came to recognize that they were ineffective and unnecessary. For example, Iowa Sen. Brad Zaun argued that his state "wouldn't have passed the [school choice] bill but for COVID," adding that "[g]roups like Moms for Liberty were down at the capitol nearly every day clamoring for school choice."[26]

Iowa's school choice bill passed in 2023. If COVID-19 was the primary factor in its passage, what took so long? The reality is that frustrated parents and local activists didn't become advocates for school choice immediately. Initially, parents just wanted their local public schools reopened. Many districts in Iowa—including in Des Moines, the largest in the state—remained closed for in-person instruction for more than six months. When it became clear that the school boards would not listen, parents turned to state lawmakers for help. Iowa Gov. Kimberly Reynolds and the state legislature ultimately forced schools to reopen. A similar dynamic played out in numerous states nationwide.

When schools reopened, however, things did not return to the status quo ante. The trust that parents had placed in their local schools had been shaken. Previously, they had assumed that the "neighborhood" public schools were primarily accountable to them. But the shutdown fight made many parents realize that the schools were more beholden to special interests operating in them, particularly the teachers' unions. The COVID-19 shutdowns had also given those parents a window into their children's classrooms via virtual instruction, and many didn't like what they saw, particularly the politicization of the classroom.

After the schools returned to in-person instruction, the parents who had led the reopening fight remained wary and engaged. Samantha Fett, then the chair of the Warren County, Iowa, chapter of Moms for Liberty, explained that her group first got involved after discovering books in local public elementary school libraries with sexually explicit scenes and images. As with the reopening fight, their first instinct was to go to the school boards with their concerns—but once again, they were rebuffed. "The public school administrators and school boards would just ignore us and hope we'd go away," Fett explained.[27]

As they had done before, the parent activists then turned to state lawmakers for relief. "The frustration we had [at] the local level, not making any progress, not getting any answers, and being pushed away, drove us to look for solutions outside the district system," said Fett.[28] This process would repeat itself, in Iowa and across the nation, over a host of issues including mask mandates, social distancing restrictions, lessons based on critical race theory and gender ideology, and policies that put males on girls' sports teams and in girls' locker rooms. Angry parents would first approach the local school board, get nowhere, then demand that state lawmakers intervene. As Iowa Senate President Amy Sinclair observed, "Schools they trusted all these years were usurping their authority as parents and they didn't like it."[29]

The political moment was ripe for the Red State Strategy. Conservative groups began explicitly arguing that school choice offered a solution to parents' concerns over issues such as critical race theory.[30] In the paper, "Time for the School Choice Movement to Embrace the Culture War," Jay P. Greene and James D. Paul analyzed survey data regarding social issues and school choice. They found that support for school choice was higher among respondents who were "skeptical about the woke agenda."[31] Greene and Paul concluded, "If education reform groups emphasized cultural problems in public schools and promote school choice as a solution—one that could benefit people on all sides of the cultural debate—the constituency for choice would likely increase."

This argument was appealing to both parents and state lawmakers. Instead of addressing each issue as it arose, school choice offered a comprehensive solution. "The legislature got tired of playing whack-a-mole with all the [culture-war] issues," explained Iowa state Senator Sinclair. "School choice solved all of them at once."[32]

Parent groups like Moms for Liberty and Parents Defending Education enthusiastically embraced school choice, which not only gave families an immediate escape hatch when their assigned public school did not reflect their values, but also gave them additional leverage when raising concerns about what was happening in their local public schools. Parents understood that public school administrators and school boards had been able to ignore them because they had been a captive audience. School choice strengthened their voice.

In 2021, a year after the COVID-19-related school closures commenced, the dam began to break for school choice. Seven states passed new choice policies, and 15 states expanded 23 existing policies. Noting that the *Wall Street Journal* had hailed 2011 as the "Year of School Choice" after 13 states enacted school choice legislation, advocates acclaimed 2021 as the "Year of Educational Choice."[33]

It wasn't just the quantity of choice policies enacted that was so impressive. It was also the quality. The language shift from "school choice" to "educational choice" reflected an important shift in the policies that states were enacting. Up until that point, nearly all the private choice policies were traditional school vouchers or tax-credit scholarships that helped parents cover tuition at a private school. But in 2021, states began to embrace K–12 education savings accounts (ESAs) that allowed families to use state funds to customize their children's education. Parents could use ESA funds on private school tuition, tutoring, textbooks, homeschool curricula, online courses, special-needs therapy, and a host of other educational products and services. In 2021, the number of states with ESA policies expanded from five to eight.

The bills enacted in 2021 were also much more expansive than prior choice policies, particularly in West Virginia, which became the first state in the nation to enact a publicly funded education choice policy open to all K–12 students. At a time when about 608,000 students were participating in private school choice programs, 19 states made an additional 3.6 million students eligible for education choice.[34] The following year, Arizona expanded eligibility for its ESA policy to all K–12 students.

Iowa, however, would have to wait. Gov. Reynolds's ESA bill for low-income families passed in the state senate in 2022 but failed in the Iowa House of Representatives after a lengthy and contentious debate. The GOP had sizable majorities in both legislative chambers, but several Republicans representing rural constituencies balked at the proposal, arguing that it would harm rural public schools. The governor kept the legislature in session past the point where they were no longer paid, but the rural legislators would not budge.

Reynolds realized she would need a new legislature. Following the Red State Strategy playbook, Reynolds endorsed several primary challenges to sitting legislators. It was a risky move. If they survived their primary challenges and won their seats—as they'd shown they could do—Reynolds's political capital would be severely diminished.

The governor's success depended on the Republican base being closer to the governor's position on school choice than the rural legislators. Again following the Red State Strategy playbook, Reynolds framed school choice as a tool to combat the radical left-wing ideology that had seeped into the public school system and to restore parental authority in education. The governor even visited rural communities and proposed school choice as a solution to controversial transgender policies that the local public schools had adopted. "We want to make sure parents understand what's involved in the bill I'm putting forward," Reynolds said of one such rural community visit. "It was an opportunity to hear from parents to hear how important it is for them to make the decision on what is the best environment for their child."[35]

The governor's gamble paid off. Eight of the nine candidates she endorsed won their primaries. That fall, Iowa voters rewarded Reynolds with a second term and expanded the Republican Party's legislative majority.

State legislators got the message. In January 2023, they moved with all deliberate speed to deliver the universal school choice bill to Reynolds's desk. They also followed the Red State Strategy playbook, tying school choice to concerns over "'woke' school curriculum, grooming, transgender students, COVID masking policies, and Critical Race Theory."[36]

By the end of 2023, seven states passed new education choice policies and eight states expanded existing choice policies, including four states (Arkansas, Iowa, Oklahoma, and Utah) that made all K–12 students eligible.[37] In 2024, several more states adopted new education choice policies, including universal eligibility policies in Alabama and Louisiana, and smaller policies in Georgia, Nebraska, and Wyoming. In February 2025, Wyoming expanded its ESA to all K–12 students, and Idaho and Tennessee also adopted universal choice policies.

A similar dynamic to Iowa has played out in Texas. Gov. Greg Abbott's ESA bill cleared the state senate in 2023, only to be blocked by rural Republicans in the state house. As Reynolds had done, Abbott endorsed pro-school choice primary challengers, successfully replaced more than a dozen incumbents, and tried again.[38] In 2025, the state legislature passed a universal-eligibility ESA bill, which Abbott proudly signed into law. By the summer of 2025, 17 states had adopted publicly funded education choice policies for which every K–12 student is eligible. Thanks to the Red State Strategy, America's education system has hit a tipping point with more than half of US K–12 students eligible for school choice.[39]

America's School Choice Future

Ironically, the hyperpartisan Red State Strategy may yet yield bipartisan results. With one-half of US students eligible for school choice, the concept is being normalized. Polls show that parents strongly support school choice. Those who have it will fight to keep it, and parents in states that lack school choice will increasingly demand it. Meanwhile, the opponents' most salient argument—that school choice destroys public schools—is already evaporating.

As the demand for school choice grows and the fears about its effects diminish, any political party that stands in the way will be punished at the ballot box. Democrats will eventually tell teachers' unions that they can support their other issues, but their electoral viability will require dropping their opposition to school choice. Seeing the writing on the wall, some prominent Democrats—most notably Pennsylvania Gov. Joshua Shapiro—have already begun to embrace school choice.[40]

Within a few generations, universal school choice will be the norm in all 50 states. Eventually, people will forget that it was ever a controversial idea at all.

Notes

1. Jay P. Greene and Frederick Hess, "Education Reform's Deep Blue Hue," *Education Next*, March 11, 2019.

2. Morris Fiorina, "Party Sorting to Blame for Political Stalemate, Says Stanford Political Scientist," *Stanford Report*, October 26, 2020; and "Political Polarization in the American Public," Pew Research Center, June 12, 2014.

3. Morris P. Fiorina, "Polarization Is Not the Problem," *Stanford Magazine*, May 2018; and Fred Dews, "A Primer on Gerrymandering and Political Polarization," Brookings Institution, July 6, 2017.

4. There were some notable exceptions, such as the dueling California ballot propositions in the mid-1990s.

5. See, for example, the results from the *Education Next* surveys.

6. *Education Next*, PEPG Survey, 2007, question 8.

7. "Results from the 2022 *Education Next* Survey," *Education Next*, August 16, 2022.

8. In sketching out this framework, I am indebted to Arnold Kling's *The Three Languages of Politics: Talking Across the Political Divides*.

9. Friedman Foundation for Educational Choice, "The ABCs of School Choice: 2016 Edition," January 2016.

10. EdChoice, "US States Ranked by Educational Choice Share, 2016," January 29, 2016.

11. Author's calculations based on "The ABCs of School Choice: 2015 Edition," Friedman Foundation for Educational Choice, January 2015; National Center for Education Statistics, "Table 203.20: Enrollment in public elementary and secondary schools, by region, state, and jurisdiction: Selected years, fall 1990 through fall 2031," Digest of Education Statistics, 2023 edition; and National Center for Education Statistics, "Table 205.10: Private Elementary and Secondary School Enrollment and Private Enrollment as a Percentage of Total Enrollment in Public and Private Schools, by Region and Grade Level: Selected Years, Fall 1995 through Fall 2021," Digest of Education Statistics, 2023 edition.

12. See, for example, Terry M. Moe, *Special Interest: Teachers Unions and America's Public Schools* (Brookings Institution Press, December 2011).

13. Lauren Anderson, "The Teacher Unions Reinvigorating Progressive Politics," *Harvard Political Review*, October 20, 2020.

14. Jay P. Greene and James D. Paul, "Does School Choice Need Bipartisan Support? An Empirical Analysis of the Legislative Record," American Enterprise Institute, September 22, 2021.

15. Greene and Paul, "Does School Choice Need Bipartisan Support?"

16. Jason Bedrick, "The Folly of Overregulating School Choice," *Education Next*, January 5, 2016; Jason Bedrick, "On Regulating School Choice: A Response to Critics," *Education Next*, January 14, 2016; and Patrick J. Wolf, "What Happened in the Bayou?," *Education Next*, August 13, 2019.

17. For more on this subject, see Jason Bedrick and Lindsey M. Burke, "Myth: School Choice Needs Regulation to Ensure Access and Quality," in *School Choice Myths: Setting the Record Straight on Education Freedom*, ed. Corey A. DeAngelis and Neal P. McCluskey (Cato Institute, 2020), pp. 129–44.

18. See, for example, Colyn Ritter et al. "2024 Schooling in America: Public Opinion on K–12 Education, Transparency, Technology, and School Choice," EdChoice, August 2024, p. 27. In 2024, support for universal ESAs was at 71 percent compared with 53 percent support for needs-based education savings accounts. Over the past decade, the EdChoice survey consistently found that support for universal school choice was about 15 to 30 percentage points higher than support for needs-based school choice.

19. This is something I witnessed multiple times in my two decades of school choice advocacy. For example, in 2021, after a legislative committee in New Hampshire amended the eligibility for the proposed Education Freedom Accounts from universal to 300 percent of the federal poverty line, one parent advocate who had been very active told the coalition that because the program would no longer benefit her children, she could no longer justify all the time spent away from them advocating for it.

20. EdChoice, "The ABCs of School Choice: 2020 Edition," January 2020.

21. The findings of these focus groups remain unpublished. The author had access to them in his role as policy director of a leading school choice organization.

22. Jay P. Greene and Frederick M. Hess, "America's Students Flounder While Education Reformers Virtue Signal," *National Review*, November 5, 2019.

23. The author was part of these strategy sessions. The Red State Strategy we devised is described at greater length in chapter 4 of Corey DeAngelis, *The Parent Revolution* (Center Street, May 2024), pp. 55–75.

24. See Corey DeAngelis and Jason Bedrick, "School Choice Teaches Iowa Republicans a Big Lesson," Fox News, June 16, 2022; Corey DeAngelis and Jason Bedrick, "Parents Wanted School Choice—and They Voted," *National Review*, July 2, 2022; Corey DeAngelis, "The School-Choice Election Wave," *Wall Street Journal*, November 10, 2022; Lindsey M. Burke and Jason Bedrick, "School Choice Is a Political Winner," *Wall Street Journal*, November 15, 2022; Jay P. Greene and Jason Bedrick, "What's Behind the Recent Surge in School-Choice Victories," *National Review*, February 4, 2023; Corey DeAngelis, "2023 Is Already a Record Year for School Choice," *Wall Street Journal*, March 10, 2023; Joshua Q. Nelson,

"Texas GOP Primary Results Highlight School Choice as a Key Issue After Struggles to Pass Legislation," Fox News, March 11, 2024; and Jay P. Greene and Jason Bedrick, "The New GOP Litmus Test on School Choice," *Daily Signal*, July 17, 2024.

25. Kelsey Koberg, "Heritage Foundation Releases Education Freedom Report Card, with Florida Ranking Highest," Fox News, September 9, 2022.

26. Jason Bedrick, "The Big School Choice Turnaround in Iowa That More States Should Follow," Fox News, February 15, 2023.

27. Bedrick, "The Big School Choice Turnaround in Iowa."

28. Bedrick, "The Big School Choice Turnaround in Iowa."

29. Bedrick, "The Big School Choice Turnaround in Iowa."

30. For example, the Heritage Foundation's Jonathan Butcher, in a paper on critical race theory, proposed that policymakers "offer education savings accounts . . . to students attending schools teaching racially discriminatory content." See Jonathan Butcher, "Rescuing Math and Science from Critical Race Theory's Racial Discrimination," Heritage Foundation, July 13, 2021. See also this paper by two Heritage Foundation scholars: Jay P. Greene and Lindsey Burke, "The Values-Based Case for School Choice Is Also the Winning Case," American Enterprise Institute, December 6, 2021.

31. Jay P. Greene and James D. Paul, "Time for the School Choice Movement to Embrace the Culture War," Heritage Foundation, February 9, 2022.

32. Bedrick, "The Big School Choice Turnaround in Iowa."

33. Jason Bedrick and Michael Q. McShane, "How 2021 Could Be the 'Year of Educational Choice,'" *Washington Examiner*, April 1, 2021; and Jason Bedrick, "The Year of Educational Choice Is Here," EdChoice, May 25, 2021.

34. Jason Bedrick and Ed Tarnowski, "How Big Was the Year of Educational Choice?," *Education Next*, August 19, 2021.

35. KCCI Des Moines, "Reynolds Meets with Parents After School Board Passes Transgender Policy," May 5, 2022.

36. Team Starting Line, "Republicans Said the Quiet Parts Out Loud During Voucher Debate," *Iowa Starting Line*, January 24, 2023.

37. Jonathan Butcher and Jason Bedrick, "2023: The Year of Education Freedom," Heritage Foundation, September 11, 2023.

38. Jason Bedrick, "Texas GOP Primary Runoff Results Bring Big Wins for School Choice," *Daily Signal*, May 30, 2024.

39. Jason Bedrick, "Texas Tips the Scales: School Choice Now Covers Half of US Kids," *Daily Signal*, April 17, 2025.

40. Stephen Caruso et al., "Inside Pennsylvania Gov. Josh Shapiro's Support for Private School Vouchers," Spotlight PA, July 26, 2024.

Index

Note: Information in figures and tables is indicated by *f* and *t*; n designates a numbered note.

About the Contributors

JASON BEDRICK is a research fellow at the Heritage Foundation's Center for Education Policy. Previously, he served as the director of policy at EdChoice and as a policy analyst with the Cato Institute's Center for Educational Freedom. He also served as a legislator in the New Hampshire House of Representatives and was an education policy research fellow at the Josiah Bartlett Center for Public Policy. He has published numerous studies on educational choice programs with numerous national- and state-level think tanks and is the coeditor and coauthor of two books, *Educational Freedom: Remembering Andrew Coulson, Debating His Ideas* and *Religious Liberty and Education: A Case Study of Yeshivas vs. New York*. His articles have been featured in the *Wall Street Journal, City Journal*, the *New York Post*, the *Boston Globe, National Review, National Affairs*, and *Education Next*, among others. Bedrick received his master's degree in public policy from the John F. Kennedy School of Government at Harvard University, where he was a fellow at the Taubman Center for State and Local Government.

ASHLEY ROGERS BERNER is the director of the Johns Hopkins Institute for Education Policy and an associate professor of education. Palgrave Macmillan released *Pluralism and American Public Education: No One Way to School* (2017), and Harvard Education Press released her new book, *Educational Pluralism and American Democracy: How to Handle Indoctrination, Promote Exposure, and Rebuild America's Schools,* in April 2024. Berner has published dozens of articles, books, book chapters, op-eds, and a widely watched TEDx Talk on citizenship formation, academic outcomes, pluralism, and the political theories of education in different national contexts. She led the design of the Institute's School Culture 360 survey and ELA and Social Studies Knowledge Maps. Berner represents the Institute's work across the country and consults regularly with international, federal, and state agencies; nongovernmental organizations; and school systems. Berner holds degrees from Davidson College (Honors AB) and from Oxford University (MLitt and DPhil in modern history).

DICK M. CARPENTER II is professor emeritus at the University of Colorado and senior director of strategic research at the Institute for Justice. His work has appeared in many academic journals, such as *Economic Development Quarterly, Criminal Justice Policy Review, Economic Affairs, Journal of Entrepreneurship and Public Policy, Fordham Urban Law Journal, International Journal of Ethics, Education and Urban Society, Urban Studies,* and *Regulation and Governance.* His research results have been quoted in such newspapers as the *New York Times, Washington Post,* and *Wall Street Journal.* His work has also been cited by the White House and the US Supreme Court. He is the coauthor of the book *Bottleneckers: Gaming the Government for Power and Private Profit.*

CHERYL FIELDS-SMITH is a professor of elementary education in the Department of Educational Theory and Practice in the College of Education at the University of Georgia. She earned her doctoral degree from Emory University in 2004 under the direction of Vanessa Siddle Walker. Her research focuses on home/school/community partnerships. In 2006, Fields-Smith was awarded a Spencer Foundation grant and became a pioneer in black homeschool research. Using bell hooks's conception of "homeplace," Fields-Smith conceptualizes black home education as a form of resistance to traditional school practices that can harm black children, such as discipline disproportionality, teacher low expectations, or bullying. Her published books include *Exploring Single Black Mothers' Resistance Through Homeschooling,* a coedited book titled *Homeschooling Black Children in the US: Theory, Practice, and Popular Culture*, and most recently *Creating Educational Justice: Learning from Black Home Educators.* Her work has been featured in major networks and other multimedia broadcasts. She is a former elementary school teacher who taught first, second, and fourth grades in her home state of Connecticut.

NICOLE STELLE GARNETT is the John P. Murphy Foundation Professor of Law at Notre Dame Law School, where she also directs the Notre Dame Education Law Project. She writes primarily on topics related to education policy and religious liberty. In addition to dozens of scholarly and popular articles on these subjects, she is the coauthor of *Lost Classroom, Lost Community: Catholic Schools' Importance in Urban America* (University of Chicago Press, 2014) and the coeditor of *The Case for Parental Choice* (Notre Dame Press, 2023). She is an elected member of the American Law Institute and a senior fellow at the Manhattan Institute. Garnett earned a BA, with distinction, from Stanford University and a JD from Yale Law School, after which she clerked for Judge Morris S. Arnold of the US Court of Appeals for the Eighth Circuit and for Associate Justice Clarence Thomas. Before joining the Notre Dame Law School faculty in 1999, she practiced law for two years at the Institute for Justice, where she helped to defend the constitutionality of the nation's first private school choice programs.

CHARLES L. GLENN is professor emeritus of educational policy at Boston University, where he served for 25 years as department chair and interim dean. Previously, he was for more than 20 years a state official in the Massachusetts Department of Elementary and Secondary Education, responsible for equal educational opportunity (race, sex, national origin) and more than $100 million of state funds for urban education. In the 1960s, he was active in the struggle for racial justice as an inner-city pastor and then worked nationwide in the war on poverty. Glenn has played a role in a dozen court cases about race, language, or school finance, most recently as amicus curiae to the US Supreme Court in *Carson v. Makin*

(2021) and *St. Isidore of Seville Catholic Virtual School v. Drummond* (2025). He has published more than a dozen books, 160 book chapters, and 200 articles in journals in North America and Europe and has consulted on education reform in Israel, Italy, Russia, Ukraine, and other countries. While the first 30 years of his career focused on equal opportunities, the past 20 have largely been concerned with religious freedom in education.

WILLIAM H. JEYNES is a professor of education at California State University, Long Beach. He graduated first in his class from Harvard University. He is also a senior fellow at the Witherspoon Institute in Princeton, New Jersey. He has served as a speaker and/or adviser for four presidential administrations as well as for several G20 foreign governments and the EU. He specializes in conducting statistical meta-analyses on a variety of public policy topics. Jeynes has more than 185 academic publications, including 18 books. His articles have appeared in journals by Columbia University, Harvard University, the University of Chicago, Cambridge University, the University of Notre Dame, the London School of Economics, and other prestigious academic journals. He received the Distinguished Scholar Award from the California Senate and the California State Assembly. He received the Distinguished Achievement Award from an arm of the American Educational Research Association. Jeynes has been interviewed or quoted by many of the world's leading newspapers and media outlets, including the *Wall Street Journal*, the Associated Press, CBS, NBC, ABC, CNN, FOX, and WGN.

MATTHEW H. LEE is a clinical assistant professor of economics at Kennesaw State University, where he conducts research for the Education Economics Center. He is also a senior fellow at the Association of Christian Schools International and has previously taught as an adjunct professor of education policy at Johns Hopkins University. He is coeditor of *Religious Liberty and Education* (Rowman & Littlefield, 2020) and coauthor of *Future Ready* (ACSI/Cardus, 2022). His peer-reviewed research has been published in the *Journal for the Scientific Study of Religion, Journal of Religion and Health, Intelligence*, and *Journal of School Choice*. His articles have been featured in *Education Next, Law & Liberty, National*

Review, *Forbes*, the *Atlanta Journal-Constitution*, and others. He earned his PhD in education policy from the University of Arkansas.

RON MATUS is director of research and special projects at Step Up for Students, the nonprofit that administers Florida's education choice programs. He joined Step Up after more than 20 years as an award-winning journalist, including 8 years as the state education reporter at the *Tampa Bay Times*. Matus leads collaborative teams on white paper projects that spotlight the historic change underway on Florida's education landscape. Recent topics include the migration of black families to school choice options beyond school districts; former public school teachers starting private schools; the steady but measured expansion of choice in rural Florida; and the rapid, ongoing rise of "a la carte learning." Matus holds a bachelor's degree in history and creative writing from Florida State University and is a graduate student in Florida Studies at the University of South Florida.

JANE SHAW STROUP (who also writes as Jane S. Shaw) is chairperson of the Raleigh-based James G. Martin Center for Academic Renewal, where she retired as president in 2015. Currently, she is an editorial consultant for the John Locke Foundation. She is a coauthor of the new edition of *Common Sense Economics* (St. Martin's Press). Before coming to North Carolina in 2006, Shaw Stroup was a senior fellow with the Property and Environment Research Center (PERC) in Bozeman, Montana. She wrote and edited many articles about what became known as free-market environmentalism. She coauthored *Facts, Not Fear: Teaching Children About the Environment* with Michael Sanera (Regnery) and coedited *A Guide to Smart Growth* with Ron Utt (Heritage Foundation). Before joining PERC, she was an associate economics editor of *Business Week* in New York City. Shaw Stroup has a bachelor's degree in English from Wellesley College and a master's degree in history from North Carolina State University. She was married to the late Richard L. Stroup.

About the Editors

NEAL P. McCLUSKEY is the director of the Cato Institute's Center for Educational Freedom. He is the author of the book *The Fractured Schoolhouse: Reexamining Education for a Free, Equal, and Harmonious Society* and is coeditor of several volumes, including *School Choice Myths: Setting the Record Straight on Education Freedom* and *Unprofitable Schooling: Examining Causes of, and Fixes for, America's Broken Ivory Tower.* McCluskey also maintains Cato's Public Schooling Battle Map, an interactive database of values and identity-based conflicts in public schools. Prior to Cato, McCluskey was a policy analyst at the Center for Education Reform, taught high-school English, covered municipal government and education as a freelance reporter, and served in the US Army. McCluskey holds an undergraduate degree from Georgetown University, where he double majored in government and English; has a master's degree in political science from Rutgers University, Newark; and holds a PhD in public policy from George Mason University.

JAMES V. SHULS is the head of the Education Liberty Branch at the Institute for Governance and Civics at Florida State University (FSU). His work focuses on education policy, school choice, and the intersection of values and education. Prior to joining FSU, Shuls served as an associate professor and the department chair of educational leadership and policy studies at the University of Missouri–St. Louis and as dean of the College of Education at Southeastern University in Lakeland, Florida. He has authored numerous academic articles, policy reports, and opinion pieces, and his research has been featured in outlets such as *Education Next*, *Phi Delta Kappan*, and the *Journal of School Choice*. Shuls is also a fellow at the Show-Me Institute, where he writes regularly on education reform topics. He holds a PhD in education policy from the University of Arkansas, a master's degree in elementary education from Missouri State University, and a bachelor's degree in elementary education from Missouri Southern State University. A former public school teacher, Shuls brings both practical classroom experience and scholarly insight to education reform debates.

About the Cato Institute

Founded in 1977, the Cato Institute is a public policy research foundation dedicated to broadening the parameters of policy debate to allow consideration of more options that are consistent with the principles of limited government, individual liberty, and peace. To that end, the Institute strives to achieve greater involvement of the intelligent, concerned lay public in questions of policy and the proper role of government.

The Institute is named for *Cato's Letters*, libertarian pamphlets that were widely read in the American Colonies in the early 18th century and played a major role in laying the philosophical foundation for the American Revolution.

Despite the achievement of the nation's Founders, today virtually no aspect of life is free from government encroachment. A pervasive intolerance for individual rights is shown by government's arbitrary intrusions into private economic transactions and its disregard for civil liberties. And while freedom around the globe has notably increased in the past several decades, many countries have moved in the opposite direction, and most governments still do not respect or safeguard the wide range of civil and economic liberties.

To address those issues, the Cato Institute undertakes an extensive publications program on the complete spectrum of policy issues. Books, monographs, and shorter studies are commissioned to examine the federal budget, Social Security, regulation, military spending, international trade, and myriad other issues.

In order to maintain its independence, the Cato Institute accepts no government funding. Contributions are received from foundations, corporations, and individuals, and other revenue is generated from the sale of publications. The Institute is a nonprofit, tax-exempt, educational foundation under Section 501(c)3 of the Internal Revenue Code.